Social Work and Social Welfare Yearbook 1

1989

Edited by
Pam Carter,
Tony Jeffs and
Mark Smith

Open University Press
Milton Keynes · Philadelphia

Open University Press
12 Cofferidge Close
Stony Stratford
Milton Keynes MK11 1BY

and
242 Cherry Street
Philadelphia, PA 19106, USA

First Published 1989

British Library Cataloguing in Publication Data

Social work and social welfare yearbook
    1. Great Britain. Welfare work
    361.3'0941

    ISBN 0–335–15876–5
    ISBN 0–335–15875–7 Pbk

Library of Congress Catalog number available

Typeset by Scarborough Typesetting Services
Printed in Great Britain by
Biddles Ltd, Guildford and Kings Lynn

Contents

Notes on editors and contributors

Ruth Adler — Research Associate, Faculty of Law, Edinburgh University. Assistant to the Lay Observer for Scotland. Secretary of the Scottish Child Law Centre.

Pam Carter — Lecturer, Department of Social Work and Social Policy, Newcastle-upon-Tyne Polytechnic.

Andrew Fenyo — Computing Officer, Personal Social Services Research Unit, University of Kent at Canterbury.

Janet Ford — Senior Lecturer in Sociology, Loughborough University.

Bob Franklin — Researcher, Centre for Television Research, University of Leeds.

Robbie Gilligan — Lecturer in Social Work, Department of Social Studies, University of Dublin, Trinity College.

Tony Jeffs — Lecturer, Department of Social Work and Social Policy, Newcastle-upon-Tyne Polytechnic.

Chris Jones — Head of the School of Community Studies, Lancashire Polytechnic, Preston.

Kathleen Jones — Professor, Department of Social Policy and Social Work, University of York.

Martin Knapp — Reader in the Economics of Social Policy and Deputy Director, Personal Social Services Research Unit, University of Kent at Canterbury.

Ruth Lister — Professor of Applied Social Studies, University of Bradford. Former Director of the Child Poverty Action Group.

James Midgley — Dean, School of Social Work, Louisiana State University.

Mike Oliver   Principal Lecturer in Special Needs, Thames Poly-
                     technic.
Eamonn Rafferty   London-based freelance journalist.
Sue Richardson   Child Abuse Consultant, Cleveland Social Services
                     Department.
Stephen Shaw   Director of the Prison Reform Trust.
Mike Simpkin   Health Liaison Officer, Health Unit, Leeds City Coun-
                     cil.
Ruth Sinclair   Principal Research Officer, Leicestershire Social Ser-
                     vices Department.
Mark Smith   Tutor at the Centre for Professional Studies in Informal
                     Education, YMCA National College, London.
Christopher Turner   Lecturer in Law, University of Edinburgh.
Lincoln Williams   Deputy Senior Youth Officer (Southwark Area), Inner
                     London Education Authority.

The views expressed are those of the contributors and should in no way be taken to represent those of their employers or other agencies with which they are connected.

Introduction

In the two years it has taken to bring this first Yearbook to fruition, major reports on community and residential care were published; proposals for a Qualifying Diploma in Social Work were finalized, submitted and then rejected by the government; social work intervention became widely debated in the media, especially in respect of child sexual abuse; and major changes in the income support system have been implemented. At one level, we should not be surprised by the scale and nature of the events that have taken place. Such movement and debate has long been a feature of this area of welfare. However, it is difficult to escape the feeling that the personal social services, whether statutory or voluntary, are faced with fundamental dilemmas concerning purpose, method, organization and essential values. The tensions that flow from these changes affect the working lives of all those in health and social welfare. Yet for practitioners, students in training, policy-makers, managers, and educators and trainers there is a paucity of appropriate material.

We have sought to balance the need for accessibility with the requirement of allowing contributors sufficient opportunity to develop sustained analysis. The Yearbook has not been constrained by a narrow focus on one area of welfare, although it is oriented towards those arenas of practice increasingly associated with social services. Our purpose has not been to provide a review of the year or a catalogue of administrative detail. These are available elsewhere. Rather we have sought to bring together a collection which will help readers to think about the direction and nature of practice. Material which:

1 updates and reviews current and potential practice developments, policy changes and research;

2 allows readers to gain or maintain a broad perspective on social welfare so
   that discussions about specialisms are better informed;
3 facilitates critical debate.

The Yearbook is a forum for analysis and dialogue. It occupies a position
somewhere between the weekly magazines which can carry only limited
analysis, substantive works which take some time to appear, and journals,
which are either more specialist or somewhat diverse in coverage. The
Yearbook format provides a means by which questions and themes can be
addressed over time. We could have filled the volume several times over, and it
is obvious that we could not hope to provide a comprehensive picture of social
work and social welfare in one volume.

   Although it has taken two years to establish the Yearbook, the contributors
have worked to short and tight deadlines in order to minimize the danger of
being overtaken by events. It would not have been possible to achieve this
without their commitment and that of everyone at the Open University Press.
Thank you.

Pam Carter
Tony Jeffs
Mark Smith

1
Wimps and bullies: press reporting of child abuse

Bob Franklin

The *Daily Mail* broke the story of what subsequently became known as the 'Cleveland affair' on 23 June 1987. The front page headline declared: 'Hand Over Your Children; Council Orders Parents of 200 Youngsters'. This first report presaged the paper's subsequent coverage; it was sensational, oversimplified, uncritically accepting of the parents' case and indifferent to any discussion of the rights of the children concerned. Six months later, the *Star* reported the death of Kimberley Carlisle with the headline 'Man Who Let Kimberley Die'. Under a photograph of the social worker concerned, the subheading announced 'Dithering Social Worker Slammed For Leaving Her With Wicked Stepdad' (*Star* 12.12.87).

These headlines illustrate a major theme in the discussion below. Press reporting of child abuse, paradoxically, rarely focuses upon the abuse of children. It quickly regresses into an attack on welfare professionals, particularly social workers who, in their turn, seem to have become a metaphor for the public sector. Although child abuse makes good newspaper copy, large parts of the press have incorporated the issue into a broader political agenda expressing the government's sustained attack on the public sector. For their part social workers symbolize state provision of services which previously were provided by the family and community and which, according to the radical right, should be again; social workers thereby undermine the traditional role of the family. Social workers are identified with the local, rather than central, state and account for a substantial proportion of its expenditure. Consequently media discussions of social workers must be viewed in the context of recent tendencies towards centralization and the diminution of local initiatives. Hostility to the public sector, especially the local state, may explain why voluntary organizations such as the NSPCC consistently receive a better hearing in the press than the statutory sector (Mawby, Fisher and Hayle 1979: 15).

Much press coverage of 'child abuse' has masked, as well as provided a vehicle for, this attack on social work and the public sector. The latter is presented as inefficient and unable to meet the demands placed upon it, while simultaneously it is allegedly repressive and illiberal. As symbols for the public sector, social workers have been portrayed in the press by two antithetical stereotypes; both are extremely negative. The first presents social workers as indecisive, and reluctant to intervene to protect children from abusing adults. The second image for the social worker is that of the authoritarian bureaucrat who, with little regard for civil liberties, 'breaks up families' by removing children into care.

Journalists routinely use key words and phrases to establish these stereotypical images. Social workers are described as 'naive, bungling, easily fobbed off and hoodwinked' (*Daily Express* 29.3.85), 'incompetent and insufficiently professional' (*Daily Telegraph* 18.12.87), 'official do-gooders' with 'no experience of the world' (*Sun* 29.3.85). In the more euphumistic prose of the *Daily Mail*, social workers are 'butterflies in a situation that demands hawks' (20.12.87).

Alternatively social workers are 'meddlers' (*Daily Express* 18.11.87), 'guided by prejudice' (*Daily Mail* 6.7.88). They are 'abusers of authority, hysterical and malignant, callow, youngsters who absorb moral-free marxoid sociological theories' (*Daily Mail* 7.7.88). In the words of Tim Devlin MP, the social services are merely, 'another organisation with the initials SS' (*Guardian* 30.6.87).

Putting aside the excessive rhetoric of press reports, these two images of social workers express something of the dilemma which social workers confront when making decisions in cases of alleged child abuse. The dilemma, moreover, reflects an unresolved tension in the social worker's job brief between the need to care for their clients, but on occasion also to control them. This point is captured neatly by Tonkin, who claimed

> 1987 was the year when the wimp became a bully. A quick shuffle of stereotypes replaced the gormless, non-judgemental social worker with the heavy booted commissar of child care, flanked on either side by magistrate and paediatrician.
>
> (Tonkin 1987: 15)

But Tonkin's remark is misleading. The image of social workers as bullies has not replaced an earlier image of the wimp; both images are presented alternatively or may even coexist within the same newspaper. In June 1987 press coverage of Cleveland presented the social worker as an authoritarian bully. By December 1987 press reports of the Kimberley Carlisle and Tyra Henry cases stereotyped social workers as wimps, but by July 1988, when Butler-Sloss reported, the bully returned with a vengeance. This seems to be an instance of the curious 'amnesia' which McIntosh identifies when media respond to essentially the same issue in a radically different way (McIntosh

1988: 10). In reality, however, it is not a matter of journalistic short-sightedness, but a journalistic viewpoint informed by a political agenda which is largely conservative and rampantly anti-public sector (Brynin 1988: 32; Goldsmiths College Media Research Group 1987: 19; Todd 1987: 2).

Journalists offer their own utilitarian analysis of their professional interest in child abuse.

> Child abuse makes good newspaper copy. There is the trial which involves 100s of column inches devoted to the details of the child's grisly end. This allows for both public conscience and appetite for horror to be satisfied at the same time. Then there is the ritual purification; the inquiry into what went wrong and the public execution of the 'guilty parties' – the social workers.
>
> (*Guardian* 23.6.87)

Whatever the reasons underlying journalists' concern with the subject, press reporting of child abuse has proved extremely significant in three arenas. It has influenced public opinion against social workers (Fry 1987: 11; Phillips 1979: 12), modified various aspects of professional practice, for example concerning social workers' willingness to apply for place of safety orders (Parton 1981: 392; Geach 1982: 15) and ultimately prompted government to introduce new policy initiatives to deal with particular social problems as defined and structured by media discussions (Geach 1982: 15; Golding and Middleton 1979: 5). The Children's Act 1975, for example, was heavily influenced by press coverage of the Maria Colwell case. A similar role is attributed to the press in influencing public opinion and government policy concerning child abuse in the USA (Nelson 1978: 28).

The press, child abuse and social workers

Research on press reporting of child abuse is scarce. In part this reflects the sensitive nature of the subject matter (McCron and Carter 1988: 69), but largely it attests to the recent 'discovery' of child abuse as a public issue. It was the death of Maria Colwell in 1973 and the establishment of a public inquiry, that triggered press interest in child abuse as a major source of stories (Hartley 1982: 38). Between 1968 and 1972 only 9 articles were published discussing child abuse and these tended to propagate the views of the NSPCC Battered Child Research Unit (Parton 1977: 84; 1979: 438; 1981:399; 1985: 97).

The few research studies which exist are diverse in methodology, objectives and conclusions, but three consensual points emerge. First, press reporting of child abuse seems to conform to what has been described as a moral panic (Golding and Middleton 1979: 5; Hartley 1982: 66; Nava 1988: 103; Parton 1981: 394). The phenomenon was initially identified by Cohen who was concerned to explain the rapid increase in press reporting of mods and rockers and the powerful public response to these social groups (Cohen 1972: 28). A necessary requirement for such 'panics' seems to be conditions of social crisis when traditional values and social institutions momentarily lose their credibility and waver under an attack, presumed or real, by a group which Cohen designates 'folk devils' (Cohen 1972: 28). The media have a central role in both creating and sustaining the panic by identifying the group to serve as 'folk devils', by isolating, defining and socially censuring them as an out group, and by restating and reaffirming the traditional social values. The latter is achieved by giving extensive and priority media access to what Hall *et al.* describe as 'the primary definers': authority figures such as judges, MPs, police officers who legitimize, but at the same time help to structure, dominant cultural values (Hall *et al.* 1978: 57). In summary the press create the labels by which social problems are publicly recognized and understood. Typically such problems are cast in manichean mould as a battle between heroes and villains, insiders and outsiders, them and us. On the inside 'is the public, including the media as vox populi, while on the outside are the threatening deviant or suspect group' (Golding and Middleton 1979: 11). What is extraordinary in this case, however, is that it is not the 'wrong-doers', the abusers, who are labelled as 'folk devils' but social workers who are cast in this role. Personifying and representing the public sector is, it seems, a more heinous crime than child abuse; press and public hostilities are appropriately severe. In the Colwell inquiry the social worker, as well as being vilified by the press, had to be protected from the public while entering and leaving the court, was questioned for twenty-five hours in evidence and eventually had to change her name to escape public and press attention (Andrew 1974: 643; Lees 1979: 15; Shearer 1979: 13).

Nava offers an innovative variant of the moral panic framework by informing it with feminist assumptions. She argues that Marietta Higgs became a symbol for feminism in press reports and, in this way, the spectre of feminism became the threatening folk devil (Nava 1988: 105). Nava's case has undoubted merit but the argument here is that it was Higgs's social function as a welfare professional, rather than her gender, which was critical to press designations of her as folk devil. Only when the primary press target is identified as the public sector, rather than feminism, can the similar press vilification of male welfare professionals, like the social worker in the Kimberley Carlisle case, be explained.

The second consensual point stresses that press coverage has tended to focus overwhelmingly upon the publication of the report of the committee of inquiry rather the the death of the child, or the criminal trial of the abuser (Hartley 1982: 43; Parton 1979: 440). In turn, newspaper reports of the inquiry have placed the role of the social worker centre stage. The major consequence of this press emphasis is that child abuse has been 'decriminalized' and redefined as a social service problem. In 1971 18 per cent of reports concerning child abuse in *The Times* mentioned social workers and/or social service departments, whereas figures for 1973, 1974, 1975, and 1976 had grown dramatically to 37 per cent, 34 per cent, 51 per cent and 48 per cent (Hartley 1982: 41). Hartley concludes that

Child abuse which had previously been reported as a criminal matter by the press came to be reported as a social service matter. Main news items about it began to focus on the activities of welfare workers and particularly social workers who apparently 'failed' to deal with the problems efficiently.

(Hartley 1982: 76)

Shearer goes further and suggests that from its inception, press reporting of child abuse has had the more covert intention of challenging what, in 1973, were the newly established and fledgling social service departments.

A number of newspapers [Shearer claimed] were simply waiting for the right issue by which they could 'give them a kick' . . . in this respect the case of Maria Colwell . . . provided an opportunity to criticise social service departments and the new profession of social work.

(Parton 1977: 113)

The final common theme in the research suggests that social workers are, at least in part, culpable for the poor press treatment they receive. They do not understand the organization or operation of the media, they use a technical language which journalists cannot translate, they fail to exploit public relations techniques to improve their image, and miss the opportunity to achieve favourable coverage in the local press which is more likely 'to praise local services' (Young 1979: 11; Rote 1979: 17; Fry 1987: 13; Phillips 1979: 12; Hills 1980: 19).

Indecisive wimps and big bad bullies

Press coverage of the Jasmine Beckford, Tyra Henry, and Kimberley Carlisle cases lampooned social workers as indecisive wimps. Press reaction to the Cleveland case, however, was very different. The target remained the same but the imagery was reversed and the social worker emerged as the authoritarian bully.

There are, of course, significant differences between these cases. First, Beckford, Henry and Carlisle illustrate press responses to physical abuse whereas Cleveland involved sexual abuse. Second, the press focus in the former cases was upon particular instances of abuse, but in Cleveland the press was unable to identify specific individuals and consequently less able to personalize the issue. Finally, the press identified the Beckford, Henry and Carlisle cases as the 'tip of an iceberg'. When the Cleveland story broke in June 1987, some reports signalled that child abuse may be widespread, although newspapers were ambiguous on this point (Nava 1988: 108). By the time Butler-Sloss reported however, newspapers were unanimous in believing the initial numbers of cases at Cleveland were an overestimate: the result of a panic or some other malfunction in the welfare system.

Press reporting of the Beckford, Henry and Carlisle cases portrayed social workers as indecisive and ineffectual, putting children at risk because of their reluctance to intervene to protect them. Even an allegedly sympathetic article in the *Listener* conceded reluctantly, 'There are lots of hopeless ones who make their colleagues cringe and who feed the stereotyped image of the bearded, denim-clad, drabbie with the two CV and silly hippy ideas' (Forsyth and Prysor-Jones 1986: 10). As mentioned above, however, the social worker's indecisiveness is, on occasions, presented in the press as a crime equivalent to the act of abuse itself. The *Star* cited Jasmine Beckford's foster parents' allegation that 'if her stepfather is a killer, so are Brent social services' (29.3.85). The *Sun* carried a picture of a social worker alongside the heading, 'They Killed The Child I Adored' (29.3.85). Social workers in the Henry and Carlisle cases were similarly castigated by the press. *The Times* headlined, 'Tyra Henry Inquiry Says Social Workers To Blame Over Murder' (18.12.87), while the *Mirror* alleged, 'Bungling social worker Martin Ruddock was blamed yesterday for the death of four year old Kimberley Carlisle' (12.12.87). The press seem to believe that only the social worker is responsible for what has happened to the child; the criminally convicted abuser is a marginal figure in their reporting. The indecisive wimp – a comic figure to be ridiculed – has a more sinister aspect; the fool is transformed into a villain. The press attack on the social worker in the Carlisle case was so severe that *The Times* felt obliged to remind its Fleet Street colleagues that, 'Whatever journalists and others may insinuate, she was not killed by her social worker . . . she was killed by a brute abetted by a woman whose sense of evil had atrophied' (*The Times* 12.12.87).

The press's habit of considering social workers culpable for the fate of their clients gives them a unique place among professionals, even though the actions of incompetent doctors, for example, might affect more directly the well-being of their patients. Social workers are always judged to be wrong, doctors rarely so, the police virtually never. Giving social workers additional powers however is no remedy for their incompetence since, according to Keith Waterhouse, senior *Daily Mail* columnist, it is good judgement rather than powers which they lack. He derides social workers for their ineffectiveness. He claims

> The depressingly usual pattern is that social workers are alerted by neighbours. They call round several times to utterly no effect but finally have a reassuring chat through the letter box with the father or stepfather who persuades them all is well.

No degree of power can substitute for such a lack of judgement. Indeed social workers' powers are already too great and consequently they are 'hated and feared by the inadequates and human clinker of the council ghettos'. Such fear and contempt can only be exacerbated by 'giving them the same power to snatch up a child almost at whim as is enjoyed by their much envied counterparts in Sweden' (*Daily Mail* 14.12.87).

An additional factor in the Tyra Henry and Jasmine Beckford cases was that the parents and children were black. Racist overtones in the press treatment of Maurice Beckford seem apparent. The *Star* carried a large, front-page picture of Beckford with the headline 'The Brute' (29.3.85). Moreover, in much the same way that local – 'loony left' – councils have been accused of discrimination against white people because of their commitments to anti-racist policies, social workers were sometimes accused of treating black people more favourably than whites. The *Mail* editorial about the Beckford case on 29 March 1985 asked

> To what extent were the social workers of Brent 'naive' and to what extent were they blinded by dogmas? What influence if any did colour have on the decisions they took? Was it of any significance that the foster mother was white, while the stepfather and natural mother were of West Indian origin?

The issue is addressed as a series of questions but in reality it forms an accusation.

How did the press react when the Cleveland crisis seemed to counter the previous imagery of social workers? It could hardly ignore the issue; indeed the extent of press interest was quite phenomenal and without precedent. The first five weeks of coverage generated 9,000 press items while 'mentions on national television news were an everyday occurrence' (Treacher 1988: 15). Coverage was sustained across a period of a year from the initial break of the story in June 1987, through the seventy-four days of the inquiry, until the publication of the Butler-Sloss report on 6 July 1988.

Four foci emerged for press reporting of Cleveland. First, the accuracy of the diagnostic technique used by paediatricians to identify sexual abuse was contested by parents, MPs, journalists and, most significantly, by paediatricians. The issue was central since without a reliable test the extent of sexual abuse could not be established. By the time Butler-Sloss reported, the press seemed enthusiastic to play down initially high estimates of sexual abuse. The *Mirror* claimed that the test may indicate only 'that a 3 year old has sat on the funnel of his toy ship at bath time' (6.7.88).

A second press concern was to expose disputes between professionals. The most celebrated of these concerned liaison between medical, social work and police professionals, and Bell's allegation of a 'conspiracy' between Higgs and Richardson to 'exclude' police personnel from investigations of sexual abuse (*Daily Mail* 30.6.87). The story achieved a high profile across all newspapers.

A third focus for press coverage was the Butler-Sloss report. Assessments varied concerning the report's merits. The *Independent* (7.7.88) described it as 'strikingly child-centred and humane, constructive and full of common sense', whereas the *Guardian* claimed there was 'a vacuum' at the heart of the report which left key questions unanswered (8.7.88). Most newspapers simply quoted the report selectively to endorse their previous editorial line. The crude and simplistic reviews typically published in the press conveyed little of the complexities which Butler-Sloss had so thoroughly detailed.

The most sustained and significant focus of the reporting concerned the confrontations between parents (usually described as 'anguished' or 'innocent') and welfare professionals (invariably described as 'zealous' or 'authoritarian') supported by the courts and armed with place of safety orders. The loudly canvassed concern was the extent to which child care procedures might threaten parental rights. This is undoubtedly a complex and important issue, but press sympathies were unequivocal. The *Mirror* headlined 'No End

To Agony for Parents In Child Sex Story'. The story reported parents leaving court, 'in tight little groups, the odd tear trickling down blank, bewildered faces'. A pregnant woman with three children in care is quoted as saying, 'if I can't get my kids back the social services will take the baby automatically and I couldn't bear that' (30.6.87).

A year later the style was much the same. With the benefit of hindsight, the problem in Cleveland was reducible to 'an outbreak of hysteria among doctors and social workers' who wished to 'seize sleeping children in the middle of the night. . . . The Higgs group' was able to act in this way because of 'the prevalence of ultra feminists and of anti family views in some medical and social work circles. . . . Persons holding such views are quite unsuited to be social workers'. Given the analysis, the solution is correspondingly simple. 'There ought to be an ideological purge to drive out those whose opinions commit them to a campaign of subversion against the family' (*Sunday Express* 10.7.88).

The ideological implications and their inconsistency are apparent. Social workers are no longer wimps failing to protect children from the terrors of the family; they are bullies attacking family life. This contrast is apparent in the press treatment of the two figures identified by the press as central to the Cleveland drama: Stuart Bell and Marietta Higgs. Their significance, as Nava argues, reflects the fact that the press uses each individual as a symbol to mobilize a distinct set of associations, values and prejudices (Nava 1988: 115). Bell speaks for traditional family values; Higgs symbolizes the forces which the press presumes seek to subvert them.

From the outset, Bell has enjoyed readier access to the press than Higgs. He is a seasoned politician with experience of media performance, the press have largely supported him against Higgs and Cleveland social services department and, unlike Higgs and Richardson, his discussions with journalists have not been constrained by concerns of breaching confidentiality.

The image of Marietta Higgs presented in the press has, from the earliest reportings, been negative. The captions under her photograph – describing her variously as 'accused' or 'slammed' or as a 'crusader' – have betrayed press commitments. At best she was 'the doctor in the child abuse storm' (*Daily Mail* 24.6.87), at worst, one of the two 'sex row plotters' (*Mirror* 30.6.87). Press attitudes hardened after the publication of the Butler-Sloss report, despite the fact that it vindicated her against many of the previous press allegations of professional and moral malpractice. On 7 July 1988 the *Mail* carried a prominent photograph of Marietta Higgs with the caption 'Not A Sign Of Regret' for, as the text explains, 'the part she played in breaking up scores of families'. Her statement to the press was described as 'defiant words', her actions inevitably as 'zealous'!

In addition to these direct accusations against her, newspaper coverage of Marietta Higgs contained more 'subtle' passages which, while overtly offering contextualizing information about her, covertly presented negative messages for the reader to decode. An article in the *Mail* on 24 June 1987 is worthy of closer examination. The paper had rung Mr Higgs at the couple's home; both are described as 'Australian born'. The text is as follows:

Mr. Higgs, 40, was speaking at the couple's rambling detached house in
Middlesbrough where he is bringing up their five children . . . while his
wife pursues her medical career, he gave up his own – he was a biologist
involved in cancer research – to concentrate on raising the family.

This short paragraph signals a number of 'unattractive' points for readers
about Marietta Higgs. She is foreign, middle class, rich, she lives in a big house,
she is married to someone who gave up his job to bring up children (what sort
of a man behaves in such a way?), she clearly places her own career before that
of her husband (even though his work was serious and valuable) and her 'duty'
as a mother to look after her children. In brief, an image is presented of
someone who defies many expectations of female behaviour, especially in the
family and stirs many deeply held prejudices. Little wonder. the *Mirror*
claimed, that as a consequence of her involvement in Cleveland, 'family life has
been struck a devastating blow' (29.6.87).

Every aspect of Higgs's behaviour was metamorphosed, in press coverage,
from virtue into vice. Reports of her giving evidence at the enquiry were
unexceptional. The *Sunday Express* claimed, 'what disturbs me about
Marietta Higgs is her calm. Her sweet, smiling reason' (11.11.87). Perhaps
journalists would be less 'disturbed' if Marietta Higgs had been 'frenzied' or
'hysterical' instead of 'calm', or perhaps 'irrational' instead of being guided by
'reason'? Such behaviour would certainly have approximated more closely to
male expectations of stereotyped female responses to stress situations. The
Sunday Times restated the *Express's* anxiety. 'No question seemed to faze or
rattle her', it claimed. 'Her voice is gentle and low. But it is a voice without
emphasis or inflection'. A different coded message is very apparent here. Higgs
is so controlled and contained in her responses as to be unnatural. She is cold,
devoid of emotion, almost inhuman, a robotic automaton: not one of us!

Even Marietta Higgs's professional practice of examining children to assess
if sexual abuse had occurred came to be defined, by the press, as sexual abuse
and the paediatrician as the abuser: a bizarre and morally repugnant inversion.
The *Mirror* claimed that the medical examination left children 'hysterical,
shouting and screaming. The doctors', it was alleged, 'examined the kids like
animals. That was the only sexual abuse' (*Mirror* 26.6.87).

By contrast reporting of Stuart Bell was extremely positive. Captions under
his photographs, as with Higgs, betrayed, press sentiments. He is treated as a
'primary definer', 'Determined To Protect Children' (*The Times* 30.6.87). He
is, in the words of the *Sunday Telegraph*, 'One of the few public figures
involved in the Cleveland case who has no need to reproach himself'. Unlike
Higgs, career is not uppermost in his mind, having stepped down from a
front-bench position to devote his energies to the support of the parents
concerned: his constituents. Moreover his actions have allegedly 'earned him
the hatred of the Labour Party's lesbians, man-haters and family haters so his
front bench prospects have probably been destroyed' (10.7.88).

The veracity of Bell's assertions was rarely challenged by the press who
present them as 'facts'. He became an indirect vehicle, in the press, for the

family and anti-public sector lobbies. Bell himself often stressed the latter commitment and his article, 'Stop The Sex Abuse Industry Now' in the *Mail* on 6 July 1988, précised his major concerns throughout the Cleveland episode. Discovering child abuse, he claimed, is currently a 'fashionable obsession', but in reality the incidence of sexual abuse is substantially less than social workers suggest. Childline receives 8,000 calls a day but 'free telephone lines . . . are open to abuse from hoaxers and children who just like the idea of a free phone call'. The preoccupation with sexual abuse, moreover, merely follows an American precedent where, in 1986, 'a million children were wrongly taken from their parents'; both assertions were, of course, unsubstantiated.

Certain groups, he alleged, have a vested interest in promoting this 'child sexual abuse bandwagon', because it represents 'jobs, money and power'. The Butler-Sloss report provides additional momentum to this 'spurious, new growth industry'. The beneficiaries are 'an ever increasing army of social workers . . . who are unskilled and guided by prejudice' and who 'already waste time on daily case conferences and squander money attending unnecessary seminars'. Campbell (1988) suggests that many of Bell's arguments were based on factual inaccuracies and were mere assertions designed to achieve political ends, but the press seemed to accept them uncritically. His advocacy of the parents' position touched a nerve end with a large number of readers. By denying the prevalence of sexual abuse, he spoke for them, calmed their anxieties and put them morally at their ease. It is worth noting Butler-Sloss's criticisms of Bell. His remarks were described as 'inflammatory' and 'intemperate' and his widely publicized allegations against various medical and welfare professionals dismissed as unfounded. Butler-Sloss, moreover, was 'sad' that Bell was 'unable in the light of the further knowledge that he clearly had, to withdraw or modify allegations which could not be substantiated' (Butler-Sloss 1988: 165).

An assessment

The Reports of inquiries into cases of child abuse have traditionally commented disparagingly on media coverage. 'The popular press', the Beckford Inquiry observed, 'ever avid for sensationalism and for evidence to buttress its innate and irrational hostility to social workers', indulged in 'gross distortions' (Blom-Cooper 1985: 288). The Carlisle Inquiry spoke of the 'verbal abuse of social workers bordering on the hysterical', which 'abounds in the popular press' (Blom-Cooper 1987: 134). In the context of these criticisms, Butler-Sloss's conclusion that press coverage involved 'inevitable selectivity' which became 'one-sided distortion' verges upon the laudatory (Butler-Sloss 1988: 169).

Others involved in the Cleveland affair were more critical. The public relations officer at Cleveland complained about bias, the publication of confidential High Court evidence, misleading phone calls, editorial blackmail (give us a story or we'll print something really nasty), and the invasion of council offices (Treacher 1988: 15). Medical staff complained about disruption of their work because of interviews being conducted on wards, at least one journalist dressing as a nurse to gain access to wards, and the blockage of the entrance to Ward 9 creating access problems for nursing and ambulance staff (Butler-Sloss 1988: 171).

The content of press reporting can be criticized on a number of counts, although they apply with varying force to the 'quality' and 'tabloid' press. Reporting was on occasions sensational and trivialized, biased in its judgements, simplistic, factually inaccurate, and seeking to scapegoat. The issue of child abuse has persistently been presented and framed within the parameters prescribed by dominant and traditional social values. Attempts to discuss the rights of children, or feminist critiques of patriarchy which tried to get beyond these narrow confines, were largely ignored.

Sensationalism and trivia are almost defining characteristics of the tabloid press and consequently many examples could be cited here. On 2 July 1988 the *Sun*, fed by Press Association leaks from the previous day, ran a headline on page 2, 'Sack Them All'. A prominent subheading on the far right of the page, directly adjacent to page 3, announced 'Care Order Boob'. The ironic juxtaposition of moral propriety and outrage on page 2 with the pornography of page 3 is undoubtedly judged 'good copy' by subeditors, but also helps explain why the Press Council receives so many complaints about the *Sun*.

The press' uncritical advocacy of the parents' case has been evident from headlines such as 'Victims Of Sex Abuse "Experts"; The Continuing Nightmare Of The Innocent Parents Who Stand Accused' (*Mail* 24.5.87). There is no evidence in the report of any attempt to establish the facts, to gain expert corroboration for any allegations or to present relevant statistical evidence. The press simply took the parents' side, interviewed them and presented their account of events as reality. This is a quick, cheap and efficient way of news-gathering, but the result is unbalanced headlines like 'They Killed Our Baby Grieving Father Accuses Social Services' (*Mail* 18.11.87).

Press coverage also oversimplifies events. Reports tend to concentrate on the immediate circumstances which 'triggered' a particular event – perhaps a child refusing to eat, or crying – rather than the background and progression of events which led to the assault (Mawby, Fisher and Hayle 1979: 15). Time constraints further exacerbate simplification. A short item on television or radio news attempts to explain issues which 'took an inquiry 3 months to investigate and 15 months to deliberate upon' (Social Worker 2 1983: 17).

In the context of the Cleveland case, press coverage has regularly misrepresented important issues and reported factual inaccuracies. The Butler-Sloss report confirmed that Marietta Higgs never diagnosed sexual abuse solely on the basis of the 'controversial' reflex anal dilation test, that the alleged 'conspiracy' between Higgs and other agencies was a fallacy and that she did not routinely check children at Middlesbrough Hospital for child abuse unless they had been referred by other agencies (Butler-Sloss 1988: 164–6). These 'allegations', however, became the central issues in press coverage and persisted after the Butler-Sloss Report was published.

Finally, press coverage was flawed by its concern to scapegoat. The need to identify individuals who could be blamed blinded the press to the complexities of both child abuse and the interaction between welfare agencies attempting to cope with it. Headlines such as 'Tyra Henry Death Inquiry Blames Social Workers' (*Mail* 19.12.87) make less demands on readers as well as journalistic resources.

Assessment so far has focused on published content of press stories but it is 'the stories that are not published and angles which are not taken which form the important subjects for analysis' (Murphy 1974: 750). Three substantive issues were not addressed by the press.

First, the inadequate financial and human resources allocated to deal with child abuse are rarely discussed in press coverage. This is a curious omission since while the recorded incidence of child abuse is rising, 'the resources to deal with it are diminishing'; this, it is claimed, 'is the real abuse' (Doran and Young 1987: 13). A draft report from the government Social Services Inspectorate on 30 June 1988 disclosed 600 cases of child abuse in London alone which were not allocated to a social worker (*Independent* 7.7.88). However by ignoring resource issues, the press is merely reflecting the practice of various inquiries into child abuse. The Carlisle Report for example stated that 'Behind issues related to a protection service lie the chronic resource implications that go way beyond any child abuse inquiry' (Philpot 1988: 15). The provision of adequate resources to deal with child abuse is surely a central issue.

Second, a series of gender-related omissions have been highlighted. particularly by feminist writers. Press coverage, they allege, has persistently evaded the key issue by failing to specify abusers as 'male' and the abused as 'female', preferring the non-gender-specific terms 'parents' and 'children'. Such terms obscure the fundamental character of sexual abuse, the reasons why it occurs and policies for its prevention; they 'amount to a deceit' (Macleod and Saraga 1988b: 15). Two recent and authoritative research studies confirm that abusers are 'overwhelmingly male' (90 per cent), while more than 80 per cent of young people abused are female (NSPCC 1988: 4–7; La Fontaine 1988: 1–2). Levels of incidence of child abuse among girls may well be even higher, depending upon how sexual abuse is defined. Feminists argue that to date definitions have been restrictive and prompted underestimates (MacLeod and Saraga 1988a: 19; Kelly 1988a: 66).

Finally, the press have framed the issue of child abuse in the Cleveland case as a battle between the state's obligation to protect children and parents' rights to exercise an equivalent paternalism. The rights of the children concerned have had a poor hearing even though their interests may be massively at odds with either their parents, the state, or both. It seems extraordinary that children who have suffered abuse by an adult must then be treated as the guilty party, removed from their families and placed in an institution; as Campbell notes, to date no other institutional response exists (Campbell and Sedley 1988: 16). Imagine the uproar if adult victims of physical or sexual abuse, rather than the abuser, were institutionalized while welfare professionals 'sorted things out at home'. The physical and sexual abuse of children reflects their powerlessness in the patriarchal family and wider society. They should not however be presented as vulnerable, passive victims of abuse needing protection but, as Kitzinger observes in her eloquent essay, 'we should replace restrictive notions of "protection" with liberating notions of "empowerment" (Kitzinger 1988: 83).

References

Andrew, C. (1974) 'The Maria Colwell Inquiry', *Social Work Today*, 4, 10 January 1974: 637–44.
Bell, S. (1988) *When Salem Came to the Boro*, London: Pan Books.
Blom-Cooper, L. (1985) *A Child in Trust: The Report of the Panel of Inquiry into the Circumstances Surrounding the Death of Jasmine Beckford*, London: Kingswood Press.
—— (1987) *A Child in Mind: The Protection of Children in a Responsible Society: The Report of the Commission of Inquiry into the Circumstances Surrounding the Death of Kimberley Carlisle*, London: Borough of Greenwich.
Brynin, M. (1988) 'The unchanging British press', *Media Information Australia*, 47: 23–37.
Butler-Sloss, E. (1988) *Report of the Inquiry into Child Abuse in Cleveland 1987*, Cm 412, London: HMSO.
Campbell, B. (1988) 'Champ or chump', *New Statesman and Society*, 15 July: 14–16.
Campbell, B. and Sedley, S. (1988) 'A family tragedy: a conversation', *Marxism Today*, July: 16–19.
Cohen, S. (1972) *Folk Devils and Moral Panics: The Creation of the Mods and Rockers*, London: MacGibbon & Kee.
Doran, C. and Young, J. (1987) 'Child abuse: the real crisis', *New Society*, 27 November: 12–14.
Forsyth, J. and Prysor-Jones, H. P. (1986) 'Society pays to keep the ugliness hidden', *Listener*, 6 February: 10–11.
Fry, A. (1987) *Media Matters; Social Work, the Press and Broadcasting*, Surrey: Reed Business Publishing.
Geach, H. (1982) 'Social work and the press', *Community Care*, 27 May: 14–16.
Golding, P. and Middleton, S. (1979) 'Making claims: news media and the Welfare State', *Media, Culture and Society*, 1: 5–21.
—— (1982) *Images of Welfare: Press and Public Attitudes to Poverty*, London: Martin Robertson.
Goldsmiths College Media Research Group (1987) *Media Coverage of London Councils: Interim Report*, London: Goldsmiths College.
Hadley, J. (1987) 'Mum's not the word', *Community Care*, 5 November: 24–6.
Hall, S., Critcher, C., Jefferson, T., Clarke, J., Roberts, B. (1978) *Policing the Crisis*, London: Macmillan.
Hartley, P. (1982) *Child Abuse, Social Work and the Press: Towards the History of a Moral Panic*, unpublished MA thesis, University of Warwick.
Hills, A. (1980) 'How the press sees you', *Social Work Today*, 11, 36, 20 May: 19–20.
Kelly, L. (1988a) 'What's in a name? Defining child abuse', *Feminist Review* 28: 65–74.
—— (1988b) 'Cleveland – Feminism and the media war', *Spare Rib*, 193: 8–12.
Kitzinger, J. (1988) 'Defending innocence: ideologies of childhood', *Feminist Review*, 28: 77–88.
La Fontaine, J. (1988) *Child Sexual Abuse*, ESRC Research Briefing, London: ESRC.
Lees, D. (1979) 'As the hurt fades', *Social Work Today*, 10, 19, 9 January: 15.
McCron, R. and Carter, R. (1988) 'Researching socially sensitive subjects: the case of

child abuse', *Annual Review of BBC Broadcasting Research Findings*, no. 13, London: BBC Research Department, pp. 69–77.

McIntosh, M. (1988) 'Introduction to an issue: family secrets as public drama', *Feminist Review*, 28: 6–16.

Mawby, R., Fisher, C. and Parkin, A. (1979) 'Press coverage of social work', *Policy and Politics*, 7, 4: 357–76.

Mawby, R., Fisher, C. and Hayle, J. (1979) 'The press and Karen Spencer', *Social Work Today*, 10, 22, 30 January: 13–16.

MacLeod, M. and Saraga, E. (1988a) 'Challenging the orthodoxy; towards a feminist theory and practice', *Feminist Review*, 28: 16–56.

—— (1988b) 'Against Orthodoxy', *New Statesman & Society* 1, 4, 15–16.

Murphy, D. (1974) 'The unfreedom of the local press', *New Society*, 19 December: 750–2.

Nava, M. (1988) 'Cleveland and the press: outrage and anxiety in the reporting of child sex abuse', *Feminist Review*, 28: 103–22.

Nelson, B. C. (1978) 'Setting the public agenda: the case of child abuse', in J.V. May and A.B. Wildavsky (eds) *The Policy Cycle*, New York: Sage.

NSPCC and Greater Manchester Authority Child Sexual Abuse Unit (1988) *Child Sexual Abuse in Greater Manchester: A Regional Profile 1st March 1987 to 29th February 1988*, Manchester, May.

Parton, N. (1977) 'the natural history of non-accidental injury to children', MA thesis, University of Essex.

—— (1979) 'the natural history of child abuse: a study in social problem definition', *British Journal of Social Work*, 9, 4: 427–51.

—— (1981) 'Child abuse, social anxiety and welfare', *British Journal of Social Work*, 11, 4: 391–414.

—— (1985) *The Politics of Child Abuse*, London: Macmillan.

Phillips, M. (1979) 'Social workers and the media: a journalist's view, *Social Work Today*, 10, 22, 30 January: 123.

Philpot, T. (1988) 'What social work must learn from Carlisle' (interview with Louis Blom-Cooper), *Community Care*, 7 January: 12–15.

Rote, G. (1979) 'How to cope with the media', *Social Work Today*, 10, 22, 30 January: 17.

Sedley, S. (1987) *Whose Child? The Report of the Public Inquiry into the Death of Tyra Henry*, London: Borough of Lambeth.

Shearer, A. (1979) 'Tragedies revisited 1: the legacy of Maria Colwell', *Social Work Today*, 10, 19, 9 January: 12–19.

Social worker 2 in the Lucie Gates Case (1983) 'Savaged by the press', *Community Care*, 445, 13 January: 16–17.

Todd, R. (1987) 'The media and the people', Hetherington Lecture delivered at London School of Economics, 14 June 1987.

Tonkin, B. (1987) 'A year of living dangerously', *Community Care*, 31 December: 15–19.

Treacher, R. (1988) 'The problem with being on the media map', *Local Government Chronicle*, 22 July: 15.

Young, R. (1979) 'Social workers and the media: a social services view', *Social Work Today*, 10, 22, 30 January: 10–11.

2
Defending the cash/care frontier: social work and the social fund

Ruth Lister

Social work and poverty

Although the sums of money involved may be relatively small compared with the social security budget as a whole, [single payments] act as an important symbol of the way in which we operate the safety net for the poorest members of society.

(SSAC [Social Security Advisory Committee] 1987: para 45)

Single payments, and the social fund that has now replaced them, have also acted as a symbol of the troubled frontier between the social security system and social services/work departments. Stevenson has warned that the social fund 'will pose major and urgent dilemmas for social workers' but noted also that 'such contemporary issues only give a topical twist to a persistent and critical theme – that of the social worker's response to poor clients as individuals and to poverty in general, as a phenomenon which they so frequently encounter' (Stevenson 1986: iii). It is important therefore to set social work's reaction to the social fund in the context of its long standing uneasy relationship with the poverty experienced by so many of its clients.

Although it can be argued that 'poverty has always been at the heart of social work and social services' (Svenson and MacPherson 1988: 41), many social workers have been reluctant to accept its centrality. Referral data have traditionally blurred rather than illuminated poverty's impact so that 'the evidence of financial and material hardship among social services users goes mainly undocumented and is largely anecdotal' (Balloch and Jones 1988: 295). It is only recently that an attempt has been made to collate the evidence that is available. The tentative conclusion reached by Becker and

MacPherson on the basis of this evidence is that about nine in ten referrals are from the unwaged and that about half are from those dependent on the means-tested safety net. 'Claimants are poor before they become clients, but more and more are becoming clients because they are poor' (Becker and MacPherson 1986: para 1.1).

At a time when the numbers dependent on supplementary benefit have reached a record of over 8 million, including over 2 million children (1987 figures), it is not surprising that the data available suggests that 'there has been and continues to be a significant increase in financially based and welfare rights oriented referrals to social workers; for a large proportion of referrals these are the prime presenting problems' (Becker and MacPherson 1986: para 3.46). Research by Hill, Iolan and Smith (1983) suggests this increase is not confined to deprived areas. Poverty can also lurk behind other 'presenting problems' more readily accepted as part of the social work task. For instance, the Social Services Select Committee report on Children in Care observed 'there is a well established link between deprivation and children coming into care. Put crudely, the majority of children in care are the children of the poor' (Social Services Committee 1984: para 36).

The ambivalence of many social workers towards dealing with the practical implications of poverty is well documented. At a fairly simplistic level, it is summed up by the refrain that it is not 'real social work'. In some cases this reflects narrow professional concerns. But research into social services' response to unemployment suggests that social workers' resistance is also 'in part connected with seeing social issues and related individual needs as two totally separate things' (Dhooge and Popay 1988: 254).

Sheer pressure of work, which encourages a reactive rather than proactive approach, has also been an increasingly important factor. It is paradoxical that at the very time when the implications of poverty for social work are being brought out in the public arena, and a greater legitimacy has been accorded to welfare rights work in social services, the ability of social services/work departments to respond is diminishing. Social workers are in retreat from taking on board these issues in their daily practice. On the one hand statutory work, especially child-care work, dominates the social services agenda. On the other hand, and not totally unconnected, the same forces that have brought the issue of poverty to the surface are also creating many of the pressures that reduce social workers' ability to respond. Large-scale long-term unem-ployment, growing dependence on social security and benefit cuts have all taken their toll. Moreover, the drastic restrictions on entitlement to single payments introduced in 1986 followed by the social fund itself have increased the sense of powerlessness that many social workers feel in the face of their clients' poverty.

It is the extra one-off payments provided by the supplementary benefits scheme, together with its chronic administrative problems, that have been the source of the main problems on the social security/social services frontier. Since the early 1970s there has been a string of documents attempting to create peaceful relations on the frontier. At fieldwork level the evidence suggests that their impact has been patchy, and that liaison arrangements have come under increasing strain (Balloch and Jones 1988; Hill, Iolan and Smith 1985; Tester 1985). At national level, Stewart and Stewart have observed that

The DHSS has concentrated increasingly on pursuing its own policy agenda, while the local authority associations have gained in confidence to resist central government pressure and have formed their own stance on clients' poverty and their relationship with the social security system.

(Stewart and Stewart 1986: 12)

The local authority associations' refusal to put their name to the new version of *Liaison in Practice*, drafted by the DHSS to take account of the advent of the social fund, marks the latest stand in their defence of the cash/care boundary against the encroachment of the DHSS.

From the local authority side a long-standing key issue has been the relationship between social security provisions and their powers to provide financial assistance under section 1 of the Child Care Act 1980 (previously the Children and Young Persons Act 1963) and under section 12 of the Social Work (Scotland) Act 1968. The power to make cash payments had been given to social services/work departments in the 1960s in response to representations from local authorities, keen to do constructive work with children and frustrated by their dealings with the National Assistance Board and their reliance on charities.

It was made clear in a Home Office Circular that it was not intended that section 1 'should be used to provide an alternative to national assistance' and that it should not be 'given in circumstances where it could more appropriately be given by the Board' (Home Office 1963: para 10). However, within a decade concern was growing about the variation in the use of these financial powers and the extent to which they were meeting the basic needs of individual clients rather than funding innovative projects. A Child Poverty Action Group (CPAG) survey of the evidence available concluded that 'in many areas, section 1 funds are being used inappropriately to provide a safety net for poor families who are refused help by the Supplementary Benefits Commission (SBC) under its powers to provide lump sum grants and emergency payments' (Lister and Emmett 1976: 31). This provoked a response from David Donnison, Chair of an SBC anxious to draw clear boundaries around the help that it was prepared to provide. An attempt was made to establish the principle, later endorsed by the Social Security Advisory Committee, that 'benefit is not payable to meet a need for which another statutory authority has a power or duty to provide' (SSAC 1985b).

Subsequent research has revealed a similar picture of enormous variations in section 1 expenditure and of a large number of section 1 payments made for basic necessities such as food and fuel where the DHSS had a responsibility. 'Really, it is compensating for breakdowns in benefit delivery – missing giros – and substituting for urgent needs payments which are particularly difficult to obtain' (Stewart and Stewart 1987b). While it appears that the 1980 cutbacks in supplementary benefit clothing grants prompted social services to turn more to charities and the WRVS rather than their own funds, the evidence suggests that the 1986 single payments cuts have had an impact on section 1 expenditure. It has been reported that since the cuts some local authorities have doubled their section 1 budgets (*Social Work Today* 16.11.87). Table 1 shows how expenditure under section 1 increased dramatically between 1985–86 and 1986–87, having dropped the previous year.

Table 2.1   Net current expenditure under section 1 of the Child Care Act 1980 – England

Year	Cash (£ million)	Constant prices (£ million)
1982–3	3.358	4.283
1983–4	4.184	4.781
1984–5	7.255	7.939
1985–6	6.561	6.775
1986–7*	8.262	8.262

Note: * provisional

Source: House of Commons Debates 1988b

A central theme of a CPAG report on the effects of the single payments cuts was

> the extent to which claimants are having to turn to other sources for help. . . . Local authority social services departments have reported a marked impact on their budgets under section 1 of the Child Care Act and section 12 of the Social Work (Scotland) Act and also on their staff's time.
> (Davies and Lister 1988: 69)

Since it is widely recognized that the single payments cuts marked the first steps towards implementation of the social fund, the implications for post-April 1988 were obvious.

Concern about the extent to which expenditure under section 1 and section 12 has underpinned the social security system has reflected more than just a desire to protect local authority budgets. There is a widely held belief that it is not the responsibility of local authorities to provide income maintenance. The use of section 1 and 12 moneys as an alternative to social security is seen as a perversion of their original preventive social work purpose and as doing nothing to challenge the inadequacies of the social security system. Important questions about the role of social workers are also at stake.

One fear, articulated most strongly by Jordan drawing on studies in Britain and the USA, has been that social workers' financial powers constitute a dangerous potential source of social control over their clients (Jordan 1974). Research indicates that 'while some social workers cheerfully accept a situation in which they may use their money-giving powers to bargain with clients, very many feel profoundly uneasy about the extent to which they possess this kind of power' (Hill and Laing 1979: 78). Similarly Becker confirmed that 'giving out money is an unpopular task' (Becker 1987).

Against this background of the troubled frontier between social services and social security, the pressure of client need on social workers, traditionally ambivalent about the implications of poverty for their work, and social workers' dislike of giving out money, it is not surprising that the prospect of the social fund has provoked feelings of frustration and near-panic among many social workers.

The social fund

The social fund encompasses two very different schemes. The first, introduced in 1987, covers maternity and funeral expenses, together with cold weather payments. The second replaced one-off supplementary benefit single payments and urgent needs payments in April 1988. This second half of the fund has been presented by ministers as a residual scheme 'to provide for exceptional circumstances and emergencies faced by a minority of claimants' (DHSS 1985: para 2.118). They have emphasized that it must be set against the background of the weekly income support scheme which replaced supplementary benefit. Few would disagree for, as SSAC pointed out, 'for large groups of claimants single payments [were] a way of offsetting too low levels of benefits' (SSAC 1985a: 3.45).

The problem is that, overall, levels of benefit remain too low. A nil-cost reform inevitably meant an exercise in rough justice in which the gains for one group of claimants were at the expense of another. The DHSS estimated that just over a third of supplementary benefit claimants would lose in real terms; independent estimates, that took account of cuts that paved the way for the April 1988 changes and the abolition of single payments, put the losses much higher. A parliamentary answer suggested that total expenditure on income support would be £60m less than that on supplementary benefit if the costs of transitional protection and compensation for 20 per cent of rates payments are ignored (House of Commons Debates 1988a).

Although families with children, the main beneficiaries of single payments, appear to have been among the gainers because of the introduction of the family premium, for those who did rely on single payments to eke out inadequate weekly benefits the gains have been largely illusory.

A number of specific changes incorporated into the income support scheme are of particular significance for social services/work departments but have been paid little attention because of preoccupation with the social fund. These include: the failure to compensate carers through the premiums system for the abolition of the long-term rate; the losses both for people with severe disabilities and for those with health-related expenses (including enuretic children) who do not qualify for the disability premium; and perhaps most worrying of all, the implications for young people leaving care of a combination of lower rates of benefit for single, childless under-25-year-olds and the removal of the right to benefit for most 16-17-year-olds (to be followed by further cutbacks in provisions for lodgers in April 1989).

This is the context then in which we have to understand a scheme which, in the majority of cases, replaces grants by loans, thereby condemning claimants to living below the minimum level set by Parliament as their loan repayments are deducted from their weekly benefit. The carrot of community care grants failed to impress the local authority and professional associations. The ADSS (Association of Directors of Social Services), for instance, argued that 'it isn't easy to view the community care grant component within the social fund as a serious initiative in community care especially when one considers the current assistance available for such needs which is being abolished' (ADSS 1987: para 40). Moreover, the community care grants, like loans, are subject to a cash limit translated into a local office budget which outweighs need in the assessment of applications and are discretionary, without even an independent right of appeal. The local authority associations summed up the views of a wide range of bodies with their observation that 'the basis on which the social fund has been constructed should have no place in a social security system' (ACC/AMA [Association of County Councils and Association of Metropolitan Authorities] 1988: para 5). In fact, it holds a key symbolic place in a social security system designed to reduce expectations of what the state will provide.

The implications for social services

The *Social Fund Manual* states that 'there will be a continuing need for constructive and close liaison between the LO [Local Office] and the social services department about the social fund' (DHSS 1987: para 1050). As well as more traditional liaison arrangements, it envisages social services departments (SSDs) providing information about numbers leaving residential care and an 'exchange of views . . . about the relative priorities of different circumstances for community care grants, and for loans' (DHSS 1987: para 1048). With regard to individual claimants it calls for discussions about arrangements for referrals between the two agencies including 'co-operation where social and financial problems are linked', and discussions about 'the circumstances in which social services departments may be consulted about social fund applications from or on behalf of their clients subject to the rules of confidentiality of both agencies'. In both cases it suggests that 'joint visits or participation in case conferences may occasionally be appropriate' (DHSS 1987: para 1050). Specific circumstances in which SSD advice should be sought are provided elsewhere in the *Manual*.

The local authority associations have warned that 'this proposed liaison lies at the heart of the Government's attempt to involve local authorities in administrative co-operation with the social fund' (ACC/AMA 1988: para 11). Concern has focused in particular on the dangers of social workers being drawn into acting as gatekeepers for the fund. The *Manual* states that 'there may be circumstances in which the advice of the social worker on the needs of a particular applicant will help the SFO to reach an informed decision' (DHSS

1987: para 1050) and the social fund claim form asks whether the applicant has a social worker and for permission to seek further information, if necessary, from the social worker. Although both the *Manual* and claim form stress that 'no added weight should be given to those cases where a social worker is involved' (DHSS 1987: para 1050) social workers themselves remain suspicious.

It would not be the first time that the social security system cast social workers in the role of gatekeepers. As Stewart and Stewart have pointed out

de facto and without consultation, social workers are already 'advising the DHSS', as Ministers put it, in at least two areas of the present social security scheme: part of the single payments for furniture regulations and exempting claimant clients from time-limits imposed on under-26-year-olds by the board and lodging regulations.

(Stewart and Stewart 1987a)

The effect, they argue, is one of 'net-widening' as claimants are labelled as clients to enhance their position *vis-à-vis* the DHSS.

Local authorities have likewise not been convinced by the Minister for Social Security's assurances that 'it is not intended that the social fund should lead to increased demand on local authority provision or force local authorities into the role of providing an income maintenance service' (Scott 1988). Scott's assurance was rather weakened when he continued

where local authorities can provide a service there will be an overlap, and we would hope for constructive local debate. We do not think it unreasonable that our local offices should try to ascertain how individual local authorities interpret their responsibilities so that all concerned can be clear about what can be provided.

(Scott 1988)

Rather than clarification, the ACC has predicted that the fund will aggravate the long-standing difficulties between the boundaries of responsibility and finance between local government and social security.

The extent to which Social Fund Officers (SFOs) will direct claimants to social services for financial help is unclear at this stage. Section 33 of the Social Security Act 1986 states that 'in determining whether to make an award to the applicant . . . an officer shall have regard to . . . the possibility that some other person or body may wholly or partly meet it'. The *Manual* advises that 'this is intended to apply primarily to crisis loans applications' and in the section on crisis loans does note that social services departments 'do not normally meet financial needs' (DHSS 1987: paras 3003, 4059). However, in the community care grants section it is made clear that 'local authorities have the major responsibility for community care, as they are able to assist people in many different ways' and that 'the Secretary of State has directed that SFOs should not award CCGs if the LA has a duty to provide assistance. However, in other circumstances, SFOs may award CCGs which complement the LA's role in community care provision' (DHSS 1987: paras 6001, 6004).

Looking into the future, the waters are muddied further by the possible implications of the White Paper on child care law and the Griffiths Report. The White Paper proposes to give local authorities a new 'broad "umbrella" power to provide services to promote the care and upbringing of children, and to help prevent the breakdown of family relationships which might eventually lead to a court order'. Under that power 'the local authority will also be able to offer financial assistance in exceptional circumstances' (DHSS 1987: para 18).

Stewart and Stewart have warned that a more general power such as this would make it harder for social workers to resist SFOs' requests (1988). Although it is arguable that the 'exceptional circumstances' proviso might be used as shield, it is likely to be less effective than one that is couched in specifically social work terms as is now the case with section 1.

The publication of the Griffiths Report has further fuelled speculation that the transfer of the social fund to local authorities themselves is on the longer-term agenda. This would fit into a wider pattern of a shift in central government responsibilities (though not power) to local government. Reports by *The Times's* public administration correspondent and *Social Services Insight* at the end of 1987 predicted that such a transfer would eventually take place (*The Times* 7.12.87; *Social Services Insight* 18.12.87). The Griffiths Report confined itself to advocating that 'the community care element of the social fund should be withdrawn from the social security system and the funds earmarked for that purpose transferred to social services authorities'. He made clear that he did 'not recommend any extension of social services authorities' limited powers to make cash payments to individuals' (Griffiths 1988: para 6.8).

Local authorities, possibly tempted at the prospect of further (albeit very limited) funds for community care policies, should be wary of a potentially poisoned chalice. It conjures up two possible scenarios. First, it could represent 'a Trojan House, preceding moves to make social services departments fully responsible for disbursing the social fund' (*Social Services Insight*, 1.4.88). Davies (1988) has pointed out that this would be a 'logical progression' from the original Green Paper's observations about the nature of the social fund; that

> approach needed in dealing with claimants who will often be experiencing stress has marked similarities with that expected of professionals, such as social workers or health care staff.
>
> (DHSS 1985: para 2.100)

This is reflected in the training course for SFOs in which six out of nine days concentrate on issues commonly found in social work training (Davies 1988). The separation of responsibility for social services and social security at central government level inevitably raises questions about the future co-ordination of community care policies. This could strengthen any pressures to transfer responsibility for the community care grant element of the social fund at least to SSDs.

The alternative scenario, which is limited to Griffiths's recommendation, is also problematic. It would mean a further £60m (at 1988 prices) hole in the social security safety net with no one-off grants for clients and non-clients alike. This would inevitably mean a further increase in the number of desperate claimants beating a path to social services' doors.

Whether or not it is the government's intention under the social fund as constituted at present to put increased demands on local authority provisions, it is likely to be the result. The then president of the ADSS summed up the fears of many authorities:

> people in distress will turn to their social services departments as providers as a last resort. We will be implored to fulfil a role for which we have neither the responsibility nor the resources and this will have serious adverse consequences on our capability of carrying out those tasks and functions which are our proper responsibility.
>
> (Kay 1987)

One consequence is likely to be the aggravation of an existing trend in which more and more social work time is taken up with trying to squeeze funds out of charities that are already 'struggling . . . to provide a safety net beneath the increasingly threadbare safety net of the supplementary benefit scheme' (Davies and Lister 1988: 69).

Time can be as precious a resource as money; for hard-pressed social workers it is the prospect of the extra pressures on their time created by more claimants seeking their help in their negotiations with the DHSS as well as direct financial help that has caused much of the angst. The danger is that, given social workers' existing ambivalence about helping clients with their material problems, this could be used as a justification for a more general retreat from welfare rights work. Yet the need for such work will not go away. Fimister has suggested that

> much of what has been, hitherto, welfare rights work as such, will now split into three. First, there will still be much welfare rights work to be done, for example around basic income support entitlement and in housing benefit and benefits for disabled people. Second, there will be a lot more chasing of grants outside of the benefit system. Third, there will almost certainly be a great deal more debt management work.
>
> (Fimister 1988: 320)

He sees the last as particularly problematic for 'if social services departments simply throw up their hands and say "this is not our job" all other forms of social services intervention will run the risk of being undermined by the corrosive influence of multiple debt'. But he warns 'debt management is not a field in which to dabble' and so there are important implications for staffing and training (Fimister 1988: 322). COSLA has recommended that Scottish authorities 'should encourage the development of appropriate money advice services' (COSLA 1988: para 3.2.6.).

Finally, hanging over social services/work departments is the spectre of increased violence. Surrey's Director of Social Services (*Social Work Today*, 31.3.88) and the local authority associations have warned that 'the violence already experienced by workers in social services and housing offices could increase further as a result of public frustration with the social fund' (ACC/AMA 1988: para 28). Even before the advent of the social fund proper, CPAG reported evidence that the 1986 single payment cutbacks had

> had a damaging effect on the relationship between advice workers and claimants as the former increasingly are in the position of having to explain why no help is now available. In this way, they are, in effect, deflecting claimants' frustration from the DHSS.
>
> (Davies and Lister 1988: 69)

From non-cooperation to determined advocacy

The initial stance taken by the local authority associations and the ADSS to the social fund was that of total non-cooperation and a refusal to enter into consultation. Once the general election was out of the way and it was clear that the social fund was not going to go away, a re-think of the meaning of non-cooperation began to take place in both the statutory and voluntary sectors. With one or two exceptions, such as Hertfordshire's Director, Herbert Laming, who has called on BASW members 'to work with social fund officers in a spirit of cooperation to get the best possible deal for those who have the least' (Laming 1988), there continued to be general opposition to liaison and co-operation on the DHSS's terms as set out in the *Social Fund Manual*. It was felt that such co-operation would amount to collusion with the fund's unacceptable principles; undermine social workers' independent advocacy role and compromise them in the eyes of their clients, as well as drawing local authorities further into the web of income maintenance provision.

The difficulty was in reaching agreement on whether and how the original non-cooperation stance should be modified. A key sticking-point was whether or not social workers and advice workers should ever help claimants secure a social fund loan. Initially NALGO and BASW both argued that they should not, on the grounds that it was not in the claimant's longer-term interests. On the other hand the main view to emerge at a meeting of the Social Security Consortium (which brings together the voluntary and local authority sectors) was that it was paternalistic to deny claimants such help if, in the event of a community care grant not being forthcoming, that was what they wanted. Eventually NALGO and BASW modified their stance, although dissatisfaction among NALGO members could still lead to the reassertion of the original non-cooperation line. At least one social services department (Liverpool) together with the Federation of Independent Advice Centres (FIAC) stuck to a formal non-cooperation line, although even here non-cooperation has been defined as total boycott. Under the FIAC guidelines, help is restricted to giving claimants information about the social fund and, in the case of those with language or literacy problems, to assisting with the filling-in of the application form.

During the autumn of 1987 there slowly emerged what came to be known as the 'determined advocacy' position (labelled 'aggressive advocacy' or 'principled engagement' in its earlier formulations). Support for the concept of determined advocacy was largely motivated by the view that 'it would be irresponsible to attempt to ignore the social fund' (ACC/AMA 1988: 4).

A threefold case for a rethinking of the meaning of non-cooperation was put by myself to the 1987 UK Social Services Conference in Glasgow. First, it was argued, total non-cooperation could provide the perfect cover for a retreat from welfare rights work by those social workers who never wanted to do it in the first place. This was not the time for social workers to turn their backs on claimant-clients' financial problems in the name of the ideologically pure line of non-cooperation. Second, if local authorities simply ignored the social fund, the DHSS would go ahead and stake out its own boundaries with local authorities ill-prepared. Third, non-cooperation, ironically, could represent the ultimate collusion with the social fund. It is only by engaging with the social fund, on the local authorities' terms, that the inadequacies of the fund could be demonstrated by monitoring and case histories. And if pressure were not put on the social fund, it would be easy for ministers to claim that it was working and that, as they had always claimed, only a small minority of claimants needed extra help. Indeed, a report in the *Sunday Times* has suggested that ministers are very worried by the likely pressure that determined advocacy could create (*Sunday Times* 28.2.88).

The fullest exposition of determined advocacy is to be found in the position statement and practice guide published by the AMA and ACC together with COSLA's Scottish version (ACC/AMA 1988; COSLA 1988). This has been modified for use by the voluntary sector in a paper published by the voluntary organizations sub-group of the Social Security Consortium.

The principles underlying determined advocacy can be summed up as follows:

1 Responsibility for income maintenance lies with the DHSS and not social services/work departments;
2 local authority fieldworkers have a responsibility to provide their clients with independent advice and advocacy in connection with the social fund and not to become involved in any way in assessment for the fund. Special assistance should be provided for those with special difficulties in understanding the fund or who are vulnerable to discrimination. However, social services departments cannot be responsible for claimants who would not otherwise have been accepted as clients by them;
3 it is for clients to decide what their needs are and how their claim to the social fund should be managed in the name of 'claimant sovereignty'.

Translating these principles into practice is inevitably difficult. The practice guide provides a framework and suggestions for how to operationalize the principles it sets out. But at the end of the day individual authorities have to decide, in the context of their existing policies and traditions, how exactly they will implement a policy of determined advocacy.

From principles to practice

As noted above, the question of where responsibility for income maintenance should lie has implications mainly for the use of section 1/12 funds. However, before looking at section 1/12 policy, it should be noted that similar issues are raised in other areas. NAPO (National Association of Probation Officers) has advised that 'probation services should clarify their financial responsibilities as set out in the Probation Rules 1984. As poverty increases there will be a knock on effect putting Befriending Funds under pressure'(NAPO 1988: para 2.2). Social services departments also have to consider the use of section 1 powers in the face of the cutback in the benefits provided for young people. Now that section 1 payments are no longer treated as income for social security purposes, it is theoretically open to them to top up income support (where still payable) or housing benefit in the case of under-18-year-olds who have left care. Under section 27 of the Child Care Act, a local authority can make a contribution to the cost of accommodation and maintenance of young people aged under 21 who have been in care since reaching the age of 16; this power is likely to take on a new significance in the harsh world of the social fund and restricted benefits for young people.

The practice guide suggests that 'authorities must adopt clear policy guidelines to clarify the use they will make of their statutory powers, in particular Section 1 of the Child Care Act 1989' (ACC/AMA 1988: para 14). The fund raises in acute form the dilemmas that have traditionally faced those local authorities anxious on the one hand to do what they can to help poor families living in their area and on the other to avoid being drawn into providing an ultimate safety net beneath the social security system. The associations warn that

> unless local authorities review their guidelines in the light of social fund priorities, they will see their expenditure on section 1 increase in an uncontrolled fashion to plug the gap left by loans and emergency grants. Local authorities cannot afford to plug that gap.
>
> (ACC/AMA 1988: para 19)

Leaving aside the reasons outlined earlier as to why local authorities should not even attempt to plug the gap, they simply do not have the funds to do so. Information is not yet available about how local authorities generally are responding but it would appear that a number are reasserting the original child-care functions of section 1 policy in their revised guidelines.

While this is arguably the appropriate response it is not unproblematic. The practice guide warns that if authorities adopt a policy of making provision for needs identified as high priority for CCGs, this 'would be to invite SFOs to save expenditure by referring clients (who they would otherwise have assisted) over to the local authority' (ACC/AMA 1988: para 19). The problem is that section 1 payments and CCGs share the same rationale of keeping people in the community and out of residential care. The practice guide also leaves unresolved a problem, traditionally associated with the social security/social services frontier identified by Fimister as 'the most distressing and undignified "ping pong" routine for claimants sent back and forth between agencies' (Fimister 1980: 37).

As well as the delineation of the scope of assistance provided under section

1/12, the local authority associations have raised the question of procedural rights – or lack of them. As rights are eroded in the social security system, the practice guide argues that 'local authorities' own guidelines should aim to guarantee the rights of clients' (ACC/AMA 1988: para 19) through the provision of written reasons and a review procedure.

The practice of determined advocacy will vary between local authorities in the same way that general welfare rights work does. It is not possible to draw up an effective policy for determined social fund advocacy in the absence of a more general welfare rights policy as some authorities have discovered. Different policies may be appropriate depending on the availability of other sources of welfare rights advice. Different policies may apply to existing or potential clients as opposed to those who approach the department purely for financial advice or assistance.

Three key problem areas can be identified in the practical application of the concept of determined advocacy. The first concerns the use of the *Social Fund Manual*. While the local authority associations disapprove of the criteria underlying the prioritization of need enshrined in the *Manual*, it is clearly unrealistic to expect advocates to undertake a self-denying ordinance and not use the *Manual* at all. It is therefore suggested that the *Manual* should be used where it helps a claim, while making clear that this does not imply acceptance of the *Manual's* criteria. At the same time, given that most of the *Manual* is discretionary, an advocate should not be deterred if the guidance does not favour a claim.

More difficult and central to the non-cooperation debate are the issues of the nature of advocacy in the face of a fixed budget and of the distinction between acting as an advocate and being drawn into the process of assessment.

It is this thin dividing line between advocacy and assessment that is likely to cause the greatest difficulties for social workers. At a management level, it means pressing and publicizing the authority's policies while refusing to be drawn into liaison arrangements aimed at helping the DHSS to draw up its local priorities. At the level of the individual fieldworker, it means being clear that in any dealings with the SFO the worker is aligned with the claimant and not the SFO. Thus, for example, BASW's social fund guidelines emphasize that 'the separate and quite distinct roles of social workers and social fund officers must be clearly understood by clients' and advise that 'whilst it may on occasion be appropriate for social workers to participate in joint visits for the purposes of advocacy or facilitation in respect of a claim, this attendance is purely as an advocate or facilitator and is on behalf of the client' (BASW Poverty Panel: 1987). The symbolic significance of walking through the door with the SFO rather than being with the client should not be under-estimated.

Where the practice of determined advocacy becomes more problematic is in the need to exclude value judgements and opinions. The practice guide concedes that

> in practice it will be impossible to sustain a distinction between hard facts and subjective value judgements. However, the role of the representative

is to communicate the claimant's understanding of the facts and his or her (the claimant's) opinions. On no account should representatives volunteer statements based on their own assessment of the facts or needs. To do so would be to assist the SFO in making an assessment of need.

(ACC/AMA 1988: para 56)

In many ways, determined advocacy is asking social workers to go against their instincts and training. There is evidence that they felt more comfortable with the discretionary pre-1980 system than they did with post-1980 regulated single payments. According to Hill and colleagues' research,

> many rather regret that they seem no longer able to plead 'hard cases' for the exercise of discretion. . . . Social workers may be able to return to the approach to work of this kind adopted before 1980, of seeking to secure help for their clients by persuading social security officers that they are deserving of the exercise of exceptional discretion in their favour. We would urge social workers to consider whether this may not be a retrogressive step. It is likely to involve the very uneven provision of help in a context in which they are likely to be drawn more and more into helping sort the 'deserving' from the 'undeserving poor'.
>
> (Hill, Iolan and Smith 1985: 26, 28)

The critical difference between discretion 1970s style and the present position is that claimants are now competing for a very limited pool of resources. As the ADSS warned, the cash limit would mean that 'we will literally be assisting one claimant/client to the potential detriment of another' (ADSS 1987). Those in favour of non-cooperation with the fund argue that in the face of a cash limit it is not possible to advocate without becoming involved in the prioritizing process. Determined advocacy on behalf of social work clients is tantamount to prioritizing them and there is a danger that if this is perceived as the route to help from the social fund, it will lead to mass clientization. Moreover, it could raise false hopes among claimant/clients when resources are finite and inadequate (see Kerney 1988: Oliver 1988).

These are clearly real dangers. In response Kent, former president of the ADSW, has argued that 'since those who are least articulate are often those in greatest need, our failure to advocate on their behalf would prevent the prioritising of applications but would allow that prioritisation to be done with those most in need at a disadvantage'. And he dismissed the argument that social workers would become engulfed with requests for help with the retort that this 'was tantamount to saying that if we provide a good service everyone will want to use it so we should not provide a good service' (Kent 1988).

There is also a longer-term strategic case for putting maximum pressure on the social fund budget, in particular the CCG budget, for 'if they don't, and if the fund is under used in this its first year, the budget will be in grave danger of being cut' (Barclay 1988). The government has stated that the first year's cash limit of £203m (of which only £60m is for CCGs) is provisional; only if maximum pressure is put on the budget during that first year is there any chance of it being increased. The very low level of expenditure on CCGs during the initial months of the fund's operation has raised fears that the budget could even be cut.

This means that, as 'determined advocates', social workers must not be influenced by the fact of a fixed budget; otherwise they will end up either prioritizing their clients and thereby acting as gatekeepers to the fund or in a state of paralysis. In the words of Burgess, who is not a supporter of determined advocacy, 'win the race you are in for each of your clients as is your duty and your instinct' (Burgess 1987).

As noted earlier, another source of dispute has been advocacy for loans. There will be occasions when a CCG has been refused or is precluded by the secretary of state's directions and where, having had the implications of the various alternative options explained, a claimant wishes to apply for a social fund loan. To refuse to support them would be inconsistent with the principle of claimant sovereignty – a variant of the traditional social work value of client self-determination – which 'makes it clear that it is for claimants to decide what their needs are, and for them to be responsible for the management of claims upon the social fund' (ACC/AMA 1988: para 46).

There are wider implications here for the way in which welfare rights work is practised. The practice guide emphasizes that 'determined advocacy does not mean taking over the client's claim, regardless of how strenuously it is pursued' (ACC/AMA 1988: para 49). The COSLA guidelines envisage clients normally negotiating with the DHSS on their own behalf according to the 'normal principles of self help' (COSLA 1988: para 3.3.5). One argument sometimes put against social workers' undertaking welfare rights work on behalf of their clients is that it could reinforce the latter's dependency. Cohen and Rushton, in their book on welfare rights and social work, addressed this issue, arguing that a radical perspective should encourage the social worker 'at least, to act jointly with the claimant, to avoid taking over from her, and look instead for ways of passing on information and expertise' (Cohen and Rushton 1982: 8). Similarly Fimister's assertion that claimants 'should have to put up neither with exclusion by an overbearing professional, nor with neglect of their case by a sanctimonious consciousness-raiser' (Fimister 1986: 22) is more pertinent than ever.

Working with claimant/clients to minimize the damage of the social fund and to press for its reform is consistent with notions of empowerment. Becker has argued that effective social work 'must allow and encourage a transfer of power, skills, resources, and knowledge, even in the confines of the casework relationship, and no matter how modest, between worker and client' (Becker 1988: 250). Going a step further, social services/work departments could encourage and facilitate community responses to the social fund such as the development of credit unions and develop the kind of political stance outlined below.

Conclusion

As the practice guide makes clear, determined advocacy is a damage limitation exercise, not a panacea. It is an attempt to adapt the best traditions of welfare advocacy to a scheme which denies claimants any rights. As such, it is inevitably imperfect and likely to give rise to problems and contradictions. The legitimacy and effectiveness of the strategy requires social services/work departments to accept three important responsibilities.

First, they must publicize the policies that they have adopted. The DHSS must know their position, as must local voluntary bodies, charities and, in so far as is possible, claimants themselves. Second, they must ensure that all relevant staff know and understand the policy. This means proper training not just about the social fund itself but also in determined advocacy. Social workers cannot be expected to tread the fine line between advocacy and assessment without such training. The likely expansion of debt work also has serious implications for training. Third, monitoring of the social fund's impact is essential. The purpose here is two-fold. Social services/work departments need to know the impact of the social fund on their own work and be able to assess quickly how determined advocacy is working in practice. Early indications suggest that determined advocacy is being interpreted to mean all things to all people and that many SSDs have successfully created barriers against the increased workloads they had anticipated. SSDs also have a wider responsibility to publicize the impact of the fund on their clients. In many cases, this will mean a review of the way in which cases are recorded, for at present it is often not possible even to say how many clients are social security claimants (see Becker and MacPherson 1988). While monitoring means more work, it is a way of addressing the sense of powerlessness experienced by many social workers in face of the social fund. If the findings are fed into the political process then, at least, those involved can feel that they are contributing to the policy process.

This raises wider questions about the 'political' role of social services/work departments and social workers and endorses the political role advocated within the Barclay Report (NISW 1982). The advent of the social fund brings a new urgency to this wider political task. There is a danger though that in defending the cash/care frontier against the expected fall-out from the social fund, social workers, already under pressure, will go further and distance themselves from the social fund's effects. If social workers and their managers are not to fail in their duty to speak out, they must be prepared to meet the challenge posed by the social fund and stand up for the claimants who turn to them for help.

References

ACC (1987) *The Social Fund Manual: Views of the Association of County Councils*, London: ACC.

ACC/AMA (1988) *Social Fund Position Statement and Practice Guide*, London: AMA/ACC.

ADSS (1987) *Response to Social Fund Manual*, London: ADSS.

Balloch, S and Jones, B. (1988) 'Social services responses to poverty', in S. Becker and S. MacPherson (eds) (1988) *Public Issues, Private Pain*, London: Insight.

Barclay, P. (1988) Speech to the Association of County Councils, reported in *Social Work Today*, 5 May: 6.

BASW Poverty Panel (1987) *Social Fund Guidelines*, Birmingham: BASW.

Becker, S. (1987) 'How much collaboration?', *Community Care*, 26 March: 23–4.

—— (1988) 'Poverty awareness', in S. Becker and S. MacPherson (eds) (1988) *Public Issues, Private Pain*, London: Insight.

Becker, S. and MacPherson, S. (1986) *Poor Clients*, Nottingham: University of Nottingham Press.

—— (eds) (1988) *Public Issues, Private Pain*, London: Insight.

Burgess, P. (1987) 'Strategies to fight the social fund', *Community Care*, 10 December: 12.

Cohen, R. and Rushton, A. (1982) *Welfare Rights*, London: Heinemann/*Community Care*.

COSLA (1987) *Responses to Social Fund Manual Consultation Paper*, London: COSLA.

—— (1988) *The Social Fund Position Statement and Practice Guide*, London: COSLA.

Davies, C. (1988) 'An unusual suggestion', *Community Care*, 28 April: 22–3.

Davies, C. and Lister, R. (1988) 'Conclusion: the disappearing safety net', in R. Cohen and M. Tarpey (eds) *Single Payments: The Disappearing Safety Net*, London: CPAG.

Dhooge, Y. and Popay, J. (1988) 'The social construction of unemployment: defining out a social work role?', in S. Becker and S. MacPherson (eds) (1988) *Public Issues, Private Pain*, London: Insight.

DHSS (1985) *Reform of Social Security, Programmes for Change*, vol. 2, Cmnd 9518, London: HMSO.

—— (1987) *Social Fund Manual*, London: HMSO.

Fimister, G. (1980) 'Frontier problems', in J. Cousins (ed) *Dear SSAC*, London: CPAG.

—— (1986) *Welfare Rights in Social Services*, London: Macmillan.

—— (1988) 'The organisation of welfare rights work in social services', in S. Becker and S. MacPherson (eds) (1988) *Public Issues, Private Pain*, London: Insight.

Griffiths, R. (1988) *Community Care: Agenda for Action*, Griffiths Report, London: HMSO.

Hill, M. and Laing, P. (1979) *Social Work and Money*, London: Allen & Unwin.

Hill, M., Iolan, F. and Smith, R. (1985) *The Relationship between Local Authority Social Services and Supplementary Benefit after the 1980 Supplementary Benefit Changes*, unpublished.

Home Office (1963) Circular 204, London: Home Office.

House of Commons Debates (1988a) *Hansard* Written Answers, 7 March, col 57.

—— (1988b) *Hansard* Written Answers, 9 March, col 244; 18 May, cols 497–8.

Jordan, B. (1974) *Poor Parents*, London: Routledge & Kegan Paul.

Kay, N. (1987) ADSS press release, 22 July.

Kent, R. (1988) Speech to ADSW conference, reported in *Social Work Today*, 28 April: 8.

Kerney, D. (1988) 'Determined advocacy or determined cooperation', *Social Work Today*, 25 February: 16–17.

Laming, H. (1988) 'Making the system work' *Social Work Today*, 14 January: 13.

Lister, R. and Emmett, T. (1976) *Under the Safety Net*, London: CPAG.

Long, M. (1988) Speech to Benefits Research Unit/Social Services Insight conference, University of Nottingham, 24 March.

NAPO (1988) *Social Fund Practice Guide*, London: NAPO.

NISW (National Institute of Social Work) (1982) *Social Workers: Their Roles and Tasks*, Barclay Report, London: Bedford Square Press.

Oliver, C. (1988) 'Forum', *Community Care*, 31 March: 16–17.

Scott, N. (1988) 'In Support of the Social Fund' *Community Care*, 7 April: 23–4.

Social Security Consortium (1988) *The Social Fund and Voluntary Organisations: How Will You Respond?*, London: NCVO.

Social Services Committee (1984) *Children in Care*, vol. 1, London: HMSO.

SSAC (1985a) *Fourth Annual Report*, London: HMSO.

—— (1985b) *The Supplementary Benefit (Single Payments) Amendment Regulations 1983* (SI 1983 no 1630) Cmnd 9468, London: HMSO.

—— (1987) *The Social Fund Manual*, London: SSAC.

Stevenson, O. (1986) Foreword to S. Becker and S. MacPherson (1986).

Stewart, G. and Stewart, J. (1986) *Boundary Changes*, London CPAG/BASW.

—— (1987a) 'Responsibility without power', *Community Care*, 19 March: 14–16.

—— (1987b) 'Getting ready for the Spirit of '88', *Social Services Insight*, 3 April: 21–3.

—— (1988) 'Shifting the safety net', in S. Becker and S MacPherson (eds) (1988) *Public Issues, Private Pain*, London: Insight.

Svenson, M and MacPherson, S. (1988) 'Real issues and unreal figures: the impact of the 1986 Social Security Act', in S. Becker and S. MacPherson (eds) (1988) *Public Issues, Private Pain*, London: Insight.

Tester, S. (1985) *Cash and Care*, London: Bedford Square Press/NCVO.

3
Social work in the
Third World:
crisis and response

James Midgley

Although the notion of crisis has now been somewhat overworked in the literature of social policy and social work, few would deny that social work in the Third World is facing a critical situation. From optimistic beginnings just three decades ago when statutory social work services were rapidly expanded and professional schools of social work were established throughout Africa, Asia, and Central and South America, problems of inadequate resource allocations, poor conditions of service, low status and morale have hampered the profession's effectiveness. In addition, concerns about the cultural relevance of social work concepts and theories, the appropriateness of social work's practice methods and the effectiveness of social work in dealing with the problems of Third World poverty have been expressed with growing frequency, causing doubts about the profession's proper role in the context of Third World development.

Although some critics have claimed that social work has little, if anything, to contribute to the developing countries, this argument has been challenged by Third World social workers. They have not only debated these concerns but also attempted to remedy the problems they face. By seeking to extricate themselves from a long-standing dependence on western ideas and prescriptions, and by modifying conventional approaches in an effort to enhance relevance and effectiveness, they have responded to the crisis.

Social workers in the West, who also face resource and morale difficulties, and who are increasingly questioning the profession's role and mission, can learn from the attempts of their colleagues in the developing countries to formulate innovative approaches that address the needs and circumstances of their societies. In a shrinking world, where local events often have global relevance, social workers from different societies can enter into a mutually supportive dialogue. The unilateral transfer of social work theories and practice methods from the industrial countries to the Third World (which long characterized professional exchanges) has now been challenged, and is being resisted. A greater receptivity to the experiences of Third World social workers can facilitate the profession's future growth and enhance its relevance to the social problems facing all contemporary societies.

The creation of Third World social work

Social work may be characterized as an institutionalized response to social problems which is dependent on professionally trained personnel who apply their knowledge and skills to deal with these problems (Butrym 1976). Social work's primary interventive method uses face-to-face encounters between professional workers and individuals (and their families) to address and, hopefully, remedy social problems at the level of personal experience. Social workers are also trained to work with small groups of people, either in therapeutic or task settings, and with local neighbourhoods and communities to enhance the quality of community life. These three activities, which are known respectively as casework, group work and community work, are the result of a historical process through which various interventive techniques coalesced into a coherent methodology and professional ethic.

Social work's early historical development is closely bound with the poor relief movement in nineteenth-century Europe and North America which sought to ameliorate the punitive implementation of the Victorian Poor Laws. By dispensing temporary relief to deserving cases, and assisting them to find alternative sources of income, it was believed that both the pauperization of the needy and the horror of the workhouse could be avoided. The deployment of predominantly middle-class women to investigate the circumstances of the poor and to devise strategies for their rehabilitation led to new career opportunities for women, who had long been denied entrance to the traditional, male-dominated professions. Their involvement also facilitated the emergence of professional education and, through the writings of Mary Richmond and others, to the formulation of principles and theories applicable to different fields of practice (Leiby 1978).

Although social work in the industrial countries emerged under similar historical circumstances and shared common features, the intellectual impetus for the development of social work as a profession came from the USA. Unlike many European countries, where social work training emerged as a vocational subject, often located at non-university institutions of further education, American proponents of social work lobbied successfully for the creation of university-based, graduate-level social work programmes (Austin 1986). By the 1930s autonomous graduate schools of social work had been established at many respected American universities and it was perhaps not surprising that, within this intellectual climate, American academics should have taken the initiative for the formulation of social work's knowledge base. American social work academics were the first to exploit the popularization of psychoanalysis and to incorporate psychodynamic theories into casework practice. They were also responsible for the fusion of casework with other interventive strategies, derived from the activities of the settlement house movement and the Charity Organization Society, to produce an unitary schema for professional practice. Their intellectual leadership was internationally recognized and by the 1950s, as American global influence increased, these ideas were exported not only to Europe but also to the newly independent Third World nations which had previously been under European colonial rule (Midgley 1981).

European imperialism had created a global system of dependence and interdependence in which trade, politics and social relationships were structured in terms of the needs and requirements of the centres of world power. The gradual emergence of nationalism, with its emotive populist appeal, led to bitter struggles for emancipation from foreign rule and the eventual emergence of newly sovereign nation states throughout Africa, Asia, and Central and South America. Globally the struggle for independence began in the Iberian colonies, many of which achieved self-determination in the early nineteenth century. As nationalist movements gained confidence and strength during the next century, European world domination was further undermined. Its final collapse was facilitated by the ignominious military defeats inflicted on the British, Dutch and French by the Japanese and Germans during the Second World War. With a growing climate of anti-imperialist opinion in the industrial countries, and increasing civil unrest and nationalist fervour in the colonies, sovereignty was assured. By the 1950s and 1960s as many more nations secured emancipation from European rule, the idea of the Third World gained currency (Midgley 1987).

The notion of the 'Third World' emerged partly in response to the derogatory characterization of the newly independent territories as 'backward' or 'underdeveloped'. The idea of a 'Third World' gave identity to these nations, and also reflected the growing unity of the formerly colonized societies since it differentiated them from the Western and Eastern power blocs, and gave common purpose to their struggles for independence and non-alignment (Worsley 1984). Today more than two-thirds of the world's nation states are loosely categorized by both social scientists and the popular media as forming the 'Third World'. Located primarily in Africa, Asia, and Central and South America, the countries of the Third World are characterized by diverse cultures, a predominantly traditional economy, rapid population growth, widespread poverty and deprivation, and a colonial history which, in spite of de-colonization, is subtly perpetuated through economic and political dependence.

Imperialism had fostered the replication of European institutions, including social service programmes, in many African, Asian, and Central and South American territories (Midgley 1981; MacPherson 1982). Although it can hardly be claimed that the provision of social services to the subjugated peoples of the colonies was a priority of the colonial governments, attempts were made to ameliorate the most glaring manifestations of need, usually in the cities where problems of juvenile delinquency, vagrancy, child neglect and begging had become more common and were regarded by European administrators and settlers alike as nuisances requiring urgent attention. Generally the type of welfare programmes introduced mirrored established practices in the different metropolitan societies. The Latin tradition of religious charity was perpetuated in the French and Iberian colonies where primary responsibility for the care of the needy was given to the church, often through formalized agreements and with the provision of state subsidies. In the British territories, on the other hand, the state intervened directly and usually its services were based on a poor law approach (Midgley 1984a): public residential facilities were used to incarcerate the needy and punitive measures, including deportation to the rural areas, imprisonment and even whippings were imposed. In addition, missionaries and voluntary organizations provided services to children and other needy groups. Generally, colonial welfare services were limited in scope, haphazardly implemented and poorly funded (Midgley 1984b). And, because of the extensive delegation of authority to colonial governors, the character of colonial welfare measures was dependent on the whim, interest or compassion of individual personalities (Hodge 1973).

In most developing countries, statutory social work services began to expand around the time of the Second World War. This was due both to domestic and exogenous developments. In many colonies it was gradually recognized that more determined efforts were required to deal with the problems of poverty and destitution that accompanied rapid urbanization and it was thought that social work would provide effective, scientific remedies. But developments in the metropolitan countries also facilitated that export of social work to the colonial territories. The expansion of social security and other social services created a new climate of opinion that legitimized state intervention in social affairs. This attitude filtered into colonial administration (which was, in any case, becoming more centralized and standardized) and, increasingly, colonial administrators were required, by the central governments, to establish social programmes that reflected domestic developments (Midgley 1984c). In the 1950s for example, the French introduced uniform social security schemes throughout their African territories, which were modelled directly on domestic legislation (Mouton 1975; Midgley 1984d). In the British empire in the 1920s, following growing concern about low educational standards among the native peoples of the colonies, state responsibility for education increased significantly and this was followed in the 1930s by attempts to expand social welfare and other social services (Mair 1944). These developments led to the creation of statutory agencies charged with the provision of social work services. Known usually as ministries or departments of social welfare, they catered for neglected children, handicapped people, young offenders, destitute elderly people and other conspicuously needy groups. With this expansion, the need for trained personnel who could staff the welfare services was more keenly felt (Hardiman and Midgley 1982).

The introduction of professional social work training programmes, initially by voluntary or religious organizations and subsequently by the international development agencies and local universities, responded to this need. Among the first Third World schools of social work were the Escuela de Trabajo Social, established in Santiago, Chile, by a private foundation in 1925 and the Tata Institute which was founded in 1936 in Bombay, India, with support from a wealthy local industrialist (Midgley 1981). Religious organizations were also active in establishing the first schools of social work in the Third World; in various countries Christian missionary groups have played a significant role in the introduction of social work education. By the 1950s and 1960s, however, governmental sponsorship became more common, often through the efforts of the United Nations and particularly UNICEF, which actively advocated the creation of professional social work training facilities in Third World countries. During this time, a variety of schools were established with support from these agencies, both as non-university institutions operated by the ministries of social welfare and as academic departments in local universities. In some cases universities took the initiative themselves, and conforming to academic trends in the industrial nations, established departments of social work that provided degree programmes in the field (Adler and Midgley 1978).

A major characteristic of the expansion of social work in the Third World in the 1950s and 1960s was the widespread adoption of American social work education and practice approaches (Midgley 1981). As was suggested earlier, American academic social workers provided much of the intellectual leadership for the emergence of social work as a profession and their influence was felt internationally. American social work educators played a leading role in the creation of the major international professional organizations; they were sought after as conference participants and academic visitors; and they were widely used as consultants to advise on the creation of educational programmes, as well as the provision of social work services. Similarly American schools of social work attracted students from all over the Third World and, in the absence of curricula designed to cater to their needs, Third World students were socialized into accepting the universality of American social work models. Nor was this regarded as problematic: the pervasive acceptance of modernization as an ideal, engendered the view that the adoption of western institutions was a prerequisite for industrial development. Social work was just one of the many technologies emanating from the West that was thought to be conducive to the efforts of Third World countries to attain modernity, progress and prosperity.

Problems of Third World social work

By the 1970s social work had been widely adopted in the Third World and it could be claimed, with justification, that the creation of social work had produced significant results. Social work services provided by governments and voluntary agencies had expanded, and had resulted in more extensive services for families, children, young offenders, physically handicapped people and other needy groups. The social work services were now more frequently administered by professionally trained social workers. With the growth of international educational opportunities, many had obtained qualifications from respected schools of social work in the USA and in other western countries. In addition, as more schools of social work in the Third World were established, more locally trained social workers became available to staff the social work services. The growth of social work education in the developing countries was indeed impressive. Statistics released by the International Association of Schools of Social Work in 1974 showed that, from small beginnings when the association's member schools were located almost exclusively in Europe and North America, membership had grown to include sixty-nine schools in Asia, twenty-five in Africa, sixty-nine in Central and South America and nine in the Middle East (Stickney and Resnick 1974). In addition, Third World social workers were finding employment with the international development agencies and more were playing leading roles in the international professional social work associations. Within a relatively short period of time, from before the Second World War when social work was almost unknown in the Third World, to the mid-1970s when educational and career opportunities for Third World social workers had multiplied, social work had clearly established itself.

While the international social work profession could take pride in the expansion and institutionalization of social work in the countries of Africa, Asia and Central and South America, there was, by the 1970s, a growing debate about social work's proper role in the context of Third World development. There was concern about the cultural appropriateness of theories and practice models which had been imported from the industrial countries; questions about social work's effectiveness in dealing with the problems of mass poverty and deprivation; criticism of social work's apparent lack of relevance to the overriding task of promoting economic and social development, and a growing disillusionment about the way Third World political leaders, civil servants and other professionals appeared to disregard the profession of social work and to neglect the social work services.

In spite of declaring a commitment to provide welfare for all, Third World political leaders have not adequately supported the social work services which, in many countries, have remained limited in scope, poorly funded and excessively concentrated on conspicuous problems of social neglect in urban areas. While social service expenditures increased rapidly in many developing countries during the 1960s and 1970s, resource allocations for ministries of social welfare were small and in some cases even declined. This greatly hampered the effective delivery of services and prevented social workers from making an effective impact. Accounts of the frustrations of social workers in countries such as Ghana (Midgley 1981) and Kenya (Weisner 1972) are indicative of these resource problems which have, as a result of growing Third World indebtedness, poor economic performance and massive public expenditure cuts, become even more severe.

The resource problem was exacerbated by a disdainful attitude towards social work by local political and administrative elites who often had a simplistic understanding of the profession's role, believing social workers to be primarily concerned with 'criminals', 'dropouts' and 'misfits' and, therefore, marginal to the developmental needs of Third World countries. As in the industrial countries, the predominance of women in the profession reinforced the stereotype of social work as an essentially altruistic activity which had little, if any, contribution to make to the task of promoting industrialization and rapid economic growth (Livingston 1969). This attitude exacerbated the limited resource allocations, low status and poor conditions of service which characterized statutory social work practice in many developing countries. In spite of the institutionalization of social work in the Third World, these attitudes have become even more prevalent as development theories based on New Right ideologies have become popular. Technocratically inclined ad-ministrators and economic planners, many of whom have been trained in the West, see little need for the social services and even regard social work as inimical to development. This has compounded the problems facing many social workers and contributed further to their comparatively low status in the governmental hierarchy, where the great majority of Third World social workers are employed.

The problems facing Third World social work cannot, however, be attributed only to low resource allocations and the antipathy of local elites. Indeed, as some have realized, these problems are also a consequence of the profession's dependence on alien educational and practice conceptions that are incompatible with the indigenous circumstances of Third World societies. Since the 1970s many more critical accounts of social work's cultural and development relevance have been published, and there is today a greater recognition that steps need to be taken to modify the profession's established approach so that both issues can be properly addressed.

With regard to the problem of cultural appropriateness, it was generally held by western social workers that modern social work is a universally relevant approach to social problems, based on principles and methods which are applicable to all societies (Aptekar 1965). This view was shared by many Third World social work academics who sought, in numerous publications, to draw analogies between indigenous religious or cultural beliefs and western social work. Writers from countries as diverse as Japan (Hasegawa 1974), Pakistan (Rashid 1967) and India (Muzumdar 1964) argued that Buddhism, Islam and the philosophy of Gandhi are highly compatible with western social work, and that this legitimizes the transfer of western social work principles, theories and interventive strategies to the Third World. Another argument, which has been referred to previously, justifies the cross-cultural transfer of social work on the ground that the accelerated modernization of the developing countries requires the adoption of institutions from societies that have already attained industrial development and economic prosperity.

Both arguments are questionable and have now been refuted. It has been recognized that the concept of modernization is little more than a euphemism for westernization and today, as many more Third World societies reassert confidence in their own cultures, the search for indigenous forms of social work intervention has gathered pace. This has been facilitated also by the publication of more critical reviews of the problems of applying western casework theories and practice models to culturally different societies. Almanzor (1967), Nagpaul (1972) and Huang (1978) are just some of the scholars who have castigated the notion of the cultural universality of social work, arguing persuasively that commonly accepted assumptions in social work are culturally biased and inapplicable to Third World societies.

With regard to the problem of developmental relevance, many Third World social workers have recognized that the profession's therapeutic, individualized approach has little scope for contributing to the amelioration of the problems of hunger, illiteracy, disease, squalor, exploitation, inequality and deprivation which accompany mass poverty in the developing countries (Khinduka 1971). However, this view has not been universally shared. While some have argued that society's problems can be dealt with effectively only if they are treated at the level of individual experience (Gore 1967), others have claimed that it is not social work's primary purpose to remedy the problems of economic and social underdevelopment. The profession's expertise, they claim, lies not in economic planning but in responding to individual need. While this response is commendably realistic, it is an argument which is likely to exacerbate the profession's low status, inadequate resource allocations and perceived irrelevance to the local needs and circumstances of Third World countries.

Although many of the problems facing the Third World social workers are unique to their economic, social and cultural circumstances, some of the difficulties encountered have been experienced in the industrial countries as well. Concerns about resource constraints, low status, the efficacy of social work intervention and the appropriateness of social work's conventional methodologies, have been expressed everywhere (Brewer and Lait 1980; National Institute for Social Work 1982; Walton 1982). Studies of the efficacy of social work intervention have not always produced encouraging results and while the issue remains controversial, there is a need to reassess social work's interventive method (Fischer 1976; Rees and Wallace 1982). There is controversy also about the relevance of individualized treatment approaches to the problems facing many of the profession's clients, particularly those living in poverty in depressed inner-city areas whose needs are material rather than emotional. Radical social work has offered a scathing critique of the relevance of the profession's traditional remedial approach and has focused on its ideological proclivity to support the maintenance of the status quo (Bailey and Brake 1975; Corrigan and Leonard 1978; Parry *et al.* 1979). As these issues have been more widely debated, Third World social workers have found that many of their problems are not isolated from those facing the profession as a whole.

By the 1980s the optimism which had accompanied social work's expansion in the Third World had waned. Critical accounts of the failures of social work to contribute effectively to the task of development, and of the cultural incompatibility of western theories and techniques, were published with increasing frequency. Faced with cuts in resources, poor conditions of service and low status, the morale of many Third World social workers declined.

Critical assessments of social work as an institution by both radical social workers on the left, and by New Right thinkers who scorned the profession's attempts to deal with the problems of social need, contributed further to a growing sense of disillusionment. The notion that social work would draw on its historical roots and respond effectively to the problems of poverty and deprivation facing millions of people throughout the Third World now seemed remote. From its confident and expectant beginnings, social work in the Third World was plunged into a crisis demanding urgent changes and innovative responses.

Responding to the crisis: enhancing relevance and efficacy

While social workers in the Third World continue to face critical problems, they have attempted to address the causes of the current crisis and to find ways of enhancing the profession's relevance and effectiveness. These attempts have been accompanied by a greater awareness of social work's deficiencies and a willingness to search for solutions. This was not always the case. Like their counterparts in the industrial countries, many Third World social workers were reluctant to examine their profession and its conventional approach to human need critically. The radical critique, as well as studies that questioned widely held assumptions in the profession, were not always welcomed. Today, however, there is a greater willingness to examine and debate problematic issues of social work in the Third World. This attitude is a result not only of a greater responsiveness to criticism, but also of a growing sense of cultural and national identity in many developing countries which is fostering greater independence among social workers and the indigenization of social work approaches.

There has been considerable progress in identifying new forms of intervention which address conventional practice problems in innovative ways. While some writers have argued that social work can best enhance its relevance to the needs and circumstances of the developing countries by engaging in population control, agricultural development, and development planning (Dasgupta 1968; Kendall 1971; Hokenstadt 1973) these activities bear little relevance either to social work's historical mission or to its available expertise. And, since these services are already dominated by other professionals, attempts by social workers to claim them as their own are likely to be opposed. Nor does it make sense for social workers to abandon their conventional commitment to working with needy children, old people or handicapped people who have long been within the profession's established expertise. The crisis of appropriateness can best be met by remedying existing practice approaches that have little relevance to the needs or circumstances of Third World nations. As Midgley (1978: 188) argued, social work's traditional responsibilities should not be abandoned but redirected.

As this argument has gained currency, attempts have been made to identify new forms of remedial intervention that respond to the needs of neglected children, dependent elderly people, physically handicapped people and other needy groups. In many countries social work has relied extensively on residential services which are often dilapidated, poorly run and custodial in character. In several countries innovative, community-based services have been developed which provide remedial services in ways that are more relevant to the economic and social conditions facing Third World countries. Midgley (1984b; 1986) has provided examples of the use of these innovative approaches from countries as disparate as Cyprus, Jamaica, Malaysia and the Philippines. In these countries social work policy-makers and service adminis-trators have provided financial resources, community-based social work assistance and co-operative endeavour to facilitate the reintegration of needy groups into the local community. The creation of co-operatives for physically handicapped people in Cyprus; the provision of domicilliary services to families with mentally handicapped children in Jamaica; training and state support for needy people, including those handicapped, to establish their own small businesses in Malaysia; and the community outreach programme to blind people in the Philippines, are just some examples of innovative and appropriate forms of remedial social work that have been adopted in the developing world.

But the need for social work programmes that transcend a remedial focus remains paramount if the crisis of social work's appropriateness and effectiveness in the Third World is to be resolved. In this regard also, there is scope for optimism as social workers in several developing countries have identified forms of intervention that contribute positively to national develop-ment. Unlike the unrealistic desire to assume new roles that bear no relation to social work's historical role in society, these activities draw on the profession's existing expertise and resources. One example of the developmental approach in Third World social work is the extensive involvement of Indian social workers in community-based child and family services. Transcending tradi-tional child welfare models of practice which focused on residential care, foster placements, adoption and the treatment of problems through casework methods, the Indian approach seeks to prevent child need and facilitate the involvement of local people in the promotion of child development. And faced with desperate conditions of poverty, special attention has been focused on nutrition and health care services to combat the appallingly high incidence of infant and child mortality that occurs not only in India but also in many other Third World countries. The central point for service delivery is a local day-care centre which is established in co-operation with the local community. Staffed by local volunteers, who are supported by nutritional, medical and educational personnel, these centres also provide health services, maternal care, literacy classes and many other activities. Social workers are usually in administrative control using their training in community work as well as other professional skills to mobilize support, co-ordinate activities and respond to family problems and needs as they arise (India, Ministry of Social Welfare 1980; Midgley 1984b).

There have also been gradual changes in the curricula offered at schools of social work in the Third World and in the use of literature and teaching materials. As the awareness of the excessive dependence on western approaches has become more acute, many schools of social work have sought to modify their educational programmes, and increasingly courses of greater local relevance have been introduced. In this regard, Third World schools of social work have been attuned to issues of cultural diversity and many offer courses which enhance an awareness as well as an understanding of the significance of cultural, ethnic and racial issues among students.

It cannot be claimed that social workers in the Third World have solved their problems; indeed many would agree that, because of the desperate conditions of economic stagnation, indebtedness, militarization and political and civil conflict facing the Third World, the crisis is still of immense and apparently intractable proportions. But the initial efforts that have been made to address the crisis are encouraging. Third World social workers have begun to focus on social problems that require urgent attention, and to experiment with innovative interventive methods; they have also made considerable progress in using community and other programmes that are compatible with Third World conditions. Given the problems of economic stagnation, rising poverty associated with de-industrialization, ethnic conflict, and controversies about the value of conventional social work approaches in the industrial countries, Third World social workers may be in a position to help their counterparts in the West identify and test innovative practice methods that respond effectively to these problems. Indeed it is not inconceivable that the unidirectional transfer of ideas which characterized social work's export from the West to the Third World in the 1950s and 1960s will be reversed.

References

Adler, Z. and Midgley, J. (1978) 'Social work education in developing countries', *Social Work Today*, 9: 16–17.

Almanzor, A. (1967) 'The profession of social work in the Philippines', in Council on Social Work Education, *An Intercultural Exploration: Universals and Differentials in Social Work Values, Functions and Practice*, New York: Council on Social Work Education.

Aptekar, H. (1965) 'Social work in cross-cultural perspective' in S. Khinduka (ed.) *Social Work in India*, Allahabad: Kitab Mahal.

Austin, D. (1986) *A History of Social Work Education*, Austin: School of Social Work.

Bailey, R. and Brake, M. (eds) (1975) *Radical Social Work*, London: Arnold.

Brewer, C. and Lait, J. (1980) *Can Social Work Survive?*, London: Temple Smith.

Butrym, Z. (1976) *The Nature of Social Work*, London: Macmillan.

Corrigan, P. and Leonard, P. (1978) *Social Work under Capitalism*, London: Macmillan.

Dasgupta, S. (1968) *Social Work and Social Change*, Boston, Mass: Porter Sargent.

Fischer, J. (1976) *The Effectiveness of Social Casework*, Springfield, Ill: Thomas.

Gore, M. (1967) 'The cultural perspective of social work in India', in Council on Social Work Education, *An Intercultural Exploration: Universals and Differentials in Social Work Values, Functions and Practice*, New York: Council on Social Work Education.

Hardiman, M. and Midgley, J. (1982) *The Social Dimensions of Development: Social Policy and Planning in the Third World*, Chichester: Wiley.

Hasegawa, H. (1974) 'Zen and social work', *Social Work and Development Newsletter*, 74: 12–13.

Hodge, P. (1973) 'Social policy: an historical perspective as seen in colonial policy', *Journal of Oriental Studies*, 11: 207–19.

Hokenstadt, M. (1973) 'Preparation for social development: issues in training for policy and planning positions', *International Social Work*, 18: 2–9.

Huang, K. (1978) 'Matching needs with services: shoes for Chinese feet', *International Social Work*, 21: 44–54.

India, Ministry of Social Welfare (1980) *Integrated Child Development Services Scheme*, New Delhi.

Leiby, J. (1978) *A History of Social Welfare and Social Work in the United States*, New York: Columbia University Press.

Livingston, A. (1969) *Social Policy in Developing Countries*, London: Routledge & Kegan Paul.

Kendall, K. (1971) (ed.) *Population Planning and Family Dynamics: A New Responsibility for Social Work*, New York: Council on Social Work Education.

Khinduka, S. (1971) 'Social work in the Third World', *Social Service Review*, 45: 62–73.

MacPherson, S. (1982) *Social Policy in the Third World*, Brighton: Harvester.

Mair, L. (1944) *Welfare in the British Colonies*, London: Royal Institute for Public Affairs.

Midgley, J. (1978) 'Developmental roles for social work in the Third World: the prospect of social planning', *Journal of Social Policy*, 7: 173–88.

—— (1981) *Professional Imperialism: Social Work in the Third World*, London: Heinemann.

—— (1984a) *Social Security, Inequality and the Third World*, Chichester: Wiley.

—— (1984b) 'Social work services in the Third World: towards the integration of remedial and developmental orientations', *Social Development Issues*, 8: 89–104.

—— (1984c) 'Poor Law principles and social assistance in the Third World: a study of the perpetuation of colonial welfare', *International Social Work*, 27: 2–12.

—— (1984d) 'Diffusion and the development of social policy: evidence from the Third World', *Journal of Social Policy*, 13: 167–84.

—— (1987) 'The Third World nations: insights into the colonial past and present contexts of development', *International Journal of Contemporary Sociology*, 24: 11–19.

Midgley, J., Hall, A., Hardiman, M. and Narine, D. (1986) *Community Participation, Social Development and the State*, London: Methuen.

Mouton, P. (1975) *Social Security in Africa*, Geneva: International Labour Organization.

Muzumdar, A. (1964) *Social Welfare in India: Mahatma Gandhi's Contribution*, London: Asia Publishing House.

Nagpaul, H. (1972) 'The diffusion of American social work education to India', *International Social Work*, 15: 3–17.

National Institute for Social Work (1982) *Social Workers: Their Roles and Tasks*, Barclay Report, London: Bedford Square Press.

Parry, N., Rustin, M. and Satyamurti, C. (1979) *Social Work, Welfare and the State*, London: Arnold.

Rashid, R. (1967) 'Social work practice in Pakistan', in Council on Social Work Education, *An Intercultural Exploration: Universals and Differentials in Social Work Values, Functions and Practice*, New York: Council on Social Work Education.

Rees, S. and Wallace, A. (1982) *Verdicts on Social Work*, London: Arnold.

Stickney, P. and Resnick, R. (1974) *World Guide to Social Work Education*, New York: International Association of Schools of Social Work.

Walton, R. (1982) *Social Work 2000*, London: Longman.

Weisner, S. (1972) *Professional Social Work in Kenya*, Lower Kabete: Kenya Institute of Administration.

Worsley, P. (1984) *The Three Worlds*, London: Weidenfeld & Nicolson.

4
A bull market for prisons?

Stephen Shaw

Asked to picture the typical prison, I suppose most people would bring to mind some grim, Victorian inner-city pile; decrepit, unhygienic and overcrowded; a 'human warehouse' or 'penal dustbin'; a prison like Armley in Leeds, Walton in Liverpool, or Strangeways in Manchester.

Or like Wandsworth in London:

> These are some of the features and risks of a lack of lavatories and washing facilities when men are locked up for 23 hours a day and not let out of cells to use wing facilities during the night. Defecation in the cell bucket, quite apart from degradation for the individual, obviously creates appalling conditions afterwards. Prisoners take avoidance action. Waste products are wrapped in paper and thrown out of the window. At Wandsworth these parcels are collected up and placed in double thickness plastic bags to be taken away by the local authority in a special skip about once a fortnight. Although every effort is taken to see the bags are sealed, there is a large pigeon population which could not only contaminate the kitchen and other parts of the prison but local residents could also be at risk. In order to solve the 'parcels' problem the fixing of wire meshes over cell windows has commenced. This of course makes things worse for the prisoners.
>
> (Wandsworth Board of Visitors 1987: 17)

Prisons in which, as the House of Commons Social Services Committee (1986: 18) has recorded, 'inmates are being kept in conditions which would not be tolerated for animals'.

However, a less familiar — but no less representative — portrait of a prison would perhaps be an ex-RAF camp with 14-year-old boys marching up and down to the paramilitary tattoo of the short, sharp shock. Or the seemingly benign red brick of the new women's prison at Holloway which, from the outside, looks deceptively like a hospital or a modern housing estate. Or the bleak, explosive-proof walls of a top-security dispersal prison, topped with wires to foul the blades of helicopters, and set incongruously amongst the rural charms of North Yorkshire or the Vale of Evesham.

While some prisons would be immediately recognizable today to the prisoners who first lodged within them 125 years ago or more, the system as a whole is one of great variety in design, regime and purpose (Stern 1987). To talk of prisons means both converted castles and country houses, hi-tech security and open prisons with roads through the middle, 'model' gaols from the nineteenth century and requisitioned army camps. Similarly to talk of prisoners is to encompass both wealthy City fraudsters and indigent fine defaulters; mothers with their babies and men who have committed grave crimes against children; Rastafarians and skinheads; people serving a few days and those who may never be released; red-bands or 'trusties' serving tea to the governor and people with severe mental illness lying naked in strip cells.

The dominant characteristic of this system – if system is the right word to describe this great variety of institutions and people within them – is expansion. Indeed the number of gaols is now growing at a faster rate than any time since the 1850s. The present government's building programme includes twenty-six new gaols, most of which will open in the early 1990s, at a cost approaching £1 billion. So-called 'redevelopment' of existing prisons will also result in much additional accommodation, for example the renovation work at Leeds will virtually double the size of the gaol and will cost as much as an entirely new institution (Shaw 1987a). Capital spending on the prisons has increased fivefold since the Conservatives came to power in 1979. Considerably more new prison officers are to be recruited than there are existing numbers of qualified probation staff.

Although the prison-building programme has already been beset by scandal and controversy – delays, cost-overruns, the absence of strategic planning, the use of obsolete and staff-intensive designs (National Audit Office 1985) – by the mid-1990s or thereabouts an extra 20,000 places will have been provided. Equally, and on the Home Office's own projections, there will be at least an extra 12,000–15,000 prisoners to fill these places. From its present level of just over 50,000, the prison population in England and Wales is expected to reach between 63,000 and 69,000 by 1996 (Home Office 1988a). Already the United Kingdom imprisons a higher proportion of its people than any other Common Market country and is vying with Austria and Turkey to become the most punitive nation in Europe. On present plans, by the end of the century we will be beginning to challenge the market leaders in incarceration in the industrialized world: the USA and the Soviet Union.

Characteristics of the prison population

What sort of prisoners will these be? One important change will be that, on present trends, the prison population will include some 5,000 life-sentence prisoners, over double the number today. The proportion of prisoners on remand awaiting trial or sentence (currently over one-fifth) is also expected to grow rapidly. However, for the most part the prison population will be made up much as it is now. Although, as we have already seen, prisoners do not form a single homogeneous grouping, certain broad generalizations can be drawn. Most of our prisoners are, and will remain, young male, white and working class; while the proportion convicted of crimes of violence is increasing, the majority have, and will have, been convicted of offences against property – burglary, fraud or forgery, and theft.

In the 1960s it was optimistically predicted that women's imprisonment would gradually disappear. In fact, the new Holloway was designed to look like a hospital exactly because it was expected to become redundant as a prison and then be converted for use by the NHS. What in practice has happened is that the number of women prisoners has grown more or less in line with the increase amongst men, remaining at about 3 per cent of the total.

Their minority status results in many women prisoners' being detained 100 miles or more from friends and family. That – and the fact that over half the women sent to prison have dependent children – is perhaps one reason why imprisonment appears to have a more destructive impact on women than it does upon men. Compared to male prisoners, women are twice as likely to be punished under the prison disciplinary system (Padel and Stevenson 1988) and the prescription of psychotropic drugs is high, albeit diminishing. Women prisoners are also more likely to be first offenders or to be held on remand. Although there are some differences in the pattern of offending between men and women which have to be taken into account, the fact that so few women prisoners have long histories of offending is indicative of sexually discriminatory sentencing practices.

Black people are hugely overrepresented in the prison population. Statistics released by the Home Office have shown that about 9 per cent of male prisoners and 17 per cent of female prisoners are of West Indian or African origin whereas they comprise less than 2 per cent of the population at large (Home Office 1988b). Compared with white defendants, black people are more likely to be remanded in custody while awaiting trial. If convicted, they receive longer prison sentences despite having on average fewer previous convictions. Within the prison system, racially discriminatory treatment of black prisoners remains routine, although it is right to say that at a formal level the Prison Department has taken racism more seriously than most public bodies, let alone most private companies. However, this formal disapproval of racism has not prevented, for example, black people being detained in general under higher conditions of security than white prisoners.

Ethnic monitoring within the prison system has been hampered in the past by a lack of co-operation from staff. However, statistics are now being generated in many institutions to ensure fairness in the allocation of work, education and the operation of prison discipline. But for the last twenty years there has been no detailed study of the demographic and socio-economic status of prisoners as a whole. For example nobody knows how many prisoners have dependent children, or are homeless, unemployed or have reading difficulties.

The development of services for prisoners – whether in gaol or on release – is accordingly hindered not only by the lack of time and resources and the competing demands of 'security' and 'control', but also by the fact that we have only a most approximate understanding of what those services should be.

We do of course know that most prisoners leave prison less able to cope in the outside world than when they entered. But to suggest – as official Home Office policy now does – that the purpose of prison is to give prisoners every opportunity to prepare effectively for their eventual release, both encompasses an apparent paradox and requires a far more rigorous and comprehensive assessment of prisoners' needs than currently exists.

A further contradiction arises from the operation of the parole system. Those prisoners who are granted parole (and who necessarily are judged to have the highest chance of making a go of things on release) receive statutory supervision from a probation officer as a requirement of their parole licence. In contrast, those prisoners turned down for parole (often because they have no home or other ties in the community) have been left to fend for themselves since voluntary after-care has been more or less abolished following implementation of the government's 1984 Statement of National Objectives and Priorities for the Probation Service.

However, it would be wrong to suppose that the comprehensive development of through-care services would increase the usefulness of the prison as an institution. Research study after research study (albeit not all of them very sophisticated) have shown that no custodial regime can demonstrate greater effectiveness as an instrument for individual reform than any other (Brody 1976). The deterrent and containment effects of incarceration are equally weak. Prisons exist as a symbol; in so far as they have any practical effect it is as part of the crime problem not as part of the solution. Through-care services can hope only to mitigate the damage to individual's lives and relationships which prison causes.

Reducing the prison population is sometimes presented as a matter of diverting from custody particular groups of prisoner; fine and maintenance defaulters, schoolchildren, pregnant women and those with small babies, mentally ill people, people with drink problems, and so on. Needless to say, such a process of diversion is wholly desirable (the cynical disregard of the plight of mentally disordered prisoners by successive administrations is nothing short of institutional cruelty). But it must also be accepted that it would not substantially affect the total number of people in prison at any one time.

To achieve that end, deep cuts are required across the board. In other words, reducing sentence lengths across a range of property crimes, notably burglary. Prison as a scarce, expensive and ultimately rather futile resource would be confined to serious violent offenders for whom the protection of the public is the paramount consideration.

Such a strategy of deep cuts does not necessarily rely upon the development of new 'alternatives to custody' in the community. The prison population is of course a simple function of throughput and the average length of sentences, and it is in the latter regard that the UK is most out-of-line with European norms. Indeed in recent years the proliferation of new 'alternatives' has been increasingly questioned by the probation service and by the penal reform lobby. It is all too easily forgotten that we already possess more 'alternatives' than most countries; all they seem to achieve is a confusion of an already complex sentencing structure. Reducing maximum sentences and establishing sentencing guidelines – perhaps through a national Sentencing Council (Ashworth 1983) – stand a better chance of success exactly because they restrict, not expand, the boundaries of judicial discretion.

Nevertheless, in the pursuit of 'alternatives' which will be acceptable to the courts, the government's 'Punishment in the Community' package (Patten 1988) will pose serious questions about the pattern and purpose of those non-custodial alternatives provided by probation and social services departments. Techniques of electronic tagging, the introduction of positive and negative requirements into probation orders, tracking, curfews, 'tough' community service, are all indications of the pressures on the non-custodial sector to take on a more openly controlling and less welfare-oriented approach.

Just as we know relatively little about prisoners' socio-economic status and needs, so it is difficult to provide an objective assessment of the quality of prison life. Certainly overcrowding has worsened and most authorities hold that regimes have also deteriorated. One of the few output measures which is available – the number of hours worked in prison workshops – shows a fall of over 60 per cent in the last decade. On the other hand, new working arrangements for prison staff introduced in 1987 and 1988 under the title 'Fresh Start' do seem to have led to a marginal improvement in prisoners' access to education.

The other feature of life inside which would also be generally accepted is that the prisons are becoming increasingly subject to outbreaks of riot, violence and disruption. The official report into the riots of 1986 – the worst ever series of prison disturbances in our history – directly linked this disorder to declining regimes and conditions (Chief Inspector of Prisons 1987). The major troubles at Bedford Prison in early 1988 were similarly prompted by the withdrawal of remand prisoners' entitlements to have their own food provided by relatives.

Most of the long-term gaols in England and Scotland have experienced serious prisoner disturbances in the last twenty years. In Scotland this remains the general pattern, with the most violent incidents taking place in Peterhead, Shotts, Glenochil and Perth, although there has also been recent unrest amongst remand prisoners in Barlinnie and Longrigged. However, riots in English prisons are no longer confined to high-security institutions. Lindholme (twice), Haverigg, Ashwell, Alma Dettingen and Rollerstone – which were the scene of some of the worst rioting in 1988 – are actually low-security establishments, the latter two being military camps converted for use as emergency overflow prisons.

While war may have been the main engine of social change in the twentieth century, prisoner disturbances have not so far proved to be turning-points in penal policy. The emphasis in the prisons upon security tasks to the detriment of regimes may be a reflection of the fact that escapes are more politically embarrassing to Home Secretaries than riots.

Juveniles

There is just one sector of the prison estate – the detention centre system for juveniles (14–16) and young adults (17–20) – which has not shared in the general current of expansionism. Paradoxically this is the sector upon which the government placed most emphasis in its law and order campaign.

The history of the detention centre is frankly a bizarre one. Introduced under the 1948 Criminal Justice Act (as a *quid pro quo*) for the abolition of the birch, the first detention centre did not open its gates until 1952. Ten years and several more all-male establishments later, a detention centre for girls was opened, only to be closed after less than seven years. This coincided with the passage of the Children and Young Persons Act 1969 which envisaged the phasing out of all custody for those under the age of 17. However, that Act was subject to a highly effective campaign of judicial and political opposition (Bottoms 1974) and key sections were not implemented. Instead, the numbers of juvenile and young adult males given detention centre orders rose quickly year-by-year into the 1980s.

By this time, a new Conservative government had been elected on a law-and-order platform which placed special emphasis upon a disciplined, paramilitary 'short, sharp shock' regime for young delinquents. Promoted in suitably bombastic terms by Home Secretary William Whitelaw, himself an ex-Guardsman ('brisk tempo . . . hard and constructive . . . respect for authority . . . drill, parades and inspections'), the shock treatment was initially introduced as an experiment at four detention centres.

However, this innovation had two wholly unexpected results. First, although the regime had no effect on reconviction rates, it turned out that many of the boys did not find the regime particularly shocking. Indeed they actually enjoyed the emphasis upon drill and physical fitness (Home Office 1984a). It made the time go by quickly and physical fitness and macho strutting were virtues which they already valued. Second – and even less predictably – the courts responded to the crude psychology of the short, sharp shock by electing massively either for non-custodial Intermediate Treatment programmes or for the longer, and allegedly more 'positive', sentence of youth custody training.

In contrast to the overcrowding in much of the rest of the system, many detention centres have been operating at only half-capacity. To its considerable embarrassment, the government has been forced to close many of its short, sharp shock institutions and convert them for other purposes. Of the original four experimental centres, two are now prisons for adult men and one is a remand centre for adult women.

The failure of the detention centre regime, and the waste of financial resources which the remaining centres represented, led the government to introduce in the Criminal Justice Act 1988 a new generic sentence of detention in a young offender institution to replace the two-tier system of detention centres and youth custody centres. However, forecasts that this presaged the end of the short-sharp-shock tactics have been misplaced. Although formal drill sessions have been dropped for some years, the government has made clear that those sentenced to shorter terms of the new generic sentence will continue to face the shock regime, while those with longer sentences will serve them in institutions based on existing youth custody centres.

In other words, there is little which is new or generic about the sentence of detention in a young offender institution. The changes will allow the government to make 'better' use of its available accommodation by resolving the twin problems of half-empty detention centres and overcrowded youth custody centres. It will also mean that the Home Office – and not the courts – will determine the regime under which a male juvenile or young offender will serve his punishment. It remains to be seen if this old wine in new bottles approach will have the effect of reversing the decline in juvenile custody which has occurred during the 1980s.

Prisoners' rights

In general, British prisoners have few rights – merely privileges which can be withheld at the discretion, or whim, of management. Thus the special privileges hitherto enjoyed by remand prisoners as a reflection of the principle that people are innocent until proven guilty have been systematically curtailed in recent years in order to cut costs. By contrast, privileges for sentenced prisoners are being gradually enhanced as an incentive to good behaviour (Home Office 1984b).

Some protection has come from the courts, both at home and in Strasbourg, the judges having dropped the traditional 'hands off' attitude to prison matters (Plotnikoff 1986). This has been particularly true in the area of correspondence, the censorship rules having been found to breach the European Convention on Human Rights. But there is nowhere to which prisoners may turn for a statement of their entitlements or the quality of life to which they should aspire.

The establishment of such a code of minimum standards (Casale 1984) now unites prison staff, the Opposition political parties and the whole penal lobby. It is opposed by the government – no doubt fearful of the cost implications – which has reneged on a promise to Parliament to issue a draft code of standards for discussion.

Government has also rejected proposals to extend prisoners' rights in other areas. For example, it has turned down plans for a fairer system of prison discipline, having first expended £250,000 on a committee of inquiry which so recommended (Home Office 1985). The Home Office is also known to be unhappy with a proposal from the Chief Inspector of Prisons for the establishment of a Prisons Ombudsman. Decisions on such critical aspects of prison life as categorization, allocation and segregation are subject to few effective safeguards or due process provisions. The 35-year-old Prison Act imposes few requirements upon prison management while most of the Standing Orders and Circular Instructions which actually contain the relevant information remain classified documents.

In 1983, in calling for a new Prison Regimes Act, the House of Commons Education, Science and Arts Committee (1983: xxx) noted with no little understatement 'that the present Prison Rules have not been found to be sufficiently forceful in their impact on prison regimes'. While rejecting the proposal for new primary legislation, the government admitted in its response that many of the Prison Rules were in need of revision. It will come as little surprise to learn that five years later not one of the Rules encompassed by the Education Committee Report has yet been updated.

The prisons are of course not alone in failing to respect the rights of those in their care (how many rights do probation clients enjoy, for example?) Yet because of their wholly dependent status, prisoners should actually enjoy new rights and protections (Richardson 1985). Moreover, as the American Federal prison authorities have appreciated, there are strong practical reasons for adopting a rights approach to prison management. It cannot of course be pretended that a prison system which did practise freedom of information and demonstrated respect for the rights of its charges would necessarily be any more successful in terms of reconviction rates. But what can be claimed is that prison conditions and regimes are likely to be improved only when prisoners have a legally enforcible right to a certain minimum standard of life. Furthermore, a safer and more peaceful prison system is one in which prisoners are guaranteed entitlements and the inevitable grievances which arise are properly and independently investigated.

Perhaps the area of prison life where standards are most at variance with those in the community at large is that of medical provision. Prisoners have no choice of doctor, are denied proprietary medicines, and receive treatment not from the NHS but from the Home Office's own doctors organized through the Prison Medical Service (Smith 1984). Crown Immunity has not been lifted from the prisons, which means that local authority environmental health officers have no powers of access or inspection.

It is for all these reasons that despite the fact that the prison population consists in the main of young men – the group who make least demands on the NHS in the community – an astonishing one prisoner in every ten asks to see the doctor every day.

The prison health issue which is currently receiving most attention is the incidence of HIV-infection. Although in April 1988 there were only fifty-three prisoners i the system who were known to be HIV-antibody-positive, and only one prisoner had died an AIDS-related death, health experts are agreed that the number of prisoners affected is actually much higher and that there is a real danger that prisoners may contract the virus while in prison as a result of sexual activity or sharing syringes. This will result from the ban on condoms (on the basis that homosexuality is illegal because prisons are not a 'private place' within the meaning of the Sexual Offences Act 1967), and the almost total absence of drug counselling which does nothing to dissuade the sharing of hypodermic needles – needles being obviously much more difficult to smuggle than the drugs themselves. It is, however, surprising that Hepatitis-B, which is actually far more contagious than HIV especially in the unhygienic conditions prevalent in many gaols, has received far less attention. The chances of both staff and prisoners contracting Hepatitis are at present far greater than the likelihood of being affected by HIV.

The scourge of gaol fever (louse-borne typhus), which in the eighteenth century spread from prisons to the courtroom and beyond, was the stimulus to the Act of 1774 which effectively first established medical care in the prisons. It is interesting to consider whether the potential cross-over of the AIDS virus two centuries later may have a similar impact upon health and health care in the prison system.

The issue of discretionary treatment and the absence of rights which causes most controversy is the operation of parole. The parole system as a whole is presently the subject of a government review chaired by the former Home Office minister, Lord Carlisle. Although abolition – which is the official policy of the National Association of Probation Officers amongst others – is unlikely to be recommended, a drastic whittling down of the parole process seems on the cards.

Parole was introduced under the Criminal Justice Act 1967 at a time when 'treatment' theories of penology reached their apogee. In introducing the measure, the then Home Secretary, Roy Jenkins, claimed that

> in a number of cases what happens is that before reaching the two-thirds point prisoners reach . . . a recognisable peak in their training at which they may respond to generous treatment, but after which, if kept in prison, they may go downhill.
>
> (*Hansard* 12 December 1966: col 70)

In other words, the theory was that parole would be granted when prisoners were at their 'peak of training', an optimum point when the effectiveness of the penal system was maximized. However, the empirical basis for such a peak has in practice been found to be lacking – as has evidence of any training at all. Indeed by 1977 the Parole Board was suggesting in its Annual Report that early release might be desirable precisely because the rehabilitative functions of imprisonment were so limited.

Academic criticism of parole has focused upon its being premised on a mythical peak of treatment and upon the realization that what is actually involved is a secretive, administrative exercise in re-sentencing (Hood 1974; Howard League 1981). The bureaucratic burden has also come under attack: make-work tasks having been created for thousands of prison and probation staff as the system is crushed under a mountain of paperwork. It is even questionable how far parole succeeds in reducing the prison population, with judges improperly adjusting their nominal sentences upwards to take account of possible early release. Within the gaols the incentive of parole does operate as a control mechanism. However, this is matched by the resentment and anxiety which is caused as a result of delay and the fact that prisoners are not even told the reasons when parole is refused.

Nevertheless none of these is the principal reason why a curtailing of parole is now in the air. Rather, it is the disastrous practical results of the present government's own tampering with the parole process.

First, parole has been virtually abolished anyway for prisoners serving in excess of five years for crimes involving sex, violence or drugs. This restriction was introduced as a get-tough measure by Leon Brittan in the wake of his personally damaging intervention in the 1983 House of Commons debate on the reintroduction of capital punishment, and has since been continued by Douglas Hurd. Applied retrospectively, and (most importantly) with nothing in its place, this removal of the prospect of parole from many long-termers has greatly increased tension in prisons in both England and Scotland.

Second, and most significant of all, as a panic measure to cut the prison population a simplified parole scheme was introduced in 1984 for medium-term prisoners and the eligibility qualification was reduced from a sentence of 19.5 months to one of 10.5 months. Yet just as restricting parole at the upper end has made management of the prisons more difficult, so its liberalization at the lower end of the spectrum has turned much Crown Court sentencing into a lottery. Until half-remission was introduced as another panic measure in 1987 for prisoners serving 12 months and under, there was little effective difference between any sentence between 9 and 18 months. Anyone receiving a sentence in this the most commonly used band in the Crown Court had a 75 per cent probability of being released on parole after 6 months had been served. Similarly ludicrous anomalies remain and the protests of the judiciary have scarcely subsided.

The best guess is that discretionary release on parole will be replaced for many prisoners by automatic release at the one-third or one-half point in the sentence. Assuming that probation supervision remains an aspect of the release process, this will have consequences for the shape of probation officers' caseloads and perhaps compel much-needed probation resources to be channelled into the neglected area of through-care and after-care. Whether compulsory supervision following a prison sentence is the element of the parole licence which currently has any direct bearing on the likelihood of reoffending is another matter however. Not all of those released from prison feel the need of assistance from a probation officer. And in reality, the level of control which the probation service can exercise over many ex-prisoners is negligible. The compulsory supervision of a much higher number of ex-prisoners than at present runs the risk of increasing the number of actions for breach of licence requirements. In turn, this could ultimately lead to many of those who have been released early subsequently being recalled to prison.

Privatization

The other change in penal practice which is now widely predicted is the greater involvement of the private sector. Yet it is only three or four years ago that proposals to privatize the prisons would have been laughed out of court. There was some interest on the extreme right of the Conservative party (Adam Smith Institute 1984) and, perhaps more surprisingly, amongst the SDP (McConville and Hall Williams 1985). However, the Home Office was said to be hostile and the penal reform lobby did not even think it worth discussing (Shaw 1987b).

Equally, when the veneer of commercial hype was scratched away, there did not actually seem to be much privatization around. In the USA fewer than 1 per cent of that country's prisoners were in privately run gaols. There was no privatized Federal prison, at most two or three privatized state prisons, and perhaps two dozen or so privately managed county gaols. Add to that paltry list a private prison in Panama and the immigration detention facilities along the Rio Grande (plus that at Harmondsworth on the edge of Heathrow Airport, privatized by the last Labour government) and that was the lot. Nowhere in the EEC could you find a private prison. Whatever else it may have been, privatization was not a spectre haunting Europe.

That anyway was how matters appeared until there occurred a conversion of almost Pauline intensity on the part of the British government. However, before detailing the radical shift in government thinking which has taken place, it is worth considering what privatization might mean in the context of the prisons. In theory of course, it could mean selling off British Prisons plc as a going concern as has been done with other state monopolies like British Gas or Telecom. It could mean subcontracting certain prison-based services like workshops or the laundry – something which has a long history in the USA and which, under certain circumstances, can commend itself to penal reformers as a method of 'normalizing' the prison environment (King and Morgan 1987). It could mean 'lease-back' or 'buy-back' arrangements which are essentially creative accountancy techniques to convert capital into revenue spending, not so very different from the mechanisms used by some London boroughs under the threat of rate-capping. Or it could mean the private management of individual institutions, again under contract to the Home Office.

The private management of institutions seemed at first to have been wholly discountenanced by the government. In January 1987 the Permanent Secretary at the Home Office told the House of Commons Expenditure Committee that no work was being undertaken into privatization. In July Douglas Hurd told the Commons:

> I do not think there is a case, and I do not believe that the House would accept a case, for auctioning or privatising the prisons or handing over the business of keeping prisoners safe to anyone other than government servants.
>
> (*Hansard* 16 July 1987: col 1299)

As late as September 1987 this message was repeated by the junior minister, Lord Caithness, in a speech to the Boards of Visitors' annual conference.

However, by March 1988, all of this had changed. A letter from the Home Office was sent to some forty companies and consortia inviting them to submit detailed proposals for the construction of new open prisons and remand centres. At the same time, heavy hints were dropped that management contracts were in the offing. In particular it looked as if a decision in principle had been taken in favour of privately run remand facilities where management is not involved in the quasi-judicial function of parole decision-making (although it is possible for remand prisoners to lose remission prospectively for breaches of prison discipline). The case for privatizing the remand sector had been heavily pressed by the Chairman of the Parole Board and Conservative peer, Lord Windlesham, by the Chair of the Parliamentary All-Party Penal Affairs Group, John Wheeler MP, and by the former Chair of the Home Affairs Select Committee, Sir Edward Gardner, who on retiring from the Commons now chairs one of the consortia in the market for private prison contracts.

Thus it was no surprise when in July 1988 a Home Office Green Paper specifically proposed the privatization of the Court and escort duties currently carried out by prison officers, plus the private management of new remand accommodation, both secure and semi-secure. It argued that there was no 'over-riding difficulty of principle which ought to rule out private sector involvement, provided that sensible practical safeguards are built into the arrangements' (Home Office 1988c: 8–9). Even before the ink on the supposedly consultative Green Paper was dry, management consultants were engaged by the Home Office to examine in detail the practical arrangements which will need to be put in place.

Several factors appear to have played a part in the government's change of mind. First, the continuing mismatch between the number of prisoners and the number of prison places. Second, the seemingly endemic industrial relations problems. Third, growing concern on the part of HM Treasury regarding the escalating costs of both the prison capital and revenue budgets. All of this led the government first to seek quicker and cheaper building methods and the possibility of raising the necessary capital through the commercial market and then to consider contracting-out the management function as well.

Interestingly however, there has also been a change of mood amongst the civil servants and on the part of some prison governors. Initially highly suspicious of privatization, they increasingly voice the view that private prisons could hardly be worse-run than the ones for which the state has had responsibility for the past century. Privatization may not be the only solution, nor even a desirable solution. On the face of it, however, it is difficult to argue that conditions in Armley, Strangeways or Wandsworth could deteriorate much further if they were in private hands.

Legal opinion holds that the Home Secretary presently has no powers under the Prison Act 1952 to subcontract the running of prisons. New legislation would be needed, therefore, before private management of institutions could be introduced. However, the eventual introduction of privately run remand facilities now seems to be as certain as anything can be. Where this would leave welfare services in prisons – and the likely response of the National Association of Probation Officers and of probation management –

is just one of the factors which the government will have to weigh up. But given talk of privatizing probation itself, plus the already burgeoning non-statutory (albeit non-profit-making) provision of non-custodial initiatives for young offenders and juveniles, opposition from within probation is not likely to prove insuperable.

The limited American experience with privately managed institutions does not suggest that, at least in the short term, the pursuit of profit necessarily results in poorer regimes and conditions for prisoners. But nor does it indicate that private affluence is the unique solution to public squalor. The state monopoly of corrections is sometimes (rather dubiously) argued to be an inalienable responsibility in a civilized society. The real issue is whether a powerful commercial lobby with a vested interest in a high prison population is a desirable alternative.

All the more so when privatization of the prisons can scarcely be presented as a way of introducing greater responsiveness to the needs of 'consumers'. There is doubtless something to be said for the view that the present state of the gaols – declining conditions and regimes combined with escalating costs and wasteful security – might be predicted of any monopoly insulated from competitive pressures. However, prisoners will not enjoy consumer sovereignty whether the gaols are publicly or privately owned. Competitive tendering for prison management contracts may result in cheaper solutions for government. But it may also mean that humane regimes, decent standards, and staff and prison safety and welfare are all further imperilled. Indeed it is plausible to argue that the threat of privatization has already been used by government as a stick with which to beat the principal prison trade union, the Prison Officers' Association.

It is obviously difficult to foresee how far privatization may have shaped the prison system by the year 2000, but other aspects are simpler to predict. Unless there are radical shifts in sentencing policy, the prisons will still be suffering from the ills which beset them today. The problems of overcrowding, industrial unrest and prisoner discord have proved endemic for the past twenty years; there is little reason to suppose they will have been rooted out in the next ten.

At the turn of the century there will be many more prisons, of course. Similarly on present sentencing trends, there will be many more prisoners to fill them. Despite the investment of over £1 billion on new gaols, thousands of prisoners will still be 'slopping out' from a plastic bucket well beyond the end of the millenium. Perhaps one-quarter or more of these prisoners will be young, black Britons.

Reviewing conditions and regimes at Leicester prison, the Board of Visitors concluded recently:

> The primary task at Leicester has become survival . . . the commitment and tolerance of most of [our staff] has been little short of miraculous. The forbearance of our warehoused inmates fortunately lasts. We regard it as increasingly irresponsible to rely on an annual miracle and luck to run a prison.
>
> (Leicester Board of Visitors 1988)

Despite the boom in prison construction, it seems likely that an annual miracle will be no less necessary in Leicester, and gaols like it, in the year 2000.

References

Adam Smith Institute (1984) *Omega Justice Policy*, London: Adam Smith Institute.
Ashworth, A. (1983) 'Reducing the prison population: the need for sentencing reform', in *A Prison System for the '80s and Beyond*, London: NACRO.
Bottoms, A. (1974) 'On the decriminalisation of the English juvenile court', in R. Hood (ed.) *Crime, Criminology and Public Policy*, London: Heinemann.
Brody, S. (1976) *The Effectiveness of Sentencing: A Review of the Literature*, London: Home Office Research Study 85.
Casale, S. (1984) *Minimum Standards for Prison Establishments*, London: NACRO.
Chief Inspector of Prisons (1987) *Report of an Inquiry by Her Majesty's Chief Inspector of Prisons for England and Wales into the Disturbances in Prison Service Establishments in England between 29 April and 2 May 1986*, London: HC Paper 42.
Home Office (1984a) *Tougher Regimes in Detention Centres*, London: HMSO.
—— (1984b) *Report of the Control Review Committee: Managing the Long-term Prison System*, London: HMSO.
—— (1985) *Report of the Committee on the Prison Disciplinary System*, Cmnd 9641, London: HMSO.
—— (1988a) *Projections of Long Term Trends in the Prison Population*, Home Office Statistical Bulletin 7/88, London: HMSO.
—— (1988b) *The Prison Population in 1987*, Home Office Statistical Bulletin 7/88, London: HMSO.
—— (1988c) *Private Sector Involvement in the Remand System*, Cm 434, London: HMSO.
Hood, R. (1974) 'Some fundamental dilemmas of the English parole system and a suggestion for an alternative structure', in D. Thomas (ed.) *Parole: Its Implications for the Criminal Justice and Penal Systems*, Cambridge: Institute of Criminology.
House of Commons Education, Science and Arts Committee (1983) *Prison Education*, London: HC Paper 45.
House of Commons Social Services Committee (1986) *Prison Medical Service*, London: HC Paper 72.
Howard League (1981) *Freedom on Licence*, London: Howard League for Penal Reform.
King, R. and Morgan, R. (1987) 'Profiting from prison', *New Society*, 23 October.
Leicester Board of Visitors (1988) *Annual Report 1987*, Leicester.
McConville, S. and Hall Williams, E. (1985) *Crime and Punishment: A Radical Rethink*, London: Tawney Society.
National Audit Office (1985) *Home Office and Property Services Agency: Programme for the Provision of Prison Places*, London: HC Paper 135.
Padel, U. and Stevenson, P. (1988) *Insiders: Women's Experience of Prison*, London: Virago.
Patten, J. (1988) 'A non-prison package', *The Times*, 7 March.
Plotnikoff, J. (1986) *Prison Rules: A Working Guide*, London: Prison Reform Trust.
Richardson, G. (1985) 'The case for prisoners' rights', in M. Maguire, J. Vagg and R. Morgan (eds) *Accountability and Prisons: Opening up a Closed World*, London: Tavistock.
Shaw, S. (1987a) *Conviction Politics: A Plan for Penal Policy*, London: Fabian Society.

—— (1987b) 'Privatization and penal reform', *Prison Report: Quarterly Newsletter of the Prison Reform Trust*, November.

Smith, R. (1984) *Prison Health Care*, London: British Medical Association.

Stern, V. (1987) *Bricks of Shame*, Harmondsworth: Penguin.

Wandsworth Board of Visitors (1987) *Annual Report 1986*, Wandsworth.

5
Policy in the Republic of Ireland: historical and current issues in child care

Robbie Gilligan

The personal social services have traditionally received little attention from the Irish state. Child care has not been an exception. There has been no major child care legislation to replace the (British) Children Act 1908 (although reforming legislation is being debated in the Oireachtas [Parliament] at the time of writing [Child Care Bill 1988]). Only recently has one government department been given a lead role in relation to child care where previously oversight had fallen between three separate departments. The only provision for child protection work had been until fairly recently, that on a limited basis of the Irish Society for the Prevention of Cruelty to Children through its inspectors.

The Irish state has tended to take something of a back seat in terms of direct provision while often carrying all or a major share of the funding burden.

> residential child care: less than 2 per cent of places are provided directly by the statutory health boards.
>
> (Department of Health 1988b)

> adoptions: only one third were arranged directly under the auspices of the statutory health boards with the balance arranged by non-statutory registered adoption societies.
>
> (Adoption Board 1988: 8–9)

The vast majority of day care places for young children are provided outside the statutory sector.

mental handicap: the state directly provides only 17.1 per cent of a total of 5,193 residential places for children and adults.

(Department of Health 1988a: 57)

This is a pattern that can also be discerned in health and education generally, although this is beginning to change. Since the early 1970s, for instance, national systems of child protection and probation have begun to emerge.

The Irish state has not seen itself as having a responsibility for the resolution of social problems. At times it may have made the task of those devoted to social improvement less difficult. In Peillon's terminology the Irish state does not have a 'managerial' or 'social democratic' ideology (Peillon 1987: 207), in relation to social problems. This rather passive role in relation to social policy is certainly not unique to Ireland. However, the particularly Irish factors which have led to this situation include the struggle for legitimacy of the state after independence from British rule in 1922; the political power of the Roman Catholic church in an overwhelmingly Catholic society; the tradition of caution and passivity in the public service; chronic economic problems; and the conservatism and anti-urban bias of the prevailing political ideology. Each of these needs to be examined in turn.

The new state's legitimacy was disputed by different elements: by those who did not wish to see the British go; by those freedom fighters who felt that the terms of their going involved too much compromise; and by some within the Roman Catholic tradition who saw any secular state (in Ireland or elsewhere) as a potential threat to their interests and influence. The new state also inherited some of the odium which had previously attached to any policies or decrees issued by the British authorities. Those far from the seat of power in Dublin, and those engaged in a largely unchanging rural economy saw little reason for allegiance to an intrusive state, despite a change of political control. Even if there had been a will to tackle social problems, the political struggle of the new state, combined with factors discussed below, meant that it had neither the capacity, nor the inclination, to attend directly to social issues such as child care.

In the prevailing political atmosphere it is hardly surprising that the new state did not choose to dissolve its inheritance of what was effectively a marriage of convenience between religious and secular authorities (see Inglis 1987). The new state came to terms with the Church by preserving or extending the influence it enjoyed during the later part of British rule. The Church retained or acquired hegemony in many spheres of moral or ideological importance. In return the state won a more qualified acceptance from the Church. Further – and vital to an understanding of the subsequent evolution of Irish social policy and provision generally – the state also gained, at no charge, services and hidden subsidies in the operation of schools, hospitals, and other care institutions. Clergy and others provided services to the state in direct care – primarily as teachers or nurses – or in middle or higher management. Many received no salary from the state, or where they did they typically ploughed this money back into the running cost of the service. These hidden subsidies insulated the state from the real cost of providing a bedrock of services.

One former element in Roman Catholic teaching – the concept of 'subsidiarity' – had a profound impact on social policy development in Ireland. According to this principle, the state should not take unto itself functions which could properly be discharged by a lower level of social organization. This principle operated to narrow the influence of the state and bolster the importance of the family and wider social groupings around it, thereby preserving the influence of the Church. Although almost forgotten outside, the influence of subsidiarity as a concept, even if unnamed, lingers stubbornly in the corridors of civil service departments. The longevity of this remnant of largely redundant Catholic thought is undoubtedly due to how well it served to reinforce the prevailing ideology.

The culture of public administration was profoundly affected by the influence of British rule and the presence of the Church on the political sidelines. Caution has been a hallmark of Irish public administration. In a sense the two great sins to be avoided were to be caught with one's hand in the till, or to cause political embarrassment to one's minister. The function of the prudent public servant was to have 'clear sight over short distances', a maxim apparently inherited from the British civil service (T. J. Barrington 1980: 31). This ethos discouraged lateral or strategic thinking. The generation of ideas took place somewhere else. One former Taoiseach (Prime Minister) – and frustrated public service reformer – lamented this tendency of some government departments 'to wait for new ideas to walk in the door' (cited in Chubb 1982: 267). This critic of lethargy did succeed in generating greater activism within the public service but only in the economic arena. In the matter of social provision, the previous inertia remains largely unchallenged. The initiative for legal reform in the areas of illegitimacy and child protection did not come originally from civil servants but from single-minded interest groups which relentlessly wore down the opposition or indifference of bureaucrats and their political readers (see, for example, CARE – Campaign for the Care of Deprived Children 1972).

Another constraint on the role of the public service in social affairs has been the serious economic problems which have tended to dog the Irish state since its foundation. With the exception of a halcyon period of economic take-off in the 1960s government spending has usually been severely curtailed by economic factors. Currently interest payments on a monumental public debt absorbs 30 pence in every pound of tax revenue (Minister for Finance 1988: 13). In addition, Ireland has one of the highest rates of unemployment in the EEC (18.3 per cent, and second only to that of Spain – Eurostat 1988: 126) due in part to the decline of existing industry in the context of an already vulnerable economic base. Of the twelve EEC countries, Ireland ranks tenth in terms of relative economic strength, with a Gross Domestic Product of 62.6 per cent of the EEC average and 60.3 per cent that of the UK (Eurostat 1988: 40). The dominant political ideology means that these fiscal and economic difficulties have replaced subsidiarity as an intellectual rationale for a minimalist role by the state in social provision, at least in the area of personal social services.

The Irish state has had great difficulty coming to terms with social problems such as crime, drugs and urban decay. Part of the reason for this is that they require a more concerted approach by the state than the current conservative political and economic consensus might permit. But there is a further factor. The true repository of Irishness is seen in the rural life-style (see O'Toole 1987). These social problems are perceived as quintessentially urban in character and therefore as alien and remote from the real concerns of Irish culture and tradition. They have not come from within this tradition, which therefore has no obligation to confront them. This anti-urban ideology also gives undue influence to rural and therefore (in an Irish context at least) conservative political concerns. While rural areas clearly have no monopoly of conservatism, and while there are a number of instances historically of radical and successful collective action in rural Ireland, the current evidence is that on a range of social and moral issues, conservative responses are found more commonly in rural, rather than urban, Ireland. For instance, in the referendum on the introduction of divorce in 1986, only the six Dublin constituencies, out of a total of forty-one, returned a majority in favour of divorce. It has been noted that in predominantly rural constituencies the opposition was strongest (Girvin 1987: 96). There is also evidence that farmers have the least liberal views of any social group on a range of questions such as divorce, homosexuality and sexual permissiveness (Fogarty, Ryan and Lee 1984: 147, 194).

Recent trends in child-care provision

The 1960s heralded remarkable developments in Ireland, as elsewhere. Economic growth, the stemming of emigration, the pressure of change on the Roman Catholic Church, the impact of a national television service, and a more critical media altered dramatically the face of Irish society. Few areas of life remained untouched. The caution and constraints of the past began to give way to a new candour and optimism. Social problems received more attention in the media and electorally. All of this was to provide a platform for developments in social policy and a stimulus for a more direct role by the state in social provision in the 1970s and 1980s.

Child care too benefited from this expansion of social provision. The impetus for change was also assisted by the lobbying of modestly resourced pressure groups which skilfully exploited emerging, if faltering, public interest in social issues. Since the late 1960s, services have significantly changed, not only because of the more favourable social climate, but also consequent upon two specific policy initiatives which had an immediate impact on child care.

The first was the work of a review body on residential child care which reported in 1970 (Committee on Reformatory and Industrial Schools 1970). The second was the regionalization of health services in 1971 with the creation of eight health boards (see Curry 1980: 145–76). Following this reorganization community care teams were created which were to provide care at a local level through integrated health and social service teams. The health board structure, and especially the community care service, was to prove a platform for many developments in child care services generally. The following is a brief sketch of the major changes that have flowed from these and other initiatives.

The professionalization of service providers

During the 1970s the state began to employ social workers directly in two newly developing services: community care (health) and probation. In the field of child protection these social workers gradually supplanted the previous role of the inspectors of the Irish Society for the Prevention of Cruelty to Children. Initially upon their establishment in 1971, health boards had commonly grant-aided the employment of social workers by social service councils (umbrella agencies for local voluntary effort). At the peak of their influence social service councils aimed to provide a range of personal social service on a generic basis (see Kennedy 1981). Soon, however, in most areas, health boards chose to set up their own social work service. Over time, the generic basis of the service inherited from the social service councils has been eroded and there is now an almost exclusive preoccupation with child protection. In the psychiatric and mental handicap services, social work staff are recruited directly. The focus on child protection is due to a relentless increase in referrals combined with a standstill or reduction in posts due to cutbacks. Social workers seem also to prefer child care because it was an area largely 'uncolonized' by other professionals in the health service.

Professionalization can also be seen in the development of training. The first full-time course in the field of residential child care was established in Kilkenny in 1971 in line with the recommendations of the Kennedy Committee which had called for training for staff in this field (Committee on Reformatory and Industrial Schools 1970: 14). By 1978 responses to a survey, from nineteen children's homes, indicated that 41.2 per cent of care staff had undergone full-time training and a further 8 per cent had received in-service training (Association of Workers with Children in Care 1979: 3). Professional social work training (CQSW) began in 1968 with a one-year post-graduate course in University College Dublin. Currently some sixty students qualify annually as professional social workers from four courses, a two-year non-graduate (University College Cork), a four-year degree (University of Dublin, Trinity College) and two one-year post-graduate diploma (University College Dublin and University College Cork) (see Kearney 1987: 12–15). While there are no up-to-date statistics available, it is this author's impression that at least 90 per cent of social workers in the child care field are now professionally qualified.

A limited rationalization of the system

There has been some progress in tackling the former fragmentation of responsibility for the child care system at central government level. Adoption has been transferred from the Department of Justice to the Department of

Health, as has almost all of the Department of Education's share of residential care. Responsibility for legislative and policy initiatives in the area of child protection is now clearly located in the Department of Health.

Children in care

The number of children in care (2,686) represents a rate of 2.3 per 1,000 children of 16 years and younger (Department of Health 1988c; Central Statistics Office 1987: 14). This total has increased by 9.81 per cent in the period 1982–7 (Department of Health 1986: 1; 1988c). There is no formal facility for the placement of children 'home on trial' in the Irish system so the figure above refers to children actually in care. When a longer view is taken, however, there has actually been a dramatic reduction in the population of children in care. In a twenty-year period the numbers have fallen by over 2,000 from 4,834 in 1968/9 (Committee on Reformatory and Industrial Schools 1970: 12).

There has also been a significant reduction in the use of compulsion in the placement of children in care. In 1968/9 40 per cent were placed on a court order (Committee on Reformatory and Industrial Schools 1970: 92, 94). By 1983 this proportion had fallen to 25.8 per cent (Department of Health 1988e: 6).

In the period 1982–7 the proportion of children in care who are fostered has increased from 52 per cent to 68 per cent. There are important regional variations in the rate of fostering, ranging from a high of 97.4 per cent in the North Western Health Board (which is responsible for 2.9 per cent of all children in care), to 59.6 per cent in the Eastern Health Board (which includes Dublin and is responsible for 38.1 per cent of all children in care), and 56.4 per cent in the South Eastern Health Boards, which accounts for 10.2 per cent of all children in care (Department of Health 1988c).

The number of places in residential children's homes fell from 1,346 in 1979 to 988 in 1987 (Task Force on Child Care Services 1981: 63–4; derived from Department of Health 1988b). These figures fit in with the longer run decline of the residential sector. In explaining this trend three factors suggest themselves. First, a declared preference for foster care in official policy; second, a general policy, in more recent years, within the health service of shifting care from institutional to community settings; and finally the withdrawal of many service providers themselves. Many religious orders have opted out of this field of work; they have done so because of a wish to concentrate on other activities and/or because of a shrinkage in their own numbers which prevents them from providing a sufficient staff presence to maintain their distinctive ethos.

The availability of social workers within health boards (since the early to mid-1970s), and the gradual shift to health boards of the responsibility for the maintenance of all children in care, has led to a streamlining of admission procedures. Previously the admission process was largely controlled by residential units themselves, who would decide unilaterally on the merits of referrals by ISPCC inspectors, the courts, gardai (police), priests or other local worthies. This undoubtedly led to an excessive rate of admission, and to a bias against foster care which languished under a separate and remote arm of local government. While inevitably there remain subtle differences in approach by different social work teams, the screening by trained professionals, and the availability, if even on a limited basis, of community-based alternatives has stemmed the flow of referrals for placement and increased the chances that these are confined and tailored to those most in need.

The last two decades have seen real improvements in the residential and foster care systems. Old institutions have been closed and replaced by smaller group homes. Since 1984 administrative responsibility for most residential care has been clearly located in the Department of Health. At the same time the financing of the residential sector was switched from a capitation system to a more satisfactory annual negotiated budget. Most care staff are by now trained, and also enjoy substantially improved pay and conditions. In the period 1978–87 staffing ratios improved from one care staff member per 4.5 children to one per 2.3 children (Association of Workers with Children in Care 1979: 9; derived from Department of Health 1988b).

The influence of the Poor Law origins of fostering – boarding-out – has gradually been purged and the system is now managed by professional social workers according to internationally accepted standards of practice. Greater rigour is applied in the selection of foster parents and group work and adult education techı ques are increasingly employed in their training and support. Placement is now open to older children, to sibling groups and to children with various forms of disability. Other recent developments include the (still somewhat tentative) use of the mass media for the purposes of recruitment and public education; the establishment of the Irish Foster Care Association in 1982; and the introduction of new statutory regulations in 1983 (Department of Health 1983).

Increase in the rate of child protection referrals

The period 1983–7 saw greatly increased demands on child protection services: the number of new referrals of suspected child abuse (physical and sexual) more than trebled from 434 to 1,646. In the same period the annual number of confirmed cases increased more than fourfold with an even more dramatic growth, by a factor of thirteen, in the number of confirmed cases which included sexual abuse (Department of Health 1985; 1988d).

Dramatic fall in rate of traditional adoption

Legal adoption came relatively late to Ireland with the enabling legislation being passed in 1952. There had been conservative opposition to its introduction due to fears that adoption could become a means of unscrupulous prosyletizing, or as a threat to the orderly succession by blood tie to land and other property. As a result of these and some constitutional difficulties, adoption was introduced on a restricted basis. It has been confined essentially to children who are illegitimate, where the natural mother consents to the adoption, and to children who are orphaned. The Adoption Act 1988 extends the facility of adoption, in certain circumstances, to legitimate children, and also opens a limited possibility of adoption orders being made without parental consent. These provisions raised legal fears of the statute being declared unconstitutional in a future appeal. For this reason the President used his powers to refer the legislation to the Supreme Court for a test of its constitutionality. Having survived this test, the Act is law and represents something of a watershed in the development of children's rights.

Since the inception of the adoption system, a total of 35,332 adoption orders were made between 1953 and 1987. The number of orders made annually is now in steady decline. From an annual average of 1,300 in the peak period of 1967–75, the number made in 1987 declined to 525. A further 190 were made in favour of relatives, in most cases the child's mother and her husband, where they had married subsequent to the child's birth and where the husband was not the child's father. This facility is increasingly exercised by couples in such circumstances because it offers legal benefits to the child, a trend which reflects the growing tendency of single mothers to keep their child rather than place for adoption (Adoption Board 1988).

Modest growth in community services

Since the early 1970s there has been modest but fairly steady expansion in the range of community services and supports available to children and their families. For example it is estimated that 20,000 children attend some 1,400 to 1,500 day-care settings (nurseries, community playgroups, private play-groups); 283 of these, serving 6,681 children, are receiving some, usually very modest, state subsidy (Dail Debates 26.11.87) – on average IR £198 per child per annum. This means that nationally 2.1 per cent of 0–4-year-olds have access to a subsidized part- or full-time day-care place; the rate of subsidy is subject to wide regional variations. The balance of running costs must be raised by the sponsoring voluntary body and the paltry public subsidy jeopardizes both fair working conditions for the almost exclusively female care staff and adequate staffing ratios.

A national home-help service was set in train in 1972 (Department of Health 1972). An intended priority for family problems has, however, largely been eclipsed by an almost exclusive focus on the elderly. In a few areas full-time home-makers or home-helps have been recruited specifically to work with families on practical problems of home management. In a small number of areas workers with training in residential child care have been assigned on an individual basis to social work teams to increase the range of supports available to families. These domiciliary child-care workers intervene inten-sively with a small number of families, working directly with children at home, and helping parents explore alternative means of child management where problems have arisen.

There has been an encouraging growth in initiatives which seek to create locally based resource centres for children and families within their own communities. These typically offer some selection of day care, group work, adult and health education, and information facilities (see for example Nic Giolla Choille 1985). One interesting variation has been the provision in two instances of residential care at neighbourhood level to local children (see for example Gilligan 1982).

Some of the impetus for these developments came from the recommendations of an official review body on child care services (Task Force on Child Care Services 1981), although some projects had in fact anticipated this thinking. Coverage is by no means comprehensive, but the wide range of sponsoring agencies – health boards, Combat Poverty Agency, religious orders, voluntary child-care agencies and others – suggests that this pattern of provision will continue to thrive.

Developments in the juvenile justice system

Although the legislative framework remains static, there have been other important changes. These have included the growth of a professional probation service on a national basis; the development of a successful juvenile liaison scheme within the garda siochana (police force); the closure of some frankly primitive residential centres; the opening of the first secure unit with thirty places under the auspices of the Department of Education, and the opening of remand and assessment centres serving the whole country; the availability of professional reports and assessments to courts to assist in disposition; and the common availability of civil and criminal legal aid to those appearing in court.

Implications of the general policy environment for child care

Scope for initiative v. uneven standards/levels of provision

Ideological distaste for a managerial role for the state in social care has positive and negative implications. On the positive side, individual practitioners and voluntary agencies have much greater room for manoeuvre. It is possible to shape street-level policies and practice appropriate to conditions in given communities. On the negative side, the inadequacy of resources may stifle these initiatives. The reliance on the voluntary sector introduces an element of lottery into provision, in that the strength of that sector waxes and wanes. A dynamic voluntary agency may provide imaginative services, but where this sector is weak, the state generally does not rush to fill the gap.

Minimum use of compulsion v. non-regulation of system

The Irish child care system exhibits a preference among decision-makers for non-coercive and less formal methods of accomplishing given objectives. These decision-makers tend to be bureaucrats rather than politicians, especially at local level in the health and social services where political control seems to be in terminal decline (see R. Barrington 1987). Negotiation and/or consensus decision-making are greatly preferred to approaches which entail compulsion or conflict. This may be seen by some, at least, as producing desirable effects. The relatively modest use of Court-ordered routes into care may be seen as one example where it is preferred to avoid polarization by seeking parental co-operation in the admission decision. Another example of minimum use of compulsion is the relatively modest rate of custodial dispositions in the juvenile justice system (Caul 1985).

On the negative side, many opportunities to legislate for or to regulate standards of practice or provision have been ignored. The operation, for example, of most of the education system, or the organization of the probation service has no legislative basis. There are also, for example, no regulations to date, governing the operation of day care (although these are now proposed in draft legislation recently published (Child Care Bill 1988). Further, the discretion left to local administrators in the absence of centrally dictated requirements means that there tend to be wide local variations in provision. One local administrator likes what social workers seem to be about and places great emphasis on expanding their service; another is more sceptical and social work is marginalized accordingly. One favours good quality day-care provision; another opposes day care as undermining the family. The avoidance of conflict has also meant, for instance, that reform of the juvenile justice system has been paralysed by a finely balanced tension between competing progressive and conservative approaches. Unless this conflict magically resolves itself, or almost as unlikely, a coherent pressure group turns up the political heat for reform, it is probable that no bureaucrat or minister will voluntarily open this Pandora's box, thus leaving the system to languish unchanged.

The constitution: civil liberties v. more limited rights for certain children and families

The Irish state has a written constitution given effect by a referendum in 1937. It was skilfully drafted to circumvent political problems in church – state relations and to help incorporate dissident political opinion still alienated from the new state. In its interpretation in the higher Courts, the constitution has proved a powerful and generally positive influence on the rights of the citizen. It is sometimes criticized by liberal thinkers because of what is seen as a Roman Catholic flavour to many of its precepts. This ethos is probably inevitable given the overwhelming Catholic complexion of the population, and the political influence of that Church, especially at the time of drafting. Among other things, the constitution envisages the family as being based on marriage, proscribes legislation for divorce, and, in a section of considerable relevance for child care, refers to the 'inalienable and imprescriptible rights' of the family (S. 41.1) which are conventionally interpreted to supersede such rights of children (S. 42.5).

The constitution has not only heavily influenced the Courts in deciding child-care cases but also circumscribed efforts at legislative reform in this area. In recent years there had been a tentative move by the Courts towards recognizing the rights of children independent of their parents, although a recent decision by the Supreme Court in *K.C. v. An Bord Uchtala ([1985] Irish Reports 375)* seems to have reversed or stemmed that trend. This judgment laid down that the state may intervene to deprive parents of their children's custody only where, for compelling physical or moral reasons, they have forfeited their right to custody. In other words clear parental fault, rather than the psychological needs of the child, considered independently of the interests of the parents, must be the test for parental loss of custody (see Duncan 1986: 76–86).

Facing the future

The Irish child-care system faces a challenging period. Social conditions are likely to produce more complex demands while political and economic policies seem likely to reduce resources available. Means of coping with the child-care implications of social problems such as AIDS, drugs, emigration and unemployment must be devised. Demographic trends such as the increase in the number of single-parent households and reconstituted families also have to be coped with. At a policy level, more resources, staff, and spending on training are required. Facilities, especially at neighbourhood level, are needed to provide relevant support to families. Better provision for adolescents both in and when they leave care should also have priority. Consolidation of legal reform in relation to child protection and new legislation in the area of juvenile justice must also be sought.

Within the child-care system itself much remains to be done. Besides absorbing the effects of legislative change, two areas require urgent attention. The first is what appears to be the growing alienation of clients – young people and families – from the system and its representatives. This is evident in increasing reports of violence and conflict in worker–client relations. To address this alienation will require, among other things, a greater involvement of clients, not only in decision-making, but also in shaping the system, whether as employees or directors of agencies, as clear voices within pressure groups, or indeed as co-sponsors of alternative services. The second issue is the extent of sexism in current provision. Tackling this will mean ensuring fair conditions for all carers and real efforts to prevent caring being viewed merely as a female preserve. It will also mean attending to the need for greatly increased numbers of day-care places. In addition the current low level of specific provision for adolescent girls in residential and community services must be confronted.

Developments in the past twenty years or so may have removed Irish child care from the administrative and political oblivion which had largely been its fate. While the state has gradually assumed a more direct, if partial, role, services still lack an adequate legislative and funding base. There are few grounds for believing that such measures will be forthcoming given the well-established political inertia in this field and the climate of fiscal crisis. Any reform, therefore, is likely to come in fits and starts, in reaction to some politically embarrassing episode. But then perhaps the fate of child care in Ireland is not, after all, so different from that in many other countries.

References

Adoption Board (1988) *Annual Report 1987*, Dublin: Stationery Office.

Association of Workers with Children in Care (1979) 'Final Report on 1978 Research Project', *AWCC NEWSLETTER*, November: 2–10.

Barrington, R. (1987) *Health, Medicine and Politics in Ireland 1900–1970*, Dublin: Institute of Public Administration.

Barrington, T. J. (1980) *The Irish Administrative System*, Dublin: Institute of Public Administration.

CARE (Campaign for the Care of Deprived Children) (1972) *Children Deprived – The CARE Memorandum on Deprived Children and Children's Services in Ireland*, Dublin: CARE.

Caul, B. (1985) 'A comparative study of the juvenile justice systems of Northern Ireland and the Republic of Ireland', unpublished Ph.D. thesis, University of Dublin, Trinity College.

Central Statistics Office (1987) *Ireland: Census 86 – Summary Population Report*, Dublin: Stationery Office.

Child Care Bill (1988) introduced to Dail Eireann by the Minister for Health, 20 May.

Chubb, B. (1982) *The Government and Politics of Ireland*, 2nd edn, London: Longman.

Committee on Reformatory and Industrial Schools (1970) *Reformatory and Industrial Schools Systems Report*, Kennedy Committee, Dublin: Stationery Office.

Curry J. (1980) *The Irish Social Services*, Dublin: Institute of Public Administration.

Department of Health (1972) 'Home help service', Circular 11/72, 20 April.

—— (1983) *Boarding Out of Children Regulations 1983*, Statutory Instrument S. I. no. 67 of 1983, Dublin: Stationery Office.

—— (1985) 'Statistics on non-accidental injury 1984 (1983)', Dublin.

—— (1986) *Children in Care 1983*, Dublin.

—— (1988a) *Health Statistics 1987*, Dublin: Stationery Office.

—— (1988b) Data provided to Richard Bruton TD in response to a parliamentary question.

—— (1988c) 'Number of children in care at 1st November 1987', personal communication.

—— (1988d) Personal communication with child care division, 12 November.

—— (1988e) *Children in Care in 1984*, Dublin.

Duncan, W. (1986) 'Family law – The child's right to a family – Parental rights in disguise', *Dublin University Law Journal*, 8.

Eurostat (1988) *Basic Statistics of the Community*, Luxembourg Office for Official Publications of the European Communities.

Fogarty, M., Ryan, L. and Lee, J. (1984) *Irish Values and Attitudes – The Irish Report of the European Value Systems Study*, Dublin: Dominican Publications.

Gilligan, R. (1982) *Children in Care in their own Community*, Dublin: Society of St Vincent de Paul.

Girvin, B. (1987) 'The divorce referendum in the Republic', June 1986, in T. Garvin and M. Laver (eds) *Irish Political Studies*, vol. 2, Galway: PSAI Press.

Inglis, T. (1987) *Moral Monopoly – The Catholic Church in Irish Society*, Dublin: Gill & Macmillan.

Kearney, N. (1987) 'The historical background', in *Social Work and Social Work Training in Ireland: Yesterday and Tomorrow*, University of Dublin, Trinity College Department of Social Studies, Occasional Paper no. 1.

Kennedy, S. (1981) *Who Should Care? – The Development of Kilkenny Social Services 1963–1980*, Dublin: Turoe Press.

Minister for Finance (1988) *Budget 1988*, presented to Dail Eireann, 27 January.

Nic Giolla Choille, T. (1985) *Evaluation Report on the Darndale Family Centre*, Dublin: Irish Society for the Prevention of Cruelty to Children.

O'Toole, F. (1987) *The Southern Question*, Letters from the New Island Series, Dublin: Raven Arts Press.

Peillon, M. (1987) 'State and society in the Republic of Ireland: a comparative study', *Administration – Journal of the Institute of Public Administration of Ireland*, 35, 2: 190–212.

Task Force on Child Care Services (1981) *Final Report*, Dublin: Stationery Office.

6
Women's experience of old age

Janet Ford and
Ruth Sinclair

Women's experience of old age is both qualitatively and quantitatively different from that of men. While all older people are subject to the discriminatory and demeaning processes of ageism, women suffer additional disadvantages because of their low status, their traditional role(s), their lack of economic power and because the majority of them live alone.

There is now a growing literature that discusses the way women's experience of old age is affected by their earlier economic and social position (Phillipson 1982; Peace 1986; Townsend 1986; Walker 1987; Fennell, Phillipson and Evers 1988). In particular, economic inequalities are carried into old age, as are the dependencies created by the way in which women's identity is shaped by their roles within the family and domestic context. Further, and in common with men, women face a pervasive ageism within society at both the individual and institutional level, an attitude that encourages a view of the old as necessarily problematic, weak, dependent and significantly less deserving than other groups in society. In so far as the world of the old is predominately the world of women they are at particular risk of the outcomes of such stereotyping; exploitation, disregard and humiliation. While emphasizing that it is social and institutional processes that constrain and construct the experience of old age (rather than some inevitable age-related physical decline) such studies and discussions have not necessarily revealed very much about how these social, economic and attitudinal constraints are received, interpreted and lived on an everyday basis by those who are old.

The major aim of this chapter is to examine the consequences of these constraints as perceived and lived out by old women. The emphasis will be upon the way women themselves talk about, consider and respond to their circumstances. Such an approach is relatively uncommon. Until fairly recently ageism discouraged a detailed focus on old women, in any arena, not just in the social sciences. However, as this stance is challenged and the number of studies placing the experience and concerns of older women in a more central light grows (for example, Mathews 1979; Evers 1984; Seabrook 1980; Ford and Sinclair 1987) it is possible to begin to link together more closely the structural and the personal. This is achieved by using the personal accounts to bring into sharp focus the consequences for older women of societal processes, institutional practices and our own attitudes and behaviour. Accounts of experience that emanate from older women also force a more central consideration of the things that matter to them, and which therefore should be adequately acknowledged in both policy and practice. Thus this chapter is not concerned to examine or discuss specific welfare provision, but rather, via an examination of the nature and experience of old age as lived, to highlight some of the issues and problems that any social policy must address.

The chapter starts with a discussion of the causes and consequences of ageism, a process that affects every aspect of the lives of the old. The implications and experience of ageism are, however, compounded by other roles, in particular gender roles, so that while demeaning for all it may be so particularly for women whose low status within society further undermines them. Subsequently consideration is given to the demographic trends that have resulted in an ageing population where 'the world of the very old is a woman's world' (Peace 1986). This is followed by a brief discussion of the economic position of older women. Against this background the main aim of the chapter is to explore some of the forms and experiences of daily living as reported and discussed by older women themselves. Three themes are presented. First, the centrality to the lives of older women of the constant tension between the need for security and the desire to maintain independence. While this dilemma may be posed most starkly over the question of where to live, it is most frequently seen in relation to the family. This is because the family and the domestic environment was and remains the major source of an older woman's identity, and because the assumption embedded in social policy and the provision of social welfare is that the family (and particularly women in the family) will remain the major providers. The second theme concerns the older woman's experience of ageism and the third examines their response to the situation they face. Although each theme is treated separately they are closely connected and together reveal some of the strategies that have been developed by older women to manage their lives in order to secure a balance between independence and support. Such strategies enable women to make for themselves as positive a life as is possible at a time when their resources – economic, physical and emotional – are reducing and their needs increasing. Finally the implications of these discussions for policies on the provision of services will be raised briefly. In particular it will be suggested that the development of detailed policies for services for elderly people will be effective only if they are part of a strong challenge to ageism within our society.

Ageism

The experiences of the old are substantially affected by societal attitudes; currently in Britain these are at best ambivalent and at worst prejudicial and discriminatory. Here the very language we use suggests our attitude to older people. They are 'over the hill', have 'time on their hands', are referred to as the 'wrinklies' and 'poor old souls'. The further discrimination associated with gender is signalled by the insult to a man that he is 'an old woman'. The view of older people is that as a group they are physically weak, non-contributing, defenceless and dependent. Such attitudes are not derived from a knowledge of old people but assigned to them on the basis of chronological age. Age acts as a role sign and ageism allows a process of systematic stereotyping and discrimination against people simply because they are a certain age. The old (those over a certain age, which is itself socially determined and historically variable) are classified together irrespective of the wide range of characteristics and capabilities they actually display, and categorized as old-fashioned, conservative and difficult. Accumulated years become a stigma, and so discrediting. The arguments against 'old' as a natural, biological category, and in support of 'old' as a socially constructed category have now been put forcibly by several writers (Townsend 1986; Mathews 1979; Jones, Ester and Binney 1987) and need not be rehearsed again here. Two other issues, however, will be explored. These concern the causes and consequences of ageism as social constructions. They are distinct but related questions.

Attention has often been directed towards the dominance of societal values concerned with productivity and achievement, and the way status and legitimacy derive from the area of paid work. Any non-compliance with these norms (whether voluntarily undertaken or imposed, say through a statutory retirement policy) removes status and legitimacy. As Parker (1980) points out, a life of leisure is not a recognized virtue in our society. Other writers stress that technological developments and demographic changes have increasingly made it necessary to restrict the numbers in the labour market and that this process has been legitimized by the creation of a powerful belief in the association of age with inevitable physical decline and diminished productivity. For old women these processes are reinforced because their reproductive role is clearly at an end while the provision of care for others, their major source of identity and status, declines as children leave home and parents or partners die. Stevenson (1987) indicates a further set of complexities and ambiguities that underpin, and are reflected in ageism, particularly with regard to women; notably our own fear of physical decline (and death) in a culture that equates youth with beauty and where women are valued for their beauty (Sontag 1972). Equally a perception of the continuing power and hold of those who brought us up so that we may retain a desire to 'diminish that power by belittling and diminishing them' (Stevenson 1987).

The consequences of ageism are several and are as real for the young as for the old. Ageism acts to deter any consideration by the young of what life will be like when they are old. This applies particularly to the lives of older women where the discriminations of gender and age make the subject matter one to be avoided. Such barriers make it more difficult for younger people to develop mutually beneficial relationships with older people. As a consequence the chance of effective action by younger people to change circumstances and attitudes that jeopardize their potential quality of later life is minimized. Further, the stereotypes make it difficult for such a group to be seen as interesting research subjects. Szinovacs in 1982, introducing the first collection of articles on women's retirement, commented that the issue had been neglected because of the 'belief that it did not constitute a salient social or research issue'. While, of women's writing in general, it has been said 'only half our lives are there, our childhoods, our youths, our forties, the last half of our lives is unknown' (MacDonald and Rich 1984). Although research interest has grown in the 1980s, with notable exceptions (for example Wenger 1984) it still tends to be focused upon specific problems experienced by old people and linked to the need to develop and expand social policies for the care of old people (see, for instance, Sinclair 1988). Such a problem-centred focus is both necessary and legitimate, but it inevitably reinforces the stereotype of the old as a problem, and by virtue of their numerical prominence, older women as the major problem.

For the old themselves ageism is damaging not only in terms of how they are perceived and so treated, but also to the extent that they internalize the public images and accept the labels. A restricted old age then becomes a self-fulfilling prophecy as older people conform to the low expectations others have of them. It has been suggested, for example by Peace (1986), that the internalization of these beliefs may then make it difficult for those in need to ask for care, and to be easily satisfied with the small benefits or services they receive (Evers 1984). Most centrally, however, ageism jeopardizes the rights, dignity, autonomy and independence of old age. 'Ageism allows the younger generation to see older people as different to themselves; they subtly cease to identify with their elders as human beings' (Butler and Lewis 1983: ix). Stevenson (1987) takes the argument further:

> Once we have defined any group of people as less interesting, less attractive, and less significant than ourselves then ugly processes are set in train by which people are perceived to need less than we do of the 'goodies', whatever they may be. In a frightening way they become less human.

Demographic trends

Acknowledgement of the widespread prevalence of ageist attitudes is relatively recent. Like much of the increase in problem-centred research and policy concerns, interest in elderly people has been forced upon society because of its rapidly changing demographic structure. During the twentieth century there has been an increase in the absolute numbers of those over 65 from 1.7 million to 8.5 million (Family Policy Study Centre 1988) but also an increase in the proportion of the population who are over 65 (from 5 per cent to 15 per cent).

These changes are a result not only of a decrease in mortality rates at all ages, but also because the general decrease in birth-rates means there are proportionally fewer children and more older people within the population.

Within this older population, women outnumber men by five to three, with the sex imbalance even more marked amongst those aged 75 and over, where women comprise more than two-thirds of the population. The preponderance of women amongst the old reflects several factors. Female life expectancy exceeds the male by approximately six years. In addition, the effects of two world wars cannot be discounted. Also important is the high proportion of older women who live alone. Women tend to marry men who are older than themselves. Women are therefore more likely to be widows than men are widowers. As age increases so does the proportion of women who are unmarried such that amongst those aged 75 years or more, 80 per cent of women are unmarried compared to 39 per cent of men. These figures are reflected in a household structure of older people. Over two-thirds of those over 65 either live alone or with their spouse, and this figure has increased significantly over the last thirty years (Dale, Evandson and Arber 1987). Of those living alone women form the majority, a proportion which further increases with age: 22 per cent of women under 75 live alone (compared to 6 per cent of men) while 58 per cent of women over 75 live alone (compared to 26 per cent of men). Only one-fifth of those over 65 live either with their families or in some form of residential care.

Economic resources of older women

Central to the experience of older women is the level and security of their economic position. This largely determines their standard of living, affecting aspects of their well-being such as housing, food, recreational activities and the purchase of assistance and 'care'. Income is a particularly good example of the situation outlined above by Stevenson, where certain groups are perceived by society to need less of 'the goodies'. For most older women (6.1 million) their sole source of income is state benefits and pensions. The low level of pension payment resulted in approximately 1.8 million pensioners claiming supplementary pensions in 1986; of these claimants 72 per cent are women (Family Policy Study Centre 1988). Other income opportunities, for example those that result from occupational pension schemes, have not as yet benefited women to the same extent as men. The nature of women's work histories and pattern of participation in the labour market means that they have had limited access to such schemes (Groves 1987). For example, Family Policy Study Centre (1988) show that 22 per cent of women received a pension from a former employer compared to 72 per cent of men. Furthermore, the benefits available to women from such schemes reflect male/female earnings differentials and hence are much lower for women than for men. Recent figures show that while the number of those now members of an occupational pension scheme has grown, the differential between the sexes remains (37 per cent of women and 65 per cent of men) so continuing the low level of provision to future women pensioners (Government Actuary 1986). Although women, as opposed to men, generally experience less drop in income on reaching pensionable age this is almost entirely due to the lower level of income available to them previously either through paid work or as dependants in a domestic context. In addition, on account of their relative longevity, women have to survive on low income over a longer period and this contributes to the increased numbers in poverty in successive age bands. The impact of age and gender on income can be seen in Table 6.1. Old women are economically disadvantaged compared to men, a position that continues their experiences from earlier years. Also, given the greater proportion of older women who live alone, this disadvantage becomes even more pronounced for women as they age.

Table 6.1   Average disposable income by age, sex and marital status, 1982

Age	Married couples (£ per week)	Lone men (£ per week)	Lone women (£ per week)
60–64	—	—	57
65–69	96	67	49
70–74	86	54	49
75+	78	47	46
All ages	88	55	49

Source: DHSS 1984: 18

The discussion so far has concentrated upon the 'objective' circumstances of old people and particularly old women. While such measures are a central component of any consideration of old age they do not address other aspects of equal importance to any understanding of the lives of older people. In particular little attention has been paid to the subjective experiences of the everyday lives of older women (Phillipson 1982). One way of achieving a more holistic understanding of old age is to adopt an approach which places the accounts of old people centre stage. Here, in the second part of the chapter, we intend to do this for older women by drawing upon the small but growing number of studies which have adopted this approach, in particular using material from interviews with older women conducted by the authors (Ford and Sinclair 1987). The discussion is organized around three themes, each of them revealed as important to the women themselves as they talked about their experience of old age.

Security and independence: relationships within the family

The majority of older women live with their partners or on their own. For many their dependence on the community is no greater than that of younger people. However, for others the degree of independence they exercise and the extent of their control over their lives varies, most frequently affected by their mobility and physical health. Many have to rely on others, for example to bring in shopping, or to help with cleaning or transport. In most instances it is the family, and particularly female kin, who provide the assistance. Older women also look to the family as a source of companionship and to confirm their sense of identity, involvement, pride and worth. For women, identity and value have most often come from the private sphere and the traditional division of labour within the family. Here a series of roles – wife, mother and grandmother – have been, and continue to be, the basis of their identity, and the commitment to caring a source of emotional security and satisfaction. This is particularly the case with the current generations of older women fewer of whom have worked consistently outside the home and so have had less opportunity to develop any alternative basis as a source of respect and personal worth. However, even now, with the increase in the number of women in the labour market the evidence points to the major source of identity remaining centred around reproduction and domestic roles rather than shifting to the productive sphere (Oakley 1982). The importance of these roles and expectations continues into old age, in part, as Mathews (1979) suggests because of the absence of alternative roles for older women.

There is clearly a wide range of responses on the part of older women to the nature of their involvement with their families. In many cases older women do not experience the relationship as problematic and often express pleasure and gratitude for the help received. 'My daughter comes on Tuesdays . . . she generally brings me a lot of grocery stuff, you see, she keeps me well stocked up . . . I've got no regrets as regards my family' (Ford and Sinclair 1987: 136–7).'My niece brings a fair amount in for me, she goes to the butchers for me for my dinners' (Ford and Sinclair 1987: 84). Although happy with these arrangements this same woman recognized some of the dangers inherent in her reliance on her family and so sought to control unwanted intrusions.

'My niece says why don't you come to us, and why don't you do this? Well I won't go. I think that if you do that you give up . . . I won't go and live with my family. I'd rather be independent and do what I can to keep myself going, the best way I can. You see, while I'm here I can do as I like. If I want to go to bed and stop there I can but in somebody else's house you couldn't do that.'

(Ford and Sinclair 1987: 86)

Another woman, interviewed by Townsend (1968), made a similar point saying that she wished to live on her own because 'I can go to bed when I like and come back when I like. There is no one to say "Where've you been?"'. Townsend adds, 'She slapped the table with laughter at the thought of this reversal of role of mother and child' (1968: 37).

Familial roles and expectations may, however, be increasingly problematic for older women (and their children) in a number of ways that can give rise to conflicts, uncertainties and disappointments. Attempts to retain a central, active familial role on the part of older women may be perceived by others as inappropriate, and so resisted, either on the grounds of an assumed or actual physical or mental deterioration, or simply because from her children's point of view her position, power and significance in their lives has diminished. One of the widows interviewed by Mathews said of her role in the family:

> I lived with my daughter while I was looking for a place. I loved doing her housework and taking care of the children, but I would forget they were my grandchildren instead of my children and I would correct them. They resented being corrected by me.
>
> (Mathews 1979: 119)

While wishing to retain a clear role in the family older women reveal in their comments that they are aware of increasingly being pushed to the periphery of their children's lives. 'I shall have to ring my daughter on Sunday. I generally do and see how she's getting on. She never rings me' (Ford and Sinclair 1987: 21). Another of the women interviewed in the same study said, 'I expect I'll spend Christmas with one of my family, I don't know which; they will sort it out and one of them will come for me. I don't expect they will fight over having me' (1987: 123). Townsend reported one woman as saying, 'When you're old you're not wanted. My daughter just puts her head in the door when she's passing. She doesn't do anything. It's very hurtful' (1968: 111), although as he noted these sentiments were not necessarily widespread in his study.

A number of studies point up the extent to which older women feel that aspects of their lives are being curtailed by their families, often unnecessarily in their view, with a consequent sense of resentment. One woman in her 80s living with her husband felt she was being excluded from day-to-day decision-making.

> 'I don't really have a say . . . there are times when I do mind when the family gang up on me. There seems to be quite a lot of that going off in our household lately. You see, they want me to do what they want. I think while I can organize the house I should be allowed to.'
>
> (Ford and Sinclair 1987: 70)

In yet another instance a woman who had a lifelong interest and commitment to a political cause spoke of how she was an embarrassment to her family.

> 'They are still ashamed of me. I'm 82 and still they are ashamed. Sometimes I feel awfully hurt. . . . They tell me not to talk about politics. I said to them, "What do you think I'm going to do; stand at the door and wave the red flag?" But they are scared I might damage the way people see them. They want to get on.'
>
> (Ford and Sinclair 1987: 100)

The nature of the conflict and adjustment faced became clear when the woman continued, 'But you see, I need both of my children. I have to have a break from being on my own. I've made a promise to myself. I've vowed not to quarrel with them' (1987: 100). While the woman who so resented her exclusion from decision-making in the household said, 'I keep quiet because I think it's better to keep the peace' (1987: 70). These women are knowingly relinquishing some of their independence and control, their rights to hold and express their views and are complying with what they feel is now expected of them in order to retain something of the companionship, help, security and sense of worth that comes from involvement in the family.

From the point of view of the older person the provision of care or support facilities by the family may also have unanticipated consequences, which in some cases can exclude or push them to the margins of family life.

'One of my boys, Charlie I think it was, he came to me one day and he said to him and Michael and their wives had all been having a talk and they all thought it would be a good idea if I had a telephone. He said then if there was ever anything wrong any time, I could ring up and they'd come over; or if I like wanted the doctor I could call him. So they had this telephone put in for me. It was, it was bloody awful. I said I didn't care if they were paying for it, it was more trouble than it was worth and they were to have it taken away. One thing was they used to ring up and tell me they couldn't come over at the weekend to see me, so they'd rung up for a chat instead. You can understand it, it made things a lot easier for them. But it got to be none of them came for weeks on end – as soon as I heard the phone ringing on a Friday night I knew who it was, it was to say they couldn't come.'

(Parker 1983: 94–5)

For those older women who need or who are perceived to need greater care this may be provided by them living with their kin, most usually their daughters; a situation that may provide additional complexities to the position and experience of older women. Considerable attention has been focused upon the relationships between the carer and the cared for and increasingly the assumption of this relationship as non-problematic has been challenged. For example Evers (1984) and Peace (1986) both point to the likely difficulties associated with the willingness of women to relinquish their maternal role and become visibly dependent upon children (or other women). There is also the possibility that children may, in providing care, treat the old woman as a child thereby increasing her dependency or generating conflicts. The study of informal care is an important topic and one of legitimate concern that has been neglected until recently. However, those studies of caring, certainly as provided within the family, have tended to result in us knowing more about how the carers (usually female) see things (Finch and Groves 1983; Ungerson 1983; Equal Opportunities Commission 1982), their physical and emotional experiences, and the stresses and costs imposed on them. Yet they leave us with relatively little documentation of the perceptions, views, experiences and responses of those who are cared for. What does it feel like to be cared for as opposed to being the carer? How do mothers respond to being mothered? What aspects of the caring process are problematic, are there things they wish they could say but don't, and why not? What brings pleasure and what is emotionally painful, and what is the price of security? In what ways, if any, do they feel diminished and powerless? How do relationships between mothers and daughters change, and what are the likely determinants of a particular relationship and responses emerging? (See for example Marsden and Abrams

1987.) The area is, however, a difficult one to research. What material exists suggests that many old women know the 'rules of the game', the 'etiquette of care', to a greater extent than often allowed or assumed. Those rules indicate the terms on which continued support is likely to be forthcoming, at least in an emotionally satisfying manner and there are costs associated with 'biting the hand that feeds' that may make externalization of certain experiences of old age a difficult task for older women. Studies of old women in residential care have consistently suggested that there are pressures to 'not complain' or to 'not appear ungrateful', and such influences are also likely to be a feature of family care. Equally in saying that old women understand the rules of the encounters, this must clearly be qualified to give recognition to their circumstances, and particularly the extent of any physical and mental deterioration which reduces these abilities.

If women find that they are increasingly on the periphery of family life, in terms of time and emotional involvement, it is important to ask about alternative sources of identity and pleasure and to gain some understanding of how they structure their days and whether they manage to find alternative means of support: a situation compounded for them as their partners, friends and acquaintances age and die. A central theme of interviews with older women is their increasing sense of isolation and loneliness (distinct although often related experiences) but also their attempts to combat these feelings and to replace the void left by their changed position in the family, and the loss of friends.

> 'Friendship is important as you get older; friendship is more solid, it's your friends you turn to in the end for support and help in getting through the long days. Your family are your mainstay, they'll come at a moment's notice if you need them; but it's the ordinary days, weeks and months that have to be got through if you've been bereaved.'
>
> (Seabrook 1980: 103)

One of Townsend's respondents who was widowed and living with her daughter and grand-daughter catches the tone of what many older widows feel.

> 'I sit here for hours . . . I get depressed and I start crying. We was always together. I can remember even his laughing . . . I sit here for hours thinking about him. I can't get over it.'
>
> (Townsend 1968: 168)

> 'I'm not really isolated, but I do feel lonely sometimes. It's just an emptiness and feeling alone. It's a hollow, and you wonder what everything is for. . . . Although my daughter lives near me she has her own life to lead . . . I try never to show them.'
>
> (Ford and Sinclair 1987: 94)

Another woman of 90 said

> 'I'm tired of being by myself. I don't know what to do . . . really it is that I can't get about, that's the only thing and I don't have anybody. I'm

lonely and I think being lonely is a kind of illness – it's a drawback at any rate.'

(Ford and Sinclair 1987: 14)

Loneliness for many old women is counteracted by activity:

'At my age you've got to fill up your life as best you can otherwise you could easily end up taking pills and tranquillizers and being very sorry for yourself. But I'm not that sort of person, or at least I hope I'm not. I like to try and keep my mind active by going to the library for books and I make a point of buying a newspaper every day to keep me up to date in the world.'

(Parker 1983: 356)

Others fill the gap by joining:

'I like company and I miss it if I'm not amongst it, that's why now I join everything I can . . . I go to everything. I get depressed when I've nothing to think about for tomorrow. If you stop in it's all work and tiredness – whereas to go out, to go to the tea shop and have a cup of tea brought to you, and you talk and you forget yourself and everything.'

(Ford and Sinclair 1987: 68)

Experiencing ageism

Ageism is the systematic stereotyping of individuals on the basis of chronological age, irrespective of their individual characteristics. As we have already argued, the stereotypes stress the decline, the dependence and the powerlessness of older people and allow us to deny them independence, autonomy and respect, and to create low expectations of them. Ageism can take many forms and is seen in a multitude of ways which range from apparently trivial disrespect through to major abuse. (See for instance Wagner Report 1988; Nye Bevan Lodge Enquiry 1987.) Gender discrimination results in a situation where older women are seen as even less deserving than other groups. Studies of older women indicate that they are aware of the substance and consequences of ageism although they do not necessarily talk about it in these terms; rather they refer to instances where their privacy is disregarded, their choices curtailed, their requests ignored, and where they feel others have little regard or few expectations of them. Because it is more in the public domain, some of the clearest and most extreme examples of ageism can be seen in the accounts of residents in institutional settings (and so apply particularly to women who make up two-thirds of the population in residential care), but as will be shown below it is inappropriate to see the problem as confined to this sphere.

'Some have no time for you . . . I find when I go out I stand on the corner trying to cross. Lots of people ignore me and don't help, but there's usually one in the end. But those youngsters, they'll throw a bike down in front of you on the pavement.'

(Ford and Sinclair 1987: 22)

In that same study a woman who walked with two sticks told us of the reluctance of people to make space for her, and of cars that hooted impatiently when she was crossing the roads. Another who lived in warden-assisted housing, where there were severe ·problems with the noise and the heating, talked of the residents being ignored and the way 'the warden doesn't care', and the way people made gestures to the old (such as warden-assisted housing) but did not then care for them. 'Just throw it up quick, let's get the old people in. We've done something for them, made a good show of it' (Ford and Sinclair 1987: 117). Another widow living in a low-rise local authority block said,

> 'Quite a lot of youngsters used to congregate just at the back. Sometimes they made remarks but they could be frightening by just being there. I spoke to them and asked why they did it to us and that we were all widows living alone. One of them told me to "Fuck off".'
>
> (Ford and Sinclair 1987: 101)

Some women, particularly those in residential care, recognize the low expectations others have of them, that often results in a lack of provision for activities, or lack of imagination in those provided. One woman was reported as saying, 'You just go and sit and perhaps talk. I do an awful lot of just sitting. . . . You spend most of your time thinking about the past, that's if you haven't dozed off. You sit and think about what's happened because you haven't got much of a future' (Ford and Sinclair 1987: 34). 'If I have to go to the Safari Park once more I'll know all the bloody monkeys by name' (DHSS 1979). Another instance reported by Wilkin and Hughes again suggests the limited expectations of the old. Asked how she spent her time a woman who had previously read a great deal but who now had deteriorating eyesight and arthritis said:

> 'Sitting looking out of the window, looking at the sky . . . sometimes I ask myself why I live so long . . . I'm like the old woman when they asked "What do you do when you don't sit?" she replied "I just sit".'
>
> (Wilkin and Hughes 1987: 180)

The authors comment that this woman could read with a magnifier but had never been offered one and had not tried large-print books. Entry to a residential home may also involve experiences that undermine adult status through a sense of a loss of personal control. For example residents may be unable to organize their time, or be denied privacy with regard to their affairs, or find themselves unable to secure certain needs or information, or be denied the means to maintain their self-identity, experiences that may often be justified in terms of institutional administration and routine.

> 'I'll tell you what happened with my pension book. They have it here, they take it when you come in to help keep you and they give you so much back as spending money. I think they decide how much you get. In fact I do not know how much the pension is now. I've told them to let me know when

it's due again. It belongs to me but they have it. They never say anything to you about it.'

(Ford and Sinclair 1987: 36)

This same woman raised the question of the public discussion of personal affairs, something she disliked intensely.

'One real trouble is if you are down at the table it echos and if anybody says anything, everybody can hear it. It's a big drawback, as you don't want everyone to hear what you've got to say. Say the Matron or anyone comes and says something to you ... well everyone is looking and listening. Their eyes and ears are always on.'

(Ford and Sinclair 1987: 35)

Several studies point to women's accounts of their loss of self-esteem through a denial of personal clothing or by being made to wait for needed personal services such as bathing or toileting (Wilkin and Hughes 1987; Evers 1984). The recognition by older women of the processes that demean and limit them are clearly expressed in this poem submitted to the Wagner Committee by a resident of a home:

> They keep you waiting
> Then suggest
> That your request
> Is most unreasonable.
> We don't let our old ladies
> Have kettles in their rooms
> They might have accidents.
> We can't allow you to have
> A tray upon your knee.
> Who says they can't allow?
> What sort of way is that to speak
> To grown up people in their 'home'?

(Wagner Report 1988: 144)

Thus it is clear that many women recognize society's attitudes towards them, and report that they experience life as demeaning, as lacking choice, as denying them control. Some also indicate a growing acceptance of society's image as their own self-image.

A challenge to ageism?

As has been indicated, the danger of ageism is that it aggregates all old people together and labels them all as problematic, dependent and uninteresting. In contrast, subjective accounts of the everyday lives of older women indicate a range of life-styles, and a variety of responses to their circumstances. Inevitably cases of extreme dependency and powerlessness exist and it is these that have often been highlighted. There are also cases such as those cited earlier in this chapter where women hold back from making demands (especially of their children) because they need and wish to retain their emotional support and family contacts. Thus, to varying degrees, they are complying with other people's expectations of them and limiting their own autonomy and control. Against the context of ageism, however, much of the process of negotiating old age, as reported by older people and often involving the small details of everyday living, can itself be interpreted as a challenge to ageism. In some cases actions may constitute a deliberate challenge to the position imposed upon them or the attitudes they meet. Mathews in her consideration of old widows provides evidence of what she refers to as non-compliance in her discussion of the relationship between a widow and her daughter-in-law.

'My daughter-in-law is a pest. Last time I went [to the Doctor] she had to take me because I didn't have anyone else. She told the Doctor, "I want her ears washed out. She doesn't hear anything I say". I whispered to him and I said "Well I'll tell you why. She says such a lot of things I don't want to hear and I just turn off". She accused me of it one time. "You just turn off when you don't want to hear something". That's what I do.'

(Mathews 1979: 132)

Other challenges may be more covert, managed with an eye to the power of those in control, as for instance in the case of a woman in a residential home who described the morning routine, and her response to it. 'We have a cup of tea about seven, and they come and give you a tablet. It's a water tablet to make you go. I don't need it, but you have to take it from them so then I put it down the sink' (Ford and Sinclair 1987: 34). However, Evers (1984) in her study of geriatric wards points out that women who overtly challenged their care as demeaning, restrictive, and so on, the 'Awkward Alices', were then controlled by being ignored, or physically relocated, actions that further reduced their significance and self-respect.

Other women may be less aware of their challenge, but nevertheless engaged in one. Often for them the framework is one of taking all steps possible to maintain their independence, as can be seen in the case of the woman with an artificial leg who made herself go out every day and cross the road even though it held up the traffic and motorists made their feelings clear to her: 'I get nervous and don't want to do it, but I can help myself keep my confidence by crossing the road regularly' (Ford and Sinclair 1987. 68). In discussing the lives of older women Rich commented that she saw in their lives 'a daily heroism . . . a depth of survival knowledge . . . often a special inventiveness and creativity' (MacDonald and Rich 1984) directed towards resolving the dilemmas of independence and security, and the pressures to passivity and submission in favour of greater personal control. The inventiveness and creativity comes in many forms. Women learn to handle the loneliness of widowhood with dignity by keeping the process a private one and so not burdening their children. Women search for better places to live, they round on those who swear at them, they learn to drive in order to maintain mobility, they climb perilously steep bus steps, in order to go to town for a day, they take up new activities, undertake courses, or continue in paid work in order to remain active and independent (Ford and Sinclair 1987).

The argument in this chapter has been that the more objective accounts of the position of old people have to be supplemented with an emphasis upon the subjective experience of old age. Such an approach provides the grounds for recognizing the diversity amongst the old and for giving due acknowledgement to the complexities of their lives. As a consequence, it challenges the assumption that equates chronological age with a particular set of stereo-typical characteristics. Such an approach also reminds us of the need to see behind policies and practices that deal with aggregate groups to the individual old person with particular needs and resources. Some of these old people will lead fulfilling and independent lives, others will need high levels of care and attention. Policies for elderly people should therefore relate to all aspects of life and include not only the provision of care and support, but also public transport, local shops and services, large-print books and notices.

Listening to and reporting the experience of old age as told by old people points up the extent of ageism in our society – an ageism which itself underpins many of our current social policies and practice. It would seem therefore that any significant improvement in policies and practices must start by recognizing and challenging ageist attitudes and implementing anti-ageist policies. Indeed there is some evidence that these first needs are now being acknowledged with the growing practice within local authorities of adopting Service Principles, although issues of implementation remain. Similarly the two major reports before the government which impact upon services for elderly people also, in varying degree, acknowledge the need for policies which will give more effective rights to those individuals in need of support and care (Wagner Report 1988; Griffiths Report 1988). These rights are clearly expressed in the Code of Practice for residential care issued by the DHSS. 'Concepts such as privacy, autonomy, individuality, esteem, choice, and responsible risk taking, provide the foundations and reference points for good practice' (Centre for Policy on Ageing 1986).

Statements of Service Principles or Codes of Practice are only a beginning. This was made very clear in the introduction to the Wagner Report.

> Unless society at large feels the same indignation as the Committee at the way in which the present system can devalue the lives of some of the people most in need of help and support – despite the dedicated work of so many – then recommendations will remain recommendations.
>
> (Wagner Report 1988: 6)

This points to the fact that it is the attitudes that prevail within the wider society, the notions that people have of the worth and value of older people, that will determine the services that are provided and the respect that is accorded to elderly people. These issues remain of overwhelming significance to women, who form the majority of the old population.

> '[Old] people notice things and they're hurt by it. . . . Old people have put into the world and worked hard . . . we shouldn't have to go down on

bended knee. We should not be subjected to a lot of things that go on. It's very unfair. I've told you before that other people write off old age and it's so unfair.'

(Ford and Sinclair 1987: 118)

References

Butler, R. M. and Lewis, M. I. (1983) *Ageing and Mental Health*, St. Louis, MO: Mosby.
Centre for Policy on Ageing (1986) *Home Life: Code of Practice for Residential Care*. London: Centre for Policy on Ageing.
Dale, A., Evandson, M. and Arber, S. (1987) 'The household structure of the elderly population in Britain, *Ageing and Society*, 7: 37–56.
DHSS (1979) *Residential Care for the Elderly in London*, London Social Work Service.
—— (1984) *Population, Pension Costs and Pensioners' Incomes*, London: HMSO.
Equal Opportunities Commission (1982) *Caring for the Elderly and Handicapped: Community Care and Women's Lives*, Manchester: Equal Opportunities Commission.
Evers, H. (1984) 'Care or custody? The experiences of women patients in long-stay geriatric wards', in B. Hutter and G. Williams (eds) *Controlling Women: the Normal and the Deviant*, London: Croom Helm.
Family Policy Study Centre (1988) *An Ageing Population*, fact sheet, London: FPSC.
Fennell, G., Phillipson, C. and Evers, H. (1988) *The Sociology of Old Age*, Milton Keynes: Open University Press.
Finch, J. and Groves, D. (1983) *A Labour of Love*, London: Routledge & Kegan Paul.
Ford, J. and Sinclair, R. (1987) *Sixty Years On: Women Talk About Old Age*, London: Women's Press.
Government Actuary (1986) *Occupational Pension Schemes*, London: HMSO.
Griffiths Report (1988) *Community Care: Agenda for Action*, London: HMSO.
Groves, D. (1987) 'Occupational pension provision and women's poverty in old age', in C. Glendinning and J. Millar (eds) *Women and Poverty in Britain*, Brighton: Wheatsheaf.
Jones, J., Ester, C. and Binney, E. (1987) 'Gender, public policy and the oldest old', *Ageing and Society*, 7: 175–302.
MacDonald, B. and Rich, C. (1984) *Look Me in the Eye*, London: Women's Press.
Marsden, D. and Abrams, S. (1987) '"Liberators", "Companions", "Intruders" and "Cuckoos in the Nest": A sociology of caring relations over the life cycle', in P. Allatt, T. Keil, A. Bryman, and B. Bytheway (eds) *Women and the Life Cycle: Transitions and Turning Points*, London: Macmillan.
Mathews, S. (1979) *The Social World of Old Women*, New York: Sage.
Nye Bevan Lodge Enquiry (1987) *Report*, London: Borough of Southwark
Oakley, A. (1982) *Subject Women*, London: Fontana.
Parker, S. (1980) *Older Workers and Retirement*, London: HMSO.
Parker, T. (1983) *The People of Providence*, London: Hutchinson.
Peace, S. (1986) 'The forgotten female: social policy and older women', in C. Phillipson and A. Walker (eds) *Ageing and Social Policy*, London: Gower.
Phillipson, C. (1982) *Capitalism and the Construction of Old Age*, London: Macmillan.
Seabrook, J. (1980) *The Way We Are: Old People Talk About Themselves*, London: Age Concern.
Sinclair, I. (ed.) (1988) *Residential Care: The Research Reviewed*, NISW, London: HMSO.
Sontag, S. (1972) 'The double standard', *Saturday Review*, 55: 29–38.

Stevenson, O. (1987) *Women in Old Age: Reflections on Policy and Practice*, inaugural lecture, University of Nottingham.

Szinovacs, M. (ed.) (1982) *Women's Retirement – Policy Implications of Research*, New York: Sage.

Townsend, P. (1968) *The Family Life of Old People*, Harmondsworth: Pelican.

—— (1986) 'Ageism and social policy', in C. Phillipson and A. Walker (eds) *Ageing and Social Policy*, London: Gower.

Ungerson, C. (1983) 'Women and caring: skills, tasks and taboos', in E. Gamarnikow, D. Morgan, J. Purvis and D. Taylorson (eds) *The Public and the Private*, London: Heinemann.

Wagner Report (1988) *Residential Care: A Positive Choice*, London: HMSO.

Walker, A. (1987) 'The poor relation: poverty among old women', in C. Glendinning and J. Miller (eds) *Women and Poverty in Britain*, Brighton: Wheatsheaf.

Wenger, G. C. (1984) *The Supportive Network*, London: Allen & Unwin.

Wilkin, D. and Hughes, B. (1987) 'Residential care of elderly people: the consumers' views', *Ageing and Society*, 7: 175–201.

7
The social work press

Eamonn Rafferty

Within the last decade the 'trade' press has established itself as one of the most lucrative aspects of publishing. Guaranteed readers arising from the nature of editorial coverage, and a virtually guaranteed income from advertisements make the trade press highly profitable, once basic criteria are met. Most of the major magazine publishing groups – EMAP, Benn, Reed, Morgan Grampian – have been consolidating their interests in this profitable 'niche' sector. Many of the magazines have loose affiliations with the professional associations to which readers belong. But increasingly publishers are going it alone, using their experience to set up new titles after initial market research into the potential volume of recruitment/sectoral advertisments and the capacity for ancillary activities – conferences, pamphlets, and other revenue activities.

For the best part these magazines are very successful publishing ventures with the readers and owners locked into a mutually satisfying *modus operandi*. This gives one side information about the job – and possibly the next – and the other the revenue. Not surprisingly there are hundreds of trade magazines which rarely appear on newsagents' shelves as the circulation is either 'controlled' or by subscription only. These titles cover occupations as diverse as accountants and nurses but invariably follow a similar editorial format of news about the job from around the country, policy debates, features and general information. Though there is no definitive information about what precisely readers want, it is assumed that a mixture of these is sufficient to satisfy a curiosity about developments within one's own job or sharpen one's perceptions about the evolving nature of the profession. It is this editorial concept which the publishers tend to play up in promoting the magazine's role within the profession; this is invariably for marketing reasons, as the more the title is seen to be in touch with the sector it is aimed at, then the better that is for revenue potential.

Ironically it is the hard-pressed public sector which is the single biggest contributor to many of the magazines' success as the bulk of recruitment advertisements come from this source; certainly it is the local authorities which provide most of the revenue for the four social work magazines: *Social Work Today*, *Community Care*, *Insight*, and *Care Weekly*. In the current economic climate one must assume that recruitment costs are increasingly facing closer scrutiny and that local authorities will be looking to rationalize their whole recruitment operation. This may be one reason why some of the social work magazines have been updating 'media packs' extolling their virtues, and including a sectoral analysis of who turns to which publication when looking for jobs. However, one of the magazines, *Insight*, failed to penetrate the advertisement market and was subsequently sold to Reed Business Publishing, the owners of *Community Care*, in 1988. This failure to generate crucial advertising revenue was ultimately the fatal blow to an already weak arrangement: the publisher, Care Matters, had no real experience of social work and the Association of Directors of Social Services, who collaborated on the venture, had no previous experience of publishing. These deficiences compounded the problems that the magazine encountered and were most obvious in its wavering editorial concept and 'thin' recruitment section.

Covering the affairs of any profession poses its own problems and social work is no different as is evidenced by the oversimplification of the issues in child abuse controversies in 1987/8 in the national media. Consequently there is a belief by some within the profession that a more 'balanced coverage' is needed as redress against these excesses. There is a suspicion, therefore, that in addition to covering the sector, the magazines are expected to shore up the bruised self-image of the profession through a series of 'friendly' positive articles. But the magazines to their credit appear to be able to resist the expectation that they are there to massage social work's collective ego.

The editorial format of the publications has evolved over the years, but it has, bar a few refinements, followed the standard model: a mixture of news, features (both in-house and contributed), guest columns, access columns, comment, reviews, practice/training, lobby and noticeboard/diary slots. There have been changes to this formula, most notably in the segmentation, so that the longer features have steadily been cut back in favour of the 1,800-word maximum article where possible. Today the magazines have a fresher design-led feeling to them, but are still produced within clearly definable parameters. This format reflects as much the requirements of production as preference, since tight schedules demand that much 'copy' is set in advance. Features are often put together sometimes well before publication, allowing the staff to concentrate on news-gathering. Only the newcomer to the scene, *Residential and Day Care Weekly*, has departed significantly from the format with its strong emphasis on news, though its tabloid format is not universally liked. The magazines are not, however, as locked into 'uniformity' as their similar editorial formats suggest. There is always an eye to innovation, particularly in the endorsement of good practice as many of the features are, in effect, descriptions of worthwhile projects. In that respect the magazines are advocates of progressive social work, but it is the occupation of this 'high moral ground' that can cause tensions within orthodox sectors of social work as the ideological sands shift. For example, towards a more penetrating analysis of race and gender and the subsequent coverage these issues receive.

The circulation of the four titles is each around the mid-20,000s, though the vast majority of subscriptions in each case are free, or 'controlled' as the publishers put it, which means one can have a free copy as long as one formally requests it and falls into a particular category (usually full-time workers, managers, final-year students and the like). These are usually updated ('verified') annually. With virtually no 'casual' sales to speak of, the magazines are left to build up circulation through subscriptions, or perhaps more appropriately retain circulation, as sales seem to have reached a plateau. Unlike conventional publications, sheer sales volume does not play such an important part as most of the income is generated from advertising. What is important is for the social work titles to be able to tell advertisers that the right people are reading the magazine.

Social Work Today has been publishing the longest – since April 1970 when it was launched as the official organ of the British Association of Social Workers (BASW). Initially it appeared as a monthly journal of academic content dissecting and discussing the current theory and practice of social work. It amalgamated a number of other existing specialist publications at the time including *Medical Social Work, Mental Welfare, ASW News* and the somewhat unlikely *Bulletin of the Association of Moral Welfare Workers*. The first issue comprised fifty-six pages, eighteen of which were advertisements; however, twenty years on and the balance of contents is still remarkably similar. The monthly format changed to fortnightly and then to the present weekly.

Historically it was *Social Work Today* that chronicled the changes in social services after reorganization in the early 1970s – the rapid expansion of generic training courses and of course the era of secondment. In that respect the magazine was singularly well-placed to report on the heady days of the new-look social work, as it was a full four years before the next title arrived. *Social Work Today* stayed in BASW ownership until it sold a 50 per cent stake to publishers Macmillans for £2 million in January 1988. It is now owned by a new company, BASW/Macmillan Ltd. Until the sale, the magazine was the major source of BASW funding giving it a revenue base to help finance its other professional activities. After the partial sale the magazine moved to London from Birmingham where it underwent a 'revamp' which helped to give it an increased air of confidence. The move to London also altered the sense of interdependency between the magazine and BASW. Whether real or apparent, *Social Work Today* seemed to shake off the BASW orthodoxy which permeated the old magazine. Even though BASW retained a page in the magazine, the umbilical cord has been cut after eighteen years. For Macmillan the part purchase made obvious strategic sense, given its other health publications and its heavy investment in social work textbooks, but it could also be justified on the acquisitive tendencies among major publishers. Whether Macmillan has some radical long-term plans for the magazine remains to be seen. It no longer has an executive as such, but still has an editorial board of about ten which is composed of leading figures from social work.

Community Care is considered by many (particularly the magazine itself) as the 'market leader' though its circulation is about the same as the rest. One might say it plays a *Sunday Times* to *Social Work Today's Observer*. Certainly it contains more articles and, by and large, more in-house news coverage. This is reflected in the weekly pagination which is often more than 100, compared to *Social Work Today's* 60s, *Insight's* 30s and *Care Weekly's* 20s. The magazine, which was launched in April 1974, is owned by Reed Business Publishing and is grouped along with the company's construction and agriculture publications. Like most of the group's titles, it enjoys a large degree of commercial autonomy and complete editorial independence. So assuming the sales target set by the group are reached, the magazine has a free hand to get on with the business.

In addition, *Community Care* is not linked formally with any of the professional associations, something which it exploits in an almost gleeful manner below the masthead – 'The independent voice of social work'. Presumably this is as much a swipe at one of the others – as a commendable point to readers. In a 'media pack', produced mainly for advertisers, it uses the results of some research to say that *Community Care* is the most widely read social work publication among all categories of workers and in a variety of settings from headquarters to residential homes; the most widely read when it came to looking for jobs. The magazine's circulation of around 27,000 includes more than 25,000 controlled subscribers. The day-to-day control of the publication rests with the full-time staff and there are seven editorial advisers who meet formally twice a year to discuss the previous six months' contents and advise on the forthcoming schedules and range of articles that are likely to be covered. These advisers are picked by the editor after consultation from other senior staff. The magazine is also engaged in a number of other activities including research monographs, training videos and practice hand-books, conferences, books and an annual competition.

Social Services Insight described itself at its launch in January 1986 as 'unambiguously a journal of social services management' and the result of discussions between the Association of Directors of Social Services (ADSS) and a venture publisher. The magazine was published 'in association' with the ADSS, which was different in practice from the relationships *Social Work Today* had with BASW. Though ADSS members were on the editorial board and it had a right of veto on the appointment of editor, to all intents the magazine had editorial independence prior to its sale to Reed. In exchange for its 'endorsement' the ADSS received £50,000 a year to help fund its secretariat, and an additional profits-related sum on a sliding scale. The magazine wandered off its original editorial format which compounded the overall problems it was then facing. During the contents analysis period for this chapter (January-April 1988) it was attempting to cover all aspects of social services. *Insight* tried to save the day then by reaffirming its original editorial format of a 'unique' analysis of social services from the management perspective and had hoped to develop this theme through additional publishing and conference activities, which would both increase the magazine's profile and provide extra revenue. It identified its priorities in an internal document in which it considered the various aspects of catering for the target readership.

> We should aim to articulate the concerns which affect social services management generally, though pitch this very much at middle management levels which will inevitably form the basis of our (reduced) readership. It means us fusing the journal's identity with the identity social services managers are striving to create for themselves.

A more pronounced concentration on the management side of social services would have inevitably meant the magazine was less attractive for the full range of recruitment advertisements, though it believed then some 35 per cent of all advertisements were for management grades. It was misplaced optimism however, if it was hoped to get the vast majority of advertisements from that sector, given that the other two mainstream titles were aggressive sellers of advertising space.

Residential and Day Care Weekly was launched in October 1987 as a venture publication for this 'over-shadowed' sector. At the time work was being completed on two reports which would have profound implications for the residential sector. The Wagner Report on Residential Care and the Griffiths Report on Community Care reported in March 1988 and gave the magazine the chance to acquire *gravitas* over its coverage. For here was a publication that could essentially and singularly articulate the issues that affected the residential and day-care sector. The magazine was acutely aware of what it believed to be the paucity of coverage of the sector when it said at its launch that, for the first time, there would be a weekly journal in which the 'everyday concerns and long-term interests' of the sector would not be 'overshadowed by field social work issues.' There were suspicions at the time that the magazine would become an apologist for the private sector. But while it is unambiguously for a 'mixed economy' there is no indication that it intends to offer unqualified support. It is in favour of the same regulatory standards being applied to both private and public homes. In addition, it sees the magazine as providing a 'forum . . . in which people working in the public, voluntary and private sectors of residential and day care can start to exchange information, ideas and opinions – a process which . . . is long overdue'.

Most of the staff journalists employed by the magazines have been formally trained and come with a breadth of experience, though some do have particular social services knowledge. In any event most soon learn about the profession and are uniquely placed to apply their journalistic skills to unravelling the policy issues that tend to dominate coverage of social services.

Significantly it is policy matters, rather than practice ones, in which the journalists are most conversant. There is nothing other than anecdotal evidence about the careers (previous and subsequent) of the journalists, but many have built upon the expertise they have gained in the social work field to move to other 'specialist' jobs or begin working in the quality freelance market: in fact many journalists now in national newspapers have worked for the magazines in the past. The journalistic style in the magazines is very much modelled on quality lines, and there is a marked absence of the tabloid approach, with straight news reporting, features analysis and explanation preferred instead.

Of the range of stories that are covered many are 'national' and, therefore, often have implications for social services departments (SSDs) throughout the country. The chances are that these pieces are covered to some extent in all the magazines, as they are 'released' through some official mechanism; what differs is usually the prominence each publication attaches to the story. Some of these trends and general similarities are examined through a content analysis of the period 1 January 1988 to 31 March 1988.

Leafing through the third issue of this period (21/22 January) revealed how the magazines treated various stories. *Community Care's* lead story was 'exclusive' and about job threats at the Central Council for Education and Training in Social Work (CCETSW). The magazine interestingly had CCETSW director Tony Hall quoted on the record as intending to discuss the issue with those involved.[1]

Social Work Today had a story on homes inspection as its lead: 'Extra money for inspecting homes unlikely to meet costs'.[2] It outlined the findings of a DHSS study on the registration costs of private residential homes. This story was also covered in *Community Care* as its second lead and both magazines quoted the same spokespersons. *Social Services Insight* decided to lead with a story that the Griffiths Report would mark a shift towards privatization, and had no reference to the registration costs story.[3] *Care Weekly's* lead for that week's issue was about a 'complaints hotline' for residential staff in Gloucestershire to pass on information about alleged abuse direct to SSD headquarters and bypass the officer-in -charge.[4] It also carried a version of the registration story as an inside page lead, but with the emphasis on fears that registration costs would rise.[5]

For that week's issue, *Insight* had ten news stories, *Social Work Today* had fourteen, *Community Care* sixteen, and *Care Weekly* twelve. There was broadly the same coverage on subsidiary news stories in the first three publications: recruitment/cash crisis in London boroughs; new job for social worker in child abuse inquiry, and warnings over the impending Social Fund.

Not surprisingly the introduction of the cash-limited, loan-based Social Fund formed the basis of many news/feature stories in the three-month contents analysis period. The ideology underpinning the new alternative to single payments was under constant criticism from all the representative bodies in social services, as was the implied role of arbiter that social workers were expected to undertake. Though the 'warning' noises about the implications of the Social Fund preceded this period, it was the approaching April introduction that concentrated many of the contributors' minds. The Social Fund was, of course, only one of the aspects of the new Social Security Act 1988. Details of this were carried in the magazines' benefits sections and supplements. The special supplement which *Community Care* carried on the Act in its 28 January issue led to 9,000 requests for additional copies – an indication of the importance social workers, teachers and administrators attached to a guide on the Act.[6] Though the details of the Act were extensively covered, it was the policy implications of the Social Fund itself which attracted much of the comment.

Under an exclusive tag, *Community Care*'s lead story on 7 January – 'Fury over Social Fund Form' – claimed that Social Fund applicants would be asked for information about their social workers.[7] The magazine said that it had a copy of a form which asked if the claimants agreed that their social worker could be contacted for further details. In the next issue, however, *Community Care* carried a story in which the DHSS denied that social workers would be asked to help in assessing claims.[8] *Social Work Today* in its 7 January issue carried a short article which said the Association of Metropolitan Authorities had agreed guidelines on how local authority agencies should co-operate over the Social Fund.[9] The magazine followed this with a two-page feature in which two contributors discussed the issue.[10] One, a welfare rights worker, was recommending that social workers pursue the principles of 'determined advocacy' as a response to the insidious features of the Social Fund. Determined advocacy put the needs of clients first, the writer argued. And this was about confrontation not collusion. On the facing page, a social services director said it was important that social workers co-operated with Social Fund officers and was critical of the guidelines BASW produced because of their 'political' content. 'Because BASW, and others, cannot decide how best to approach the Social Fund, the guidelines drift between political and profes-sional statements and are therefore contradictory or full of ambiguity'.[11] The article ended by saying that as long as the Social Fund existed 'there is a need to work with Social Fund officers in a spirit of co-operation to get the best possible deal for clients.' Understandably in the following week's issue some letter writers objected to this 'accommodation' over the Social Fund.[12]

Social Services Insight reported on allegations made by Labour social services spokesperson Robin Cook that there was political bias in the allocation of Social Fund cash.[13] In its issue of 22 January, *Insight* reported warnings from the AMA and ACC that there could be threats of violence against social services staff once the Social Fund was introduced.[14] This warning was also carried in *Community Care*,[15] but *Social Work Today* emphasized the 'extended services' both associations said would be needed after the introduction of the Fund.[16]

Insight's cover story on 29 January was a profile of Social Fund commis-sioner Rosalind Mackworth.[17] Ms Mackworth, a solicitor, was appointed to the part-time post for a three-year period and had particular responsibility for appointing Social Fund inspectors. In their corresponding issues, *Social Work*

Today and *Community Care* both had short stories on the Fund. *Community Care* claimed the DHSS itself was concerned that the Social Fund would not work,[18] while *Social Work Today* reported on a DHSS invitation to social services directors to discuss the Fund's implementation.[19] In the next week's issues both *Community Care* and *Insight* reported as their main stories that NALGO – the main social work union – had decided not to ballot its members on possible non-cooperation with the Social Fund and its officers. *Community Care* reported that the NALGO ballot had been 'postponed' and its branches circulated instead with the local authority produced guidelines on the Fund.[20] *Insight* added that the move had been clearly influenced by indications that branches would not support any industrial action over the issue.[21] *Social Work Today* followed the report with news that NALGO would monitor local authorities to ensure the guidelines were followed.[22]

In the issues to the end of March the Social Fund again featured heavily in the magazines. *Insight* reported in its 'Lobby' section on Parliament moves by the Opposition to block the passage of the Fund.[23] The motion was heavily defeated or as the magazine drily reported *Hansard* as recording: 'The question was accordingly negatived.'

In the three-months content analysis the magazines kept a broad similarity in their news stories. Not surprisingly it was the problems of cuts, staff shortages, and increasingly the problem of violence against social workers that featured heavily in coverage. *Insight* reported on 15 January that 500 social services staff in Nottingham had been issued with personal 'shrill' alarms as a measure against increasing violence.[24] Not that the problem was confined solely to staff, as *Care Weekly* reported the previous week on a plan to issue people in sheltered housing with anti-mugging devices.[25] This was followed by an article in *Social Work Today* on how Rochdale and Staffordshire SSDs had agreed packages to protect staff from violent attacks.[26] In Staffordshire the department was to introduce training courses, while Rochdale promised both to prosecute attackers and make a note about violent tendencies of clients on their files. The Rochdale moves were also reported in *Community Care*'s corresponding issue.[27] Because the magazines have a similar editorial format and style, coverage of the main articles bear close resemblance. Perhaps one might give more prominence to a story, or give it a stronger position in the page, but for the best part the similarities are strong, even to the point where it might be possible to 'swap' stories among magazines without detection by the casual reader.

All the titles have an editorial or comment slot which invariably discusses and takes a stance on major news issues of the week. Most of the editorials are written 'in house' by the editor or a senior member of the editorial staff. *Social Work Today*, however, varies its in-house editorials (Comment) with those commissioned from outside (Opinion) but again the theme is on a current news topic.

All the editorials bear a close ideological relationship in that they tend to be supportive of organized social work and seek to remove those impediments which militate against it – financial restraints, inadequate training, legal anomalies, and so on. In many cases the magazines inhabit the high moral ground of aspirational social work. It may be frustrating at times to social workers in the field who are working with inadequate resources to be told about the importance of some principle or another. But by and large they are protective of social work, particularly from other parts of the media, even going as far to carry stories on how best to deal with a hostile press. *Community Care* has also published a book, *Media Matters*, and organized a conference on the subject.

On one of the major issues, the Griffiths Report into community care, all the magazines carried an editorial on its findings. *Community Care* urged readers to 'check out' the report which it felt had endorsed the role of the local authority as a 'glorified travel agency' not a municipal powerhouse: 'Today's practitioners and tomorrow's carebrokers should welcome the principle that the needs of individuals matter more than the theology of local government'.[28] Under the heading of 'Will government rise to Griffiths challenge?' *Social Work Today* said that, if implemented, the review 'would provide a basis for much more effective service'.[29] It considered a recommendation for a minister to oversee community care as 'significant' and welcomed the strengthening of the local authority role that the report envisaged, even if this was 'discomforting' for the government. *Care Weekly* was, however, more guarded in its review and wondered whether paradoxically the transfer of any finance currently spent on private residential care would ultimately 'lure' social workers into administering part of the Social Fund. In its editorial 'Heading into Mrs T's lap' the magazine argued that the debate within local authorities needed to consider 'whether Sir Roy's proposals add up to two steps forward and one backwards; or one in the right direction, and two into the lap of Mrs Thatcher'.[30] *Insight*, under the headline of 'hammering the message home' said that the Audit Commission was clear – something had to be done.[31] 'Let everyone keep hammering that home until the Government faces up to the message.'

It is the features section of the magazines that give the greatest access to contributors: practitioners, researchers, teachers and academics. Although the expectation is that contributed articles should be as far as possible 'innovatory' or definitive in some way, in practice many are likely to be anecdotal and experiential. There is nothing objectionable to this as many well-written pieces have their origins in the carefully chronicled experiences of some unusual, but not unique, project whose chances of replication elsewhere are enhanced by publication. There are those – particularly within some of the publications themselves – who believe that the very specialist nature of many of these articles means they are unlikely to appeal to others. Just how the magazines can maintain a balance of coverage across the diverse nature of social work is something that preoccupies senior editorial staff. All the magazines use regular 'names' who are prominent in social work or social policy. But the majority of contributed features are from occasional writers: for some it may be their first published article. People write for a variety of reasons whether it offers the chance to bring to a wider readership some important experiences of views, or even if one is merely alert to the self-publicity. In any event, the magazines are well used to receiving unsolicited articles: one gets about forty a month. There is a fairly well-developed routine in the magazines for dealing with these and indeed other articles. If they are very bad – 'beyond redemption' – they are rejected; if good in literacy form but the editor is unsure of its merits then sometimes they are sent to outside specialists for 'assessment'. Alternatively some articles are reworked in-house or returned for alterations under guidance. Two of the magazines now have guidelines for contributors so as to help when writing.

In the three months from January to March 1988, more than 200 feature articles were contributed to the four titles covering a wide range of topics, to the extent that it would be difficult to recognize a definite pattern. Some were clearly many months in preparation, others had the touch of spontaneity, or one in a series. A random look at some of the features from that period unveils a rich tableau of social work experiences.

June Gordon wrote in *Social Work Today* on 4 February about an intermittent relief admission scheme which gave the families of elderly people a break from caring by offering hospital placements for four weeks out of twelve in some cases.[32] In an article in *Community Care* very firmly outside the orthodoxy of social work, John Pinnock, a former social worker and convicted sex offender, described the lack of facilities in prison to help sex offenders.[33] He recalled that by the time he received help he was suicidal. This article was strikingly different from others: here was a former practitioner recalling woeful experiences as a consumer of social work.

In another provocative article, Peter Day argued the importance that sociology played in social work training against a prevailing view that it was of little value.[34] Karen Oppenheimer in *Care Weekly* turned the spotlight on to the problem of alcohol abuse among the elderly residents in care homes.[35] She illustrated by example how a pattern of abuse could emerge and what the proper social work responses should be, bearing in mind the need to balance intervention with clients' rights to exercise control over their own lives.

There are many different components in the publishing of social work magazines, and in this highly impressionistic account, some of these have been examined. What is clear is that the diffuse and often complex nature of social work practice needs constant information, reflection, encouragement, criticism and general discussion. In that respect there is an almost symbiotic relationship between those needs and the now totally commercial nature of the publications. In the final analysis, however, it is the commercial aspects which obviously count: *Insight* sold up having found the struggle for revenue too much. So ultimately the market regulates the magazines; but it is not impossible that they will be there to witness the time when the market will regulate social work as well. Most of the magazines would prefer not to think of such a scenario – not least because in any subsequent 'value for money' scrutiny, national recruitment advertising might be more closely considered. It is not impossible that new publications will appear in the future, though prospective publishers should be chastened by the *Insight* experience. If new ones do appear the chances are that they will be launched by existing magazine groups, on a go-it-alone basis rather than some nebulous arrangement *à la* ADSS. However, this scenario does not take into account the possible changes in the production of magazines – particularly desk top publishing which would theoretically allow smaller groups to produce commercial magazines of a high standard. Whatever unfurls, the commercial pressures of publishing will not escape either existing or new titles. The market has a tendency to regulate the business in a ruthless fashion. Look how *New Society*, which a decade ago was a prominent social policy magazine and jobs forum, became absorbed within the *New Statesman*. And *Voluntary Action*, originally a magazine in its own right, then a *New Society* supplement, was dropped from the merged publication. But not all the 'trailblazers' from the 1970s have become casualties in the 1980s as the *Guardian* demonstrates. Its innovative editorial coverage from that era has now become subsumed into a very successful medium for recruitment advertising, where social work jobs form part of public appointments. This almost inexorable rise of the *Guardian*'s recruitment advertising section and the entry of the *Sunday Times* into this sector must, at the very least, give the social work magazines the occasional palpitation. If the future is to be successful for them, then a commercial strategy must be developed in case jobs advertising dries up, and one in which editorial plays an essential part. That may well mean more editorial supplements or even advertising features with all the potential problems that entails.

References

Note: a different referencing system has been utilized in this chapter because of the obvious difficulties in listing by writer's name.

1 *Community Care*, 21 January 1988, 695: 1.
2 *Social Work Today*, 21 January 1988, 19, 20: 2.
3 *Social Services Insight*, 22 January 1988, 3, 3: 3.
4 *Care Weekly*, 22 January 1988, 15: 1.
5 ibid., 15: 5.
6 *Community Care*, 28 January 1988, 696 (Social Security Act).
7 *Community Care*, 7 January 1988, 693: 1.
8 *Community Care*, 14 January 1988, 694: 2.
9 *Social Work Today*, 7 January 1988, 19, 18: 3.
10 *Social Work Today*, 14 January 1988, 19, 19: 12–13.
11 ibid.
12 *Social Work Today*, January 1988, 19, 21: 11.
13 *Social Services Insight*, 8 January 1988, 3, 1: 4.
14 *Social Services Insight*, 22 January 1988, 3, 3: 4.
15 *Community Care*, 21 January 1988, 695: 2.
16 *Social Work Today*, 21 January 1988, 19, 20: 5.
17 *Social Services Insight*, 29 January 1988, 3, 4: 4.
18 *Community Care*, 28 January 1988, 696: 3.
19 *Social Work Today*, 28 January 1988, 19, 21: 4.
20 *Community Care*, 4 February 1988, 697: 1.
21 *Social Services Insight*, 5 February 1988, 3, 5: 3.

22 *Social Work Today*, 11 February 1988 19, 23: 2.
23 *Social Services Insight*, 26 February 1988, 3, 8: 9.
24 *Social Services Insight*, 15 January 1988, 3, 2: 6.
25 *Care Weekly*, 8 January 1988, 13: 3.
26 *Social Work Today*, 11 February 1988, 19, 23: 4.
27 *Community Care*, 11 February 1988, 698: 4.
28 *Community Care*, 24 March 1988, 704: 11.
29 *Social Work Today*, 17 March 1988, 19, 28: 5.
30 *Care Weekly*, 18 March 1988, 23, 7.
31 *Social Services Insight*, 18 March 1988, 3, 11: 10.
32 *Social Work Today*, 4 February 1988, 19, 22: 12.
33 *Community Care*, 4 February 1988, 697: 26.
34 *Social Services Insight*, 5 February 1988, 3, 5: 16.
35 *Care Weekly*, 4 March 1988, 21: 7.

8
Community care: old problems and new answers

Kathleen Jones

The policy of community care developed in the 1960s. As a statement of intent, it is readily acceptable. Human beings ought to live in community with one another; disabled people ought to be cared for.

Britain was one of the leaders in a movement which has swept round much of the world. Community care policies are discussed in the USA, in Italy, in Scandinavia, in Malaysia, in Australia and New Zealand, in China. The only countries which have not moved away from institutional care are the Third World countries which never built institutions in the first place, and the countries of the Soviet bloc, which still seek, in strict Marxist terms, for collective solutions to individual problems; but even the Soviet bloc may succumb under the influence of *glasnost*.

So community care makes good sense in theory, and is being implemented in many countries; but does it work? In asking this question, we are moving from statements of intent to questions about administrative fact and service delivery. At the end of the 1980s there are two distinct views.

The first view is that the gloomy institutions of the Victorian period are being run down and will soon be reduced to piles of bricks and mortar. Disabled and chronically sick people can lead normal lives in a homely environment, free of bureaucratic restraint and hospital routine, supported by a network of health and social services, with their families, friends and neighbours. The 'medical model' of care can be largely replaced by a social model which respects their individuality and allows them to lead their own way of life.

The second view is that this is all very well in theory, but in practice, successive governments have paid lip-service to the policy without providing the resources to make it a success. 'A caring community' may have seemed possible in the 1960s; but in the harsher social world of the 1980s, cuts in public sector finance and the lack of positive planning have led to a policy in disarray and a massive growth in unmet need.

So who introduced the policy, and why? What evidence do we have that it works, or fails to work? And what needs to be done now?

The origins of community care

The policy of community care first came to prominence in Britain in 1963, with the publication of *Health and Welfare: the Development of Community Care* (Ministry of Health 1963). This government Blue Book referred to categories of patients who might be better cared for outside hospital: mentally ill, mentally handicapped, and physically handicapped, including frail and infirm elderly patients. Hospital admission would be necessary only for very short periods. Much of the care could be provided on a day basis, or in their own homes, with the support of a medico-social team.

The policy was a result of major re-planning in the Hospital Service, set out in another Blue Book in the previous year (Ministry of Health 1962). The new district general hospitals were to provide an intensive 'white coat' service concentrated on medical assessment and short periods of treatment. If the rising costs of acute medicine and surgery were to be met, chronic care would have to be dealt with elsewhere. Expensive hospital beds could not be taken up by long-term patients.

Recent developments in pharmacology had increased the costs of treatment, but had also made it possible in many cases to shorten the length of hospital stay. For instance, the antibiotics virtually removed the risk of infection after surgery or childbirth. The new psychotropic drugs (sedatives, tranquillizers and 'pep' pills) controlled the symptoms of many kinds of mental illness (though they suppressed the symptoms rather than curing them, and some had unpleasant and disabling side-effects). So GPs could handle most prescribing, and local authorities could provide nursing and social care.

In fact the new policy was a reversion to an older one. The care of mentally ill, mentally and physically handicapped and elderly infirm people had nearly been left out of the NHS in the first place. In the planning stages in the early 1940s, the local authorities had fought hard to keep these services rather than having them taken over by a centralized NHS. Geriatricians and psychiatrists had fought harder to get them removed from local authority jurisdiction, in order to improve the prestige of services which had been chronically understaffed and underfunded by comparison with the acute sector of medicine. Now that this aim had been achieved, they were for the most part keen supporters of a move into the new district general hospitals, which involved a more intensive use of their skills in specialist units, and prepared to leave the problems of chronicity to GPs, district nurses and social workers.

Few voices were raised to question how the new policy would operate. One which was raised to some effect was that of Richard Titmuss, Head of the

Department of Social Science and Administration at the London School of Economics:

> If English social history is any guide, confusion has often been the mother of complacency . . . What some hope will exist is suddenly thought by many to exist. All kinds of wild and unlovely weeds are changed, by statutory magic and comforting appellation, into the most attractive and domesticated flowers.
>
> (NIMH 1961)

This key speech contained three main points: first, official statements on community care had made a sizeable jump from the ideal to the actual, but merely talking about a service did not bring it into existence. Second, community care could not be achieved merely by government pronouncements and Acts of Parliament. It would take new thinking, new training and new administrative patterns to translate it into action. His description of the 'cottage garden of community care' left no doubt that he saw the dangers of the new policy developing into a downgrading measure for the chronic services, rather than as a truly progressive measure. Third, the test of the government's intentions was whether it was prepared to recognize that a good community care service was going to cost more, not less, than centralized hospital services.

Titmuss therefore called for a clear commitment to increased finance and new training schemes if the government 'meant business'. This commitment was not forthcoming.

Sociology and anti-psychiatry

Few academic observers shared these sober reactions. The social sciences were engaged in the 1960s in an all-out attack on institutional care. The period saw a spate of books on the evils of institutions, which were regarded primarily as power structures oppressing the poor.

One of the outstanding contributions in sociology came from Goffman (1961), whose study *Asylums* introduced a new kind of analysis of institutions. He taught us about 'the total institution' – all-encompassing, replacing personal values and personal living with a machine-like routine. He orginated cross-service analysis, pointing out the common features in mental hospitals, old people's homes, prisons, concentration camps, army barracks, monasteries and convents and other places for 'batch living'. He introduced the idea of 'binary management', in which a staff world and an inmate world could be found 'jogging along together with points of official contact, but little mutual penetration', and described in detail the 'mortification of the self' resulting from admission procedures designed to turn ordinary people into 'inmates'.

This small but very influential book brought an immediate response – both from those who were determined to abolish institutional life, and from the managers of institutions who were determined to reform them from inside. At one conference at Oxford in 1965, three prison governors and five splendid

Mothers Superior from Irish convents sat in the front row, and applauded every criticism.

A cult figure in the new movement was Michel Foucault of the Collège de France in Paris. Foucault, originally a psychologist, developed a structuralist approach to institutions, claiming that he could analyse the underlying similarities which lay beneath apparently disparate events. (His title, Professor of the Archaeology of Knowledge, was his own choice.) In *Madness and Civilisation* (1967), Foucault developed the theme of social control in a capitalist society, and the ways in which mental hospitals encapsulated their patients as a means of preventing social unrest. In *Discipline and Punish* (1977) he took the same theme further, claiming that prisons, factories and other institutions were similarly 'carceral cities' existing for the purposes of oppression. Mental hospitals did not exist to cure mental patients, and prisons did not exist to reform criminals. Both were highly visible warnings to the rest of society not to indulge in behaviour unacceptable to the ruling classes.

Structuralists have an arbitrary way with history – they crunch together ideas and events from different periods and even different centuries. It is not always clear whether Foucault is talking about life in the 1960s and 1970s, or life before the French Revolution of 1789. Indeed he shrugs away the differences. Social change is no more than a mirage, short of the great Marxist revolution with which he threatens his readers.

Foucault's ideas probably had the most direct impact in Trieste, where Professor Franco Basaglia, medical director of the old San Giovanni mental hospital, worked in the 1970s. An inscription on the walls of the Casa Rosa Luxembourg (formerly the medical quarters at San Giovanni) reads 'Asile = usine = école' – a mental hospital is the same as a factory is the same as a school – a testimony to Foucauldian views. Basaglia worked first to reform the Trieste Mental Health Service, replacing hospital care with sheltered housing, group flats and 'psycho-social centres' where patients could find friendship and understanding as well as treatment; then to found a movement, Psichiatria Democratica, to spread the movement to other parts of Italy; and finally to create a pressure group which would change the law for the whole of Italy. Law no. 180 of 1978 – usually referred to as 'the 180' – was passed after a public campaign which included press, television and radio, and an exhibition which has since toured many other countries. The use of imagery – the model horse which was pushed through the hospital gates on the day when they were flung wide, the ship which was repaired and sailed with a cargo of staff and patients on the Adriatic, the 'before and after' pictures which showed patients released from dismal incarceration smiling, kissing, getting sun-tanned and sitting in deckchairs like ordinary people – was very powerful. The new law has not been a success in most parts of Italy (Jones and Poletti 1985; 1986), but the campaign was an outstanding exercise in public relations.

Back in the USA Szasz had struck a quite different note from these left-wing critics of institutions. In a stream of very readable books, including *The Myth of Mental Illness* (1961), *Law, Liberty and Psychiatry* (1963), *The Manufacture of Madness* (1971), and *Schizophrenia: The Sacred Symbol of Psychiatry*

(1979), he put forward a 'hard right' thesis which fitted better with Republican thinking than with the liberal thinking of Democrats. Mental illness was a myth, invented by psychiatrists. Everybody had 'problems in living', but people had to take responsibility for their own lives. Christianity had led to a slave mentality – a dependence on the state which needed to be fought in the name of liberty. 'Institutional psychiatry' – by which Szasz meant psychiatric services administered by the state; he included the new Community Mental Health Centres in his strictures as well as the old mental hospitals – should be abolished. The only safeguard for the patient lay in the cash nexus. Patients who paid for a psychiatrist's services to help with their 'problems in living' retained their independence. It was not clear what would happen to people who could not afford to pay for treatment – but then, if mental illness was a 'myth', why should they need it?

This bracing philosophy was very popular with the right-wing American Council for Civil Liberties, for whom 'liberty' meant freedom from state interference. Curiously the sheer readability of these and other books secured Szasz a large following among left-wing students, who warmed to his comparisons of psychiatric examination with the practices of the Spanish Inquisition, and his account of the sufferings of the poet Sylvia Plath, but had little understanding of the political philosophy which lay behind his writing.

So what was happening in Britain? Two major developments which contributed to the growing ideological attack on institutional care were the anti-psychiatry movement associated with the name of R.D. Laing, and the Fabian movement in empirical social research. Laing, a psychiatrist working from the Tavistock Clinic, saw schizophrenia as a social construct – a means by which individuals responded to intolerable social pressures. Many of these pressures were held to originate within the family – one family member, usually a son or daughter, being scapegoated for all the problems of the family circle. *Sanity, Madness and the Family* (Laing and Esterson 1964) consists of a number of case studies on this theme.

Laing was not much concerned with community care – in fact his horror of family life and of the evils which 'society' inflicted on individuals suggest that he was not impressed with its potential; but he contributed to the growing belief that mental illness was not real 'illness', and therefore that an elaborate range of hospital services was unnecessary. Laing's comments on 'senescent capitalism' suggest that, like Foucault, he was looking forward to the Marxist Revolution as the one cleansing agent for society.

Empirical social scientists extended the movement against the institution into other fields of study, and provided a more direct case for community care. Notable works in the 1960s were Peter Townsend's *The Last Refuge* (1962), and Pauline Morris's *Put Away* (1969). Townsend developed a powerful plea for the development of community care in *The Last Refuge* (1962), pointing out that Aneurin Bevan's pledge to the House of Commons in 1948 – 'the workhouse is to go' had not been fulfilled, since many former workhouses were still in use, and in a squalid state. Routines were depersonalized, and residents often reduced to a pathetic dependency. Townsend's sense of social outrage was buttressed by detailed statistical work, telling quotations from individual old people's experience, and a scathing indictment of official inaction. *Put Away* is a major study of mental handicap hospitals, in which Pauline Morris challenged the assumption that mentally handicapped people needed hospitals staffed primarily by doctors and nurses, and argued for the development of care and training rather than 'treatment'.

This very brief account of some outstanding texts does not deal with much other interesting literature of the period – for instance the literature of the Radical Criminology movement, traced in Taylor, Walton and Young's *The New Criminology* (1973), or the sociological attack on the concept of 'madness' (Scull 1977). The intellectual movement against institutional care is confused and confusing. Ideas rebound back and forth across the Atlantic and the English Channel, are applied from very different political perspectives, develop in different social contexts, and are related to different groups of people. The literature is often not about 'community care': many writers seem to have been frankly abolitionist, taking the view that once the institutions were abolished, the problems would no longer exist (Jones and Fowles 1984).

The move to action

Peter Townsend and Pauline Morris had been concerned to reveal actual shortcomings and to make some recommendations for action. By the late 1960s the Fabian Society, the intellectual arm of the Labour party, had embarked on an active campaign for the revelation of institutional scandals. The key document in the translation from academic analysis to public debate is *Sans Everything* (Robb 1967), a series of detailed allegations about the treatment of old people in hospital. A group of well-known Fabians had personally investigated the treatment in a geriatric ward of an elderly lady, Miss Wills, and had taken depositions on abuses from a number of other people, including members of hospital staff. Some of the allegations were not very well founded, and the government rebuttal was able to point out some inconsistencies and inaccuracies. Nevertheless, the mud stuck; the effect of the allegations, which received a good deal of publicity at the time, was to alert British reformers to the potential of public debate.

Soon after, the *News of the World* published a shocking account of conditions in the Ely Hospital, Cardiff – a large mental handicap hospital. This let loose a flood of popular journalism concerned with the conditions under which mentally ill, mentally handicapped and elderly infirm people lived in institutions. In the years which followed, hardly a hospital in the country which provided services for these groups escaped allegations and public inquiry. The story is told in detail in J.P. Martin's *Hospitals in Trouble* (1984). While some of the allegations were not substantiated, others were, and some led eventually to criminal convictions. The media-inspired interest had its effect, but stopped abruptly in the early 1970s. New administrative machinery in the form of the Office of the Health Service Commissioner and later the Mental Health Act Commission provided regular channels for complaint and the redress of abuse, but the work they did and the abuses they remedied were no longer news. Press, television and radio have only a short span of interest, and efforts to remedy the situation had less dramatic impact than scandals. Journalists and programme producers looked for new sensations elsewhere.

Government statements on community care

So there was a powerful movement to destroy the institutions, but what was to be put in their place? The original Community Care Blue Book (Ministry of Health 1963) had put the onus on the local authorities, but annual reports in the succeeding years indicated that the transfer from hospital was proceeding slowly; health authorities were prepared to hand over long-term patients, but still had the bulk of the funding, the land, the buildings and the staff. Local authorities often dragged their feet in taking up extra responsibilities without the money to go with them. But the blueprint for change in the key fields of mental handicap, mental illness and the care of the infirm elderly was set out in three major government documents.

Better Services for the Mentally Handicapped (DHSS 1971) proposed that in future hospitals would be used for active treatment programmes, not residential care. Psychiatrists would be increasingly responsible for genetic counselling, early detection and assessment. There would be an extension of day care and out-patient work. Local authorities would provide residential accommodation in 'homes, not hostels', and other means of care such as foster care, group homes and flats would be developed with social work support. It should be noted that this plan was written in the post-Seebohm era, when local authority social services departments were being set up for the first time, and social work services were expanding rapidly both in scope and in numbers of staff. Social workers were expected to be able to take over many new responsibilities.

The mental handicap programme involved a heavy capital cost, and was expected to take ten to fifteen years. Hospital beds for adults would be cut by 50 per cent, and residential provision would increase seven-fold (from a very limited base). The key concept behind this move was 'normalization', a policy developed originally for mentally handicapped people in Copenhagen in the 1960s (Wolfensberger 1972). Mentally handicapped people were to be regarded as ordinary citizens, and to be able to use the general range of health, educational and social services, rather than being segregated in a second-class service. Normalization is essentially a pragmatic idea, and it has obvious limits. While mildly mentally handicapped people may benefit from not being labelled as 'different', and from being treated in all respects like the rest of the population, those with serious handicaps still need special consideration and special services. The danger has been that the removal of negative discrimination for the first group may result in failure to provide positive discrimination for the second. Some local authority social services departments have taken normalization to the point of avoiding the term 'mental handicap' altogether, and running services for 'people with learning difficulties'. While this emphasis on the educational component of care is welcome, the total denial of the medical and nursing component emphasizes rather than overcomes the split between health and social services.

Better Services for the Mentally Ill was published by the DHSS in 1975. It had to be admitted that developments had not taken place entirely according to plan. Mental hospitals had begun to reduce their populations, but the expected closures had not taken place: on the contrary, hospital admission rates had continued to rise, and the volume of work had increased. Psychiatric units in district general hospitals had not replaced mental hospital accommodation. Hospital staffing was often 'less than adequate' and community facilities were 'minimal'. There was little hope of 'the kind of service we would like even within a 25-year planning horizon'.

Some new solution had to be found, and it was located not in the local authority services, but in general practice, in the form of the 'primary care team'. The family doctor, the health visitor, the district nurse and the social worker were to form an interdisciplinary team. The doctors were apparently expected to learn all these different skills by osmosis, since it was stated that they would 'increasingly have the pooled knowledge of the members of the . . . team'. Health visitor and district nurse already had special responsibilities which took them into patients' homes, and so were in a good position to detect signs of mental illness. The sections on social services and social work practice were somewhat vague, though it was hoped that the social worker would be able to contribute to 'the identification of social and psychological problems'.

The concept of the 'primary care team' worked for physical illness and disability, but has not been a success in relation to mental illness, for a number of reasons. First, general practitioners, health visitors and district nurses receive very little training in psychiatric care. The bias of their training is towards biological explanations of physical symptoms. Second, the special responsibilities of health visitors and district nurses are primarily for post-operative cases, children and old people. The onset of schizophrenia, the major cause of serious mental illness, is in early adult life; the idea that this could somehow be dealt with in passing while a baby or a grandmother was being visited is hardly practical. Many mentally ill people have very tenuous family or community links, and live alone. Further, there are not enough social workers for every general practice in the country to have one. Though some excellent demonstration team-work has been undertaken by social workers in general practice, the massive increase in social work education and training which would make this possible has never been seriously envisaged.

Growing Older (DHSS 1982) is addressed to the whole community – 'those who will grow old tomorrow as well as those who are elderly today'. It deals with the problems of an ageing population; 'by the end of the century, the number of people aged 75 and over is expected to increase by about one-fifth, and the number aged 85 and over by no less than one half'. Retirement should be seen as 'a time of opportunity', not a time for dependency. Pensions and housing provision should deal with the needs of the fit elderly, community care provision being concentrated on those who were disabled or infirm. This was already happening; at one time, people had entered local authority homes for the elderly in their 60s, but now the average age of admission was 'approaching 82'.

The health and social services and a variety of private and voluntary organizations were maintaining 'a multiplicity of organizations and arrangements for infirm old people in the community. The aim must be to develop 'local networks of provision' between the many caring agencies. A further government paper, entitled *The Rising Tide* (DHSS 1982), deals with the problem of mental illness in old age. This report from the Health Advisory Service looks somewhat gloomily on the increased numbers of people likely to develop mental infirmity in old age, and urges health and social service authorities to take action. 'It is no longer good enough to try to muddle through . . .'

The Rising Tide asks a great many questions ('What is the contribution of Social Services/voluntary organisations/Community Health Councils?') but assumes that these are to be answered at local level, and that the central government's role is confined to 'norms and guidelines'. There are injunctions to 'good organization and planning', 'flexible financing' and 'a vision of what needs to be done', and a statement that 'if we do not meet the challenges, we shall have some very angry grandchildren', but no positive recommendations or provisions for extra resources follow.

In all these government statements, the emphasis is on plurality of provision, local decision-making, and co-ordination, collaboration and co-operation to create what is hoped for – 'an effective service'. To put it bluntly, government is evading responsibility by pushing it down to the local level. Strictly speaking *co-ordination* refers to machinery set up (in the form of committees, joint administration and so on) to streamline the efforts of particular services. *Collaboration* refers to ways of working together – joint consultation, agreement about overlapping responsibilities, joint planning. *Co-operation* refers to practice – individual professionals working together. In the past ten or fifteen years the three terms have often been used interchangeably to describe a process which is highly desirable, but much more difficult than it seems.

Government exhortation has continued. *Joint Care Planning* (DHSS 1977) introduced a limited scheme of joint finance for co-ordinated ventures; but since the money available was only for pump-priming, and the financial responsibility reverted to the local authority after an initial period, most local authorities, increasingly pressurized by mounting responsibilities and funding cuts, were not very responsive. The document stated that health and social services should 'secure the best balance of services and make the most effective use of the resources available', but the resources made available were very small.

Collaboration in Community Care introduced an imperative note:

although it is now self-evident that health and social welfare are inextricably interwoven, there is often a lack of contact between health and social services . . . the obvious and most important implication is that services need to collaborate.

(DHSS 1978)

Why was this so difficult? One reason was, and is, that health authorities and local authorities are very differently constituted. A district health authority deals only with health matters, and is part of a centralized chain of command, stretching through the regional health authority to the DHSS in London. A local authority is an omnibus authority, dealing with a whole range of local services: rating and valuation, roads, libraries, parks, housing and other local needs in addition to social services, and all centralized on the Town Hall. For these, they receive a block grant from central government, and local councillors allocate funds to the various departments. Social services generally do not rate a high priority. Health and local authorities differ in scope, financing and determination of priorities. They have different budgeting patterns, different planning cycles, different working styles, and workers with different professional backgrounds.

If we add to these difficulties in the health and social services the even more complex problems of communicating with general practitioners, a variety of voluntary organizations which often work in isolation from one another, and the limited contacts with the growing private sector, it is easy to see that official exhortation is a good deal easier than practice.

The growth of public concern

The Thatcher years since 1979 have seen a considerable growth in the problems, and an increasing government reluctance to take any firm action. The importance of leaving decisions to be made at local level has been repeatedly stressed. DHSS lays down guidelines (basically prescriptions for good service) but takes little action to provide the necessary money, to promote the necessary re-training of staff, or to investigate the failures in care.

It was left to the House of Commons Social Services Committee, consisting of Members of Parliament, to sound a warning note. This Committee's second report (HCSS 1985) pointed out energetically that 'community care' had become a 'catch-all phrase' which was 'virtually meaningless'. What it often implied was a policy of saving money by getting people out of hospital, transferring them from the care of professional staff by putting extra burdens on family members (often women) and volunteers. The point had been reached where 'the rhetoric of community care had to be matched by action'.

The services were both 'under-financed and under-staffed'. To remove hospital facilities without first building up alternative services was 'putting the cart before the horse'. The Committee was concerned at the growth in homelessness among mentally ill and mentally handicapped people, and at the increasing frequency with which the Courts sent such people to prison because there was no longer any secure hospital accommodation available for them.

This indictment was all the more powerful because it came from an all-party group of MPs, in which Conservative back-benchers played an active part. Less than a year later, it was followed by a closely reasoned document from the Audit Commission for Local Authorities in England and Wales (1986). This body, which is concerned with financial responsibilities rather than policy issues, put forward a devastating critique: government was spending some £6 billion a year on long-term care for the elderly, mentally ill, mentally and physically handicapped people, and it was not getting value for money. Local authorities, subject to limitations on Rate Support Grants, rate-capping and restriction of the Public Sector Borrowing Requirement, were 'often penalised ... for building the very community services which government policy favoured'. The result of the squeeze on both hospital and local authority care had been the very rapid growth of the private sector, much of which was supported out of public funds.

The way in which this was achieved was through Supplementary Benefit payments (now Income Support) for private residential and nursing home care. Residential or nursing home fees were met when a resident's own resources did not exceed £3,000. The cost could exceed £200 a week for each individual. In many cases, people in need of care could be given better care in their own homes at a considerably lower cost if local authority services were expanded. The situation was marked by 'policy conflicts and perverse incentives'.

Conservative ideology was at the cross-roads. The government was committed to reducing public expenditure and to limiting the powers of local authorities. It was generally in favour of the development of the private sector. But it appeared that public expenditure was rising instead of being reduced, and that very large sums were going into the relatively unmonitored and unsupervised private sector. And since private sector care consisted largely of homes, patients being moved out of hospital were often going to forms of care no less institutional than those they had left.

Faced with this bundle of dilemmas, the government appointed an industrialist, Sir Roy Griffiths of Sainsbury's, to receive evidence and to make recommendations within a few months.

The Griffiths Report

The Audit Commission had suggested splitting community care: health authorities to have the 'lead responsibility' for the care of mentally ill people, local authorities for mentally and physically handicapped people, and a joint authority to be responsible for elderly people. This joint authority would have its own budget, and a 'community care manager' would have the power to buy in services 'from whichever public or private agency he sees fit'. The proposal to split the consumer groups was soon recognized to be impracticable: three different kinds of authority would be unnecessarily cumbersome, but the proposal for a 'community care manager' who could buy in from a range of services took root, and formed the basis of Griffiths's recommendations.

The chief question was how to attach the local community care manager for all three groups to the existing services. Attachment to the NHS was hardly feasible when the health districts were increasingly divesting themselves of any responsibility for long-term care. Attachment to local authorities meant increasing their power at a time when government was concerned to decrease it. A free-standing Community Care Service, though attractive, would be costly, and involve building up yet another bureaucracy. After taking evidence from a wide range of organizations and individuals, Griffiths produced his report (DHSS 1988).

His introductory letter to the Secretary of State was polite but scathing:

> community care has been talked of for thirty years, and in few areas can the gap between political rhetoric and policy on one hand, or between policy and reality in the field on the other hand have been so great.

At central government level, there was 'a feeling that community care is a poor relation, everybody's distant relative but nobody's baby'. At the local level,

> many Social Service Departments and voluntary groups grappling with the problems . . . feel that the Israelites faced with the requirement to make bricks without straw had a comparatively routine and possible task.

Sir Roy's recommendations were precise and to the point: 'the one option which is not tenable is to do nothing'. At central government level, there should be a Minister for Community Care to provide a clear focus, and save the service from being 'nobody's baby'. At local level, the only feasible option was to make the local authorities responsible for the service, providing additional funding for it by means of a 50 per cent earmarked grant. A community care manager would be responsible for all three types of clients, and would buy services 'according to where they can be provided most efficiently and economically'. Each client would have 'a clear package of care', perhaps made up of elements from different services.

'I have the occasional sinking feeling', he wrote, 'that there is nothing so outdated as to provide today's solution to today's problem'. He warned the Secretary of State that this was 'no Rubik Cube which will be perfectly solved if one can get the various components appropriately related'. The recommendations for a Minister of State, a local budget and 'packages of community care' were widely welcomed, but there are some political hurdles to be faced. The proposal to extend the powers and responsibilities of local authorities was intensely unpopular in Downing Street, while the prospect of a return to earmarked grants (the local authorities had escaped from this form of central control at the end of the 1950s) was equally unpopular with the local authorities.

And there, at the time of writing, the matter rests. The DHSS accepted the Report, and informed the waiting reporters that it would be bringing forward its own proposals in due course. We are still waiting.

Summing up

Has any other country done better? Probably the Scandinavian countries have, at least in the few large towns. (Community care inevitably works better in large centres of population than in the rural areas.) Sweden and Denmark have had a steady political will to social reform. Norway, a comparatively late starter, has had the advantage of enormous oil revenues in recent years.

Elsewhere, the same problems are recurring with appalling regularity in country after country: the problems of inadequate finance, lack of structure, poor co-ordination, professional conflict, an unregulated and expanding private sector absorbing an increasing proportion of public funds.

At the level of service delivery (or non-delivery) there are the problems of lonely and isolated people eking out a minimal existence in flats or bed-sits; of homeless people incapable of caring for themselves roaming the streets, haunting the railway stations and airports (when officialdom allows them to) and sleeping over hot air vents or in dark alleys; of people being sent to prison by the Courts because, although they clearly need treatment rather then punishment, there is no suitable hospital accommodation for them; of families under almost intolerable strain. These problems are not peculiar to Britain. They occur in the USA and Canada and Australia and New Zealand and most of Europe – including Italy, where the 'Italian Experience' never reached beyond a few northern cities.

There are some lively experiments to be found – hostels, boarding-out schemes, group homes and flats, 'core and cluster' schemes (in which accommodation is grouped round a small central service facility), community mental health centres, community units for the elderly. But these are frequently no more than demonstration models, totally inadequate to meet the need as hospitals are emptied. There is growing evidence of two kinds of distortion in provision: first, the clients with the mildest problems are the easiest to 'normalize' (this concept has now spread from mental handicap to other areas of community care), and may get more than their share of what provision there is – clients who are dirty, violent or unresponsive are less popular; second, the areas with the greatest problems are the poorest areas – community care is more likely to be adequate in the stockbroker belt than in the decaying inner cities.

Where do social workers stand in relation to community care? Many are struggling with the current situation, helping confused and inadequate clients to cope with the exigencies of the Income Support scheme and changes in housing benefits, looking forward with apprehension to the effects of the Poll Tax, explaining why a disabled client can only have half an hour of home help a day. Many social services departments do not regard community care as a high priority, as other public demands, such as coping with child abuse, are heaped upon them. In the late 1960s and early 1970s social workers were expected to take on much of the work of community care; but in recent years, there has been less government enthusiasm for the profession, and responsibilities seem to have been diverted to family doctors and community nurses.

It would be satisfying to be able to end this review of community care with some statistics which would quantify the two views described on pp. 103–4: just how many old, mentally handicapped and mentally ill people are in need? How many hospital, local authority and private home places are available for them? How many workers are there? But the fact is that we simply do not know. The disappearance of specialized services and specialized workers also means the disappearance of specialized statistics, and government statistical services have been sharply reduced.

We can only conclude with Griffiths that 'the one option that is not tenable is to do nothing'.

References

Audit Commission (1986) *Making a Reality of Community Care*, London: HMSO.
DHSS (1971) *Better Services for the Mentally Handicapped*, Cmnd 4683, London: HMSO.
—— (1975) *Better Services for the Mentally Ill*, Cmnd 6233, London: HMSO.
—— (1977) *Joint Care Planning: Health and Local Authorities*, Circular HC(77)17, LAC (77) 10, London: DHSS.
—— (1978) *Collaboration in Community Care*, Central Health Services Council, London: HMSO.
—— (1982) *Growing Older*, London: HMSO.
—— (1983) *The Rising Tide*, London: HMSO.
—— (1988) *Community Care: Agenda for Action*, Griffiths Report, London: HMSO.
Foucault, M. (1967) *Madness and Civilization: A History of Insanity*, London: Tavistock.
—— (1977) *Discipline and Punish: The Birth of the Prison*, Harmondsworth: Allen Lane.
Goffman, E. (1961) *Asylums*, New York: Doubleday.
HCSS (1985) *Community Care*, Second Report of the House of Commons Social Services Committee, London: HMSO.
Jones, K. and Fowles, A. J. (1984) *Ideas on Institutions*, London: Routledge & Kegan Paul.
Jones, K. and Poletti, A. (1985) 'Understanding the "Italian Experience"', *British Journal of Psychiatry*, 146: 341–7.
—— (1986) 'The "Italian Experience" reconsidered,' *British Journal of Psychiatry*, 148: 144–50.
Laing, R. D. and Esterson, A. (1964) *Sanity, Madness and the Family*, London: Tavistock.
Martin, J. P. (1984) *Hospitals in Trouble*, Oxford: Blackwell.
Ministry of Health (1962) *A Hospital Plan for England and Wales*, Cmnd 1604, London: HMSO.
Ministry of Health (1963) *Health and Welfare: The Development of Community Care*, Cmnd 1973, London: HMSO.
Morris, P. (1969) *Put Away: A Sociological Study of Institutions for the Mentally Retarded*, London: RKP.
NIMH (1961) Report of the Annual Conference of the National Association for Mental Health, speech by Professor R. M. Titmuss, reproduced in R. M. Titmuss (1968) *Commitment to Welfare*, London Allen & Unwin, ch. IX.
Robb, B. (ed.) (1967) *Sans Everything: A Case to Answer*, London: Nelson.
Scull, A. T. (1977) *Decarceration: Community Treatment and the Deviant: A Radical View*, Englewood Cliffs, NJ: Prentice-Hall.
Szasz, T. S. (1961) *The Myth of Mental Illness*, New York: Dell.
—— (1963) *Law, Liberty and Psychiatry*, London: Macmillan.
—— (1971) *The Manufacture of Madness: A Comparative Study of the Inquisition and the Mental Health Movement*, London: Routledge & Kegan Paul.
—— (1979) *Schizophrenia: The Sacred Symbol of Psychiatry*, Oxford: Oxford University Press.

Taylor, I., Walton, R. and Young, J. (1973) *The New Criminology*, London: Routledge & Kegan Paul.

Townsend, P. (1962) *The Last Refuge: A Survey of Residential Institutions and Homes for the Aged in England and Wales*, London: Routledge & Kegan Paul.

Wolfensberger, W. (1972) *The Principle of Normalisation in Human Services*, Toronto: Canadian National Institute for the Mentally Retarded.

9
Child sexual abuse: the challenge for the organization

Sue Richardson

This chapter will explore some of the organizational issues posed by the rapid increase in referrals of cases of child sexual abuse. It is aimed at managers and practitioners in the 'average' local authority, under pressure of shrinking resources, subject to conflicting priorities and without the necessary expertise readily available. The challenge facing these organizations concerns their ability to manage rapid change. Such change has implications for inter-agency work and survival at both organizational and professional levels.

Many writers on organizations argue that the accelerating rate of change is the largest single problem of the age. In the past 'small occasional adjustments' (Ackoff 1981: 3) have been a sufficient form of adaptation. Peters describes dramatically how this world no longer exists. In his 'chaotic new world' where 'every variable is up for grabs' (Peters 1987: 45), the pace of change threatens to outstrip the ability to adapt. Toffler (1971) described the inability to respond effectively and its associated paralysis as *Future Shock*.

The growth in detection of child sexual abuse is an example of this type of change-context. Finkelhor (1984: 200) comments that 'The problem has emerged in the human service realm rather suddenly'. The American Humane Association (1984) records that reports more than doubled between 1976 and 1982. A similar trend has been observed in the UK. A survey of one hundred local authorities carried out on behalf of directors of social services (ADSS 1987a) found that detection had quadrupled over five years, with particularly sharp rises in certain geographical areas. NSPCC figures are of an unprecedented 137 per cent increase in registered cases during 1986, falling, but maintaining the trend of increase (21 per cent) in 1987. Many professionals believe there is an inevitable degree of under-reporting behind these figures. However, experience in different countries confirms that once the fifth of

Kempe and Kempe's (1978) six stages of the process of community recognition of child abuse has been reached, reporting is likely to maintain an increased level. The stages begin with denial, proceed to recognition and management of physical abuse, followed by emotional abuse and neglect, prior to acknowledgement in the fifth stage of sexual abuse. The sixth stage is seen as one where loving and preventive care is guaranteed to every child. If the fifth stage has indeed been reached, this suggests that Peter's (1987) scenario of permanent tumult and crisis is the future reality for agencies charged with the responsibility of dealing with this problem.

The nature of these agencies provides a further problem since their structures can best be described as 'ultrastable' (Pugh 1986: 142). In other words 'they find it difficult to change, not because of inertia but because they run like mad to stay in the same place' (Pugh 1986: 142). General systems theory provides an understanding of resistance to change as a natural and vital phenomenon due to homeostatic mechanisms which serve to keep systems in a stable state. As a result it is often the case that organizations 'continue to be managed and organized much as they were before the awareness of their bombardment by change was widespread' (Ackoff 1978: 141). Paradoxically as Ackoff points out, 'Their resistance to change tends to be proportional to the need for it. The more turbulent their environment, the more equilibrium they seek' (Ackoff 1978: 141).

Both Ackoff and Peters are of the opinion that only flexible and highly adaptable organizations can survive a turbulent environment where the only possible equilibrium is 'dynamic – like that obtained by an airplane flying in a storm, not like that of the Rock of Gibraltar' (Ackoff 1981: 4). Since the local authority can more easily be compared to the latter than the former, the challenge posed by the rapid emergence of child sexual abuse is enormous.

The difficulties are compounded when other features of rapid change are examined. One key element is that some of the forces producing the change are external to the organization and it is not, therefore, in full control. The activity of outside agencies, other professionals and the community at large is crucial to child protection work. Any of these sources can singly, or in combination, generate a momentum which is capable of overwhelming existing resources. The *Report of the Inquiry into Child Abuse in Cleveland* observes:

> On the ground during the crisis, the social workers did their best under great pressure and stressful conditions. Their resources of manpower, skill and experience were inadequate to deal with the height of the crisis.
>
> (Butler-Sloss 1988: 85)

The report accepts as a summary of the general situation the comments of the President of the ADSS that 'the Cleveland case, of course, begs the question of how any Department would cope logistically under a high bombardment rate' (Butler-Sloss 1988: 85). Although the boundary between external and internal forces cannot always be neatly defined, many social services departments have generated their own internal forces for change through, for example, training, increased awareness and the introduction of specialist posts. Technically internal pressures are more amenable to planning and control. However in the management of child abuse the crucial factor is the multidisciplinary system, whose whole is greater than the sum of its parts.

Another effect of an increase in the pace of change is a reduction in the time available for planning and diagnosis. Most management models emphasize the importance of the diagnostic phase where the problem can be clearly formulated, the need for change established and thought through. Those most affected by the change need to be consulted to reduce their resistance. The planning and consultation process itself helps to lay foundations by building working relationships. The Bexley Joint Investigative Project (Metropolitan Police and Bexley London Borough 1987) is an example of where a planned approach to child sexual abuse was possible, helping to rebuild police – social worker relationships in the wake of the Lucy Gates Inquiry (Gates 1982).[1] Relationships previously regarded as good had been 'rudely shattered' (Charnley 1987) following the death of this 2-year-old child in 1979 and damaged further by criticisms of social workers made in public by a police officer. The report of the inquiry recommended that active steps be taken to restore inter-agency relationships. The project is often quoted as an example of successful adaptation in a fraught area of work. Although the number of referrals was much greater than anticipated, they remained within the system's capacity to cope. This may well relate to the establishment, via the planning process, of sufficient ownership of child sexual abuse as a multidisciplinary problem.

The explosion of child sexual abuse referrals during 1987 in Cleveland which led to a judicial inquiry provides the most dramatic example of disruption to the developmental stages which help to keep change manageable. The process of returning responsibility to the wider system, described by Manning, Cameron and Burrell (1987) as 'bounceback' in response to the overload inevitability felt by the small group of 'experts' or individuals initially willing to involve themselves, took place over a very short time-scale with insufficient space for planning. Although Cleveland may well be seen as an extreme example, it illustrates the kind of pressures to which the public services can be subject without warning and which call into question dominant management models. These models are drawn largely from the world of industry and commerce where their limitations have also been acknowledged. Goodman and associates (1982) question definitions based on assumptions that change will be planned and intentional, rather than occur randomly, through evolutionary processes, via adaptation and other mechanisms. In *The Healing Webb* Pilisuk and Parks comment on how the language of 'diagnoses and prescriptions' does not answer the needs of what we know of 'human interdependence' (1986: 142). Child sexual abuse probably best fits Ackoff's description of

> those decisions which cannot be modeled and therefore must be made by decision makers using whatever internal and external resources are available to them. These are usually the most complex problems – ones

that are strategic and normative rather than tactical and operational and involve human choice behaviour in some way.

(Ackoff 1978: 200)

In management terms sexual abuse is a 'mess', the term used by Ackoff (1974: 21) to describe complex, interdependent situations where the problem is without clear boundaries and not necessarily amenable to straightforward problem-solving. Stevenson has identified some of the difficulties of multi-disciplinary work where differences in attitudes, values, status and organizational priorities are some of the factors which combine to sink 'the good ship co-operation' (Stevenson 1988: 6). To add to the planners' nightmare, a review of the available research confirms that it is effectively impossible to establish accurate basic data on the size of the problem due to methodological problems and the secrecy with which it is surrounded (La Fontaine 1988).

While our over-burdened services struggle to respond, it is far from clear who owns the problem. When recommending a national committee to advise the government on child abuse issues, the NSPCC director, Alan Gilmour, stated that 'there is no one to pick up the ball and run with it' (*Community Care*, News Focus 24.4.88). As a result, the recommendations of child abuse inquiries are never fully implemented and ownership tends to rest with particular agencies, primarily social service departments or with individual professionals who choose to involve themselves. For example, the Jasmine Beckford Report was 'convinced that nothing shorter than a period of three years is required for the professional training of social workers' (Beckford 1985: 204). Yet this very proposal, following a lengthy review by CCETSW, was rejected by the government in 1988.

Polarization and scapegoating are some of the dangers of lack of ownership throughout the system. This process may relate not only to the prevalence of denial and strong emotional reactions but also to a reluctance to face the social and political implications of an examination of 'our defensive myth of the cereal packet norm of family life' (Freeman 1987–8). Feminist theory expands on why the threat, inherent to child sexual abuse, to dominant ideologies of the family are so strongly resisted. MacLeod and Saraga suggest that prevailing theories of causation, such as family dysfunction, are more comfortable to professionals and public alike since 'it calms the collective anxiety about the "family" which erupts, as in the furore over Cleveland, when the reality of sexual abuse of children emerges' (MacLeod and Saraga 1988: 17). The popularity of this type of analysis is related to the most glaring feature of child abuse: 'it is something that, overwhelmingly, men do to children' (1988: 16). There is therefore a need to address gender and the associated issue of male power. Such a task is particularly difficult for local authority employees whose function is based on prevailing views of the status quo.

The concept of ownership should also take the needs and rights of parents into account. Parents should be the professional's first allies in the protection of children from any form of abuse. However, many parents will inevitably resist owning that there is a problem of sexual abuse in their family. Adults have the means to ally with powerful public figures, which can lead into a process of public denial, leaving ownership with the statutory authorities and isolated professionals. This can establish a context of conflict and confrontation in which it is extremely difficult to safeguard children's interests.

Situations of escalation are a common occurrence and have identifiable patterns of behaviour. Most organizations become trapped in this dynamic since they tend to lack sensing mechanisms to alert them to the need for corrective action (Staw 1982). Conflict in the public and professional arena appears to be a key feature of the context in which decisions regarding child sexual abuse are made. As Finkelhor's research shows, the problem falls into 'competing professional and institutional domains characterized by insularity and a high degree of disagreement concerning methods of intervention and case management' (Finkelhor 1984). Evidence to the Cleveland Judicial Inquiry illustrated the absence of any consensus on which to build a framework for practice. The concept of conflicts-by-proxy (Furniss 1983), a process in which professionals and their systems themselves begin to mirror specific aspects of family conflicts, widens the complexity which has to be considered.

The context of conflict surrounding professional practice is visible in the crucial area of the legal system. The uncertainty and confusion surrounding child care law is now the subject of proposals for change. It is unlikely, however, that some of the dilemmas most specific to child sexual abuse will be easily resolved. In response to a request from Dr Bentovim in the High Court regarding the conduct of interviews with children for evidential purposes, Justice Latey outlined the dilemma as follows:

> there is 'an inter-face', as it has been described, between the needs of clinical therapeutic methods and the needs of the courts in legal proceedings. In doing what has been found so far to be best to meet the needs of the former, methods may be necessary which defeat or do not best meet the needs of the latter.
>
> (Latey 1987: 294)

While making some suggestions how this could be addressed, he nevertheless stated 'whether there can ever be a total reconciliation of the clinical and forensic needs, I, for one, do not know' (Latey 1987: 294).

It is important to acknowledge that there is little to be gained by an improved legal framework and heightened rights-consciousness unless resource allocation is addressed (Freeman 1987–8). Many child abuse inquiry reports refer to staff shortages, work overload, poor accommodation and inadequate administrative support (DHSS 1982). None has taken a comprehensive view of resource issues. They have focused instead on individual performance and procedural arrangements. This is despite the fact that some reports, for example Cleveland (Butler-Sloss 1988) and Carlisle, (1987), themselves acknowledge that recommendations on training require 'additional resources' (Butler-Sloss 1988: 225). Both the Kimberley Carlisle (Carlisle 1987) and Tyra Henry (Henry 1987) inquiry reports were issued in late 1987 amidst a national staffing crisis, particularly acute in the London boroughs, where services were claimed to be at breaking-point on the evidence of an ADSS survey (ADSS 1987b).

The political context behind the resource issue is rarely considered in the professional journals. An article entitled 'Falling apart at the seams' (Oppenheim 1988) identifies the political nature of spending cuts which have led to an increasing inability to deliver services. Even more care is the kind of description by McCarthy in *Social Work Today* (23.1.87; 7.1.88) of the development of a political philosophy which has eroded the powers of local government and placed the maintenance of welfare second to the growth of the economy. The resource-intensive demands faced by organizations who must respond to the rise in child sexual abuse work are therefore, having to be faced in a hostile political climate.

The 'widening gulf between the professional objectives or concerns of social work and the state's requirements' (Jones 1983: 112) and attendant changes can be related to the dilemmas of formulating a strategy in relation to child sexual abuse. Jones decribes how the result of having to struggle with impossible demands and too few resources is that there has been an inevitable shift in focus from treatment and rehabilitation to service provision, resource rationing and social containment. This comment is even more true now than in the early 1980s. For example, eight months after the subject of a formal inquiry into the death of Tyra Henry, Lambeth Social Services Department was struggling with a large financial deficit to maintain basic services and had over one hundred unallocated child abuse cases (*Social Work Today*, News Feature 25.8.88). The above process has been accompanied by the 'bureaucratization' of social service departments which, while growing in size, have established policies and structures which induce conformity and reduce professional autonomy. This trend can be seen in child protection work, where the response to a series of child abuse tragedies has been to emphasize the need for procedures and the establishment of inter-agency conformity.

The challenge of child protection work can act as a stimulus to the growth of professional autonomy, identity and expertise. There is bound to be a tension between the organization's need for control and the conditions in which professionals can survive and work creatively. Lateral thinkers like Ackoff (1978) and De Bono (1972) have drawn attention to the presence of creative problem-solving abilities in children which many adults need to re-contact. Such creativity is encouraged by few organizations where, because of inherent resistance to change, 'the creative problem solver is not likely to be successful unless he is also competent, communicative, and, most of all, courageous' (Ackoff 1978: 17). Peters describes the importance of the role of the 'committed champion' on whose innovative ideas progress depends. Yet, due to the disruption the ideas cause the champion is 'anathema to everything that civil, organized corporate endeavour stands for' (Peters 1987: 248). The importance of personal commitment amongst small groups of individuals in advancing the management of child sexual abuse is recognized by specialists in this field such as MacFarlane and Waterman (1986) and Sgroi (1984). As a result of MacFarlane's observation that most successful examples of collaboration were the result of such groups rather than formal policy changes, Finkelhor suggests that 'the opportunity exists for creative restructuring of service systems by individual workers who are willing to take the initiative' (Finkelhor 1984). It is, however also recognized that, due to the emotive nature of the issue, there is always a risk of provoking serious public disquiet, political opposition and personal attack. This has been a common experience in the USA and has been illustrated in the UK by events in Cleveland.

The role of the media in creating a 'moral panic' out of child sexual abuse plays a significant part in this process. (See Franklin in Chapter 1 of this volume.) Much has been written on how a stereotypical model of reporting has been established since the Maria Colwell Inquiry in 1974. This has created new 'folk devils' by focusing on general and individual failings in the welfare services rather than on the nature of the problem (Hartley 1985). Parton (1985) develops the theory of the role of moral panics in obscuring the social and political issues which need to be addressed. The media, by their ability to produce and reinforce dominant views of familial and agency inadequacy, have helped to create a climate in which welfare services are being eroded. The Butler-Sloss Report commented on how, in Cleveland, the media 'became a factor in the continuance of the crisis' (1988: 169). The report spoke of the need for responsible reporting in the awareness that its impact 'can have a disproportionate influence on those caught up in such a crisis, and may create uncertainty, confusion and injustice' (1988: 171). Cleveland well illustrates how a lost media battle can leave professionals isolated and at risk of severe public censure.

A further analysis is that of a breakdown in the informal contract between 'the state and the professional community' (Hoggett 1984: 19). It is suggested that this contract consists of a reciprocal agreement whereby each legitimizes and reinforces the other's function within established dominant values. One of the benefits is that the professions are generally left to regulate their own concerns in 'policy communities which are largely insulated from the political arena' (Hoggett 1984: 20). The price is that resources are controlled within the political arena. This is not necessarily a problem unless the consensus breaks down. 'Subversive paradigms' are threatening to this consensus, dissidents being dealt with 'via a process of marginalization and recoupment' (1984: 21). Hoggett uses the example of the anti-psychiatry movement to illustrate both processes, recoupment ensuring a future influence in a neutered form. In my opinion, a similar process is at work in recent and current upheavals around establishing an orthodoxy for the management of child sexual abuse. An example is the acceptance in the Cleveland Inquiry Report of the significance of a range of anal findings as giving rise to suspicion of sexual abuse although not conclusively diagnostic: a consensus view incorporating elements of what had been a bitter controversy (Butler-Sloss 1988: 186–93).

Given the extremely fraught context just described, how can organizations best adapt? Staw (1982) argues that measures to increase adaptability are more crucial than looking for the 'right' form of organization or policy. The first step, whether it is to change the culture of ICI (Harvey-Jones 1988) or the ability of social service departments to respond to the challenge of child sexual abuse, is to establish a shared perspective and belief system: create a climate in which the need for change is accepted and understood. In my view, despite the intervention of the Butler-Sloss Report, changes in attitude to the management of child sexual abuse are a very different matter to procedural or legislative changes and are likely to take longer, especially under conditions of continuing conflict. The debate which is needed to establish shared core values on which to base practice may be difficult to hold if organizations are in overload and under pressure to implement 'solutions'.

A corollary of rapid change is an increase in the dimension and complexity of the problem (Ackoff 1981). Complex problems, due to the number of variables involved, are rarely amenable to simple solutions. There is a danger that a wrongly applied solution may itself become the problem (Watzawick, Weakland and Fisch 1974). An example is the pressure on local authorities to divert resources into child abuse work at the expense of other services, such as hospital social work and child guidance teams. The Cleveland Inquiry was held in response to concern that the 'solutions' adopted in the management of cases had created a worse predicament. It is a matter of opinion whether some of the suggested means of rebalancing, for example by modifying previous advice always to believe the child, may also prove to be solutions with their own problems.

It is misleading to think that there are any permanent solutions to a problem as complex as child sexual abuse, especially when all agencies are at a relatively early stage of knowledge and development. Since the fit of any strategies is likely to change more quickly than the organizations which adopt them, I would suggest that the management response should contain three key features. First, top levels of management in particular should take responsibility for owning the organization's problems in relation to child sexual abuse. They should do this together with other key agencies, rather than leave the dilemmas with appointed experts or isolated professionals. Second, there should be a commitment to persevering long enough to seeing change through. The process of change will not take care of itself and requires active management. Third, a commitment should be made to providing a context which empowers staff to find creative solutions. This includes consideration of the organization's responsibility to the care and nurturance of staff, the provision of team work and skilled supervision, and a review of salaries and service conditions. Much courage is demanded of children and families to disclose and survive the trauma of child sexual abuse. It may be that higher than usual levels of courage are required of organizations if they are to enable their staff to survive the stress of case management.

To conclude, I should like to highlight the following issues for consideration for the future. It is vital that the enormous task of tackling the widespread social problem of child sexual abuse proceeds from a coherent theoretical base. Bentovim has pointed to the problems of neutrality in establishing our position since 'we cannot avoid taking a stance with respect to the issue of violence towards and sexual abuse of children' (Bentovim 1987: 384). He further acknowledges that research on theoretical models has to extend beyond the family to the social system, in order to find the most helpful ways of applying what approaches we have. It would, however, be naive to think that it is possible to stop at analysis without considering the need for social change. At this point the issue becomes political, something which makes many professionals feel uncomfortable. One of the pioneers of our understanding of child abuse, Alfred White Franklin, accepted that tackling the problem posed a challenge to the organization of society. In his view, this was a dangerous target. 'If the eradication of child abuse needs a really radical alteration of society, this possibly is too high a price to pay' (Franklin 1977: 272). Herein is a fundamental dilemma which I do not feel that professionals, along with the rest of the community, can continue to avoid without rendering the task even more Herculean.

To find the strength to address every aspect of the task, it is essential that professionals seek as wide a network of alliances as possible. This has to involve changing our concept of professionalism, one characteristic of which is that the consumer is rarely involved 'as an active subject' (Hoggett 1984: 22). Campbell in analysing events in Cleveland describes how professionals were vulnerable as a result of being isolated 'within professional networks rather than social alliances' (1988: 21). She locates this in the wider political culture in which women and their community networks were wholly marginalized in the public debate (1988: 167). Sexual abuse is one of the major types of trauma which can best be healed with the help of other survivors. If as professionals we need to be empowered, we should address ourselves to how this can be achieved in concert with those who have suffered abuse. Our task should be to enable people to go beyond survival to a point where they can contribute directly to others from their experiences. Not only is this healing for both the giver and the recipient, but also the combination of professional and self-help can be the most powerful. In her book *Cry Hard and Swim* (1987), Spring vividly describes her own experience of recontacting herself as a person via this process following an abusive childhood. Her book also shows that it is essential to have some anchor points and some hope to survive a very arduous experience. It is not always easy to see the positives while living through the whirlwind of change. Systemic thinkers such as Ackoff (1978) suggest that many problems are the result of incorrect assumptions and self-imposed constraints. If we can reframe our view of change from a problematic to a potentially liberating process, then we may be better able not only to tolerate but also to welcome the disruption for the opportunities it brings.

Note

1 In referencing child abuse inquiry reports I have followed the convention of the NSPCC library and referred to them by the name of the child .

References

Ackoff, R. L. (1974) *Redesigning the Future: A Systems Approach to Societal Problems*, New York: Wiley.

—— (1978) *The Art of Problem Solving: Accompanied by Ackoff's Fables*, New York: Wiley.

—— (1981) *Creating the Corporate Future*, New York: Wiley.

ADSS (1987a) *Child Abuse: Incidence of Registration for Child Abuse Between 1985 and 1986*, London: ADSS.

—— (1987b) *The London Workforce Study*, London: ADSS.

American Humane Association (1984) *Trends in Child Abuse and Neglect: A National Perspective*, Denver, Col: AHA.

Beckford (1985) *A Child in Trust: The Report of the Panel of Inquiry into the Circumstances Surrounding the Death of Jasmine Beckford*, London: Borough of Brent.

Bentovim, A. (1987) 'Physical and sexual abuse of children – the role of the family therapist', *Journal of Family Therapy*, 9, 4, November: 383–8.

Butler-Sloss, E. (1988) *Report of the Inquiry into Child Abuse in Cleveland 1987*, London: HMSO.

Campbell, B. (1988) *Unofficial Secrets: Child Sexual Abuse – The Cleveland Case*, London: Virago.

Carlisle (1987) *A Child in Mind: Protection of Children in a Responsible Society: The Report of the Commission of Inquiry into the Circumstances Surrounding the Death of Kimberley Carlisle*, London: Borough of Greenwich.

Charnley, H. (1987) *Child Sexual Abuse: Joint Investigative Project*, Evaluation Report of Metropolitan Police and Bexley London Borough.

De Bono, E. (1972) *Children Solve Problems*, Harmondsworth: Penguin.

DHSS (1982) *Child Abuse: A Study of Inquiry Reports 1973 to 1981*, London: HMSO.

Finkelhor, D. (1984) *Child Sexual Abuse: New Theory and Research*, London: Collier Macmillan.

Franklin, A. W. (ed.) (1977) *The Challenge of Child Abuse*, London: Academic Press.

Freeman, M. D. A. (1987–8) 'Taking children's rights seriously', *Children and Society*, 4: 299–319.

Furniss, T. (1983) 'Mutual influence and interlocking professional family process in the treatment of child sexual abuse and incest', *Child Abuse and Neglect*, 7: 207–23.

Gates (1982) *Report of the Panel of Inquiry by Bexley County Council*, London: Borough of Bexley.

Goodman, P. S. and associates (1982) *Change in Organizations*, London: Jossey-Bass.

Hartley, P. (1985) *Child Abuse, Social Work and the Press: Towards the History of a Moral Panic*, University of Warwick, Department of Applied Social Studies.

Harvey-Jones, J. (1988) *Making it Happen*, London: Collins.

Henry (1987) *Whose Child? the Report of the Panel Appointed to Inquire into the Death of Tyra Henry*, London: Borough of Lambeth.

Hoggett, P. (1984) 'Decentralization, Labourism and the professionalised state apparatus', in R. Hambleton and P. Hoggett (eds) *The Politics of Decentralization: Theory and Practice of a Radical Local Initiative*, University of Bristol, School for Advanced Urban Studies.

Jones, C. (1983) *State Social Work and the Working Class*, London: Macmillan.

Kempe, R. S. and Kempe, C. H. (1978) *Child Abuse*, London: Fontana/Open Books.

La Fontaine, J. (1988) *Child Sexual Abuse: An ESRC Research Briefing*, London: Economic and Social Research Council.

Latey, J. (1987) 'Re M (a minor): child abuse evidence', *Family Law Reports*, Special Issue, 4: 293–6.

MacFarlane, K. and Waterman, J. (1986) *Sexual Abuse of Young Children: Evaluation and Treatment*, Guildford Publications.

MacLeod, M. and Saraga, E. (1988) 'Challenging the orthodoxy: towards a feminist theory and practice', *Feminist Review*, 28, Spring: 16–55.

Manning, B., Cameron, D, and Burrell, S. (1987) 'Facing up to the truth', *Community Care*, 26 November.

Metropolitan Police and Bexley London Borough (1987) *Child Sexual Abuse: Joint Investigative Programme: Final Report*, London: HMSO.

NSPCC (1986) *Child Abuse in 1986*, Research Briefing 8, London: NSPCC.

—— (1987) *Child Abuse in 1987*, Research Briefing 9, London: NSPCC.

Oppenheim, J. (1988) 'Falling apart at the seams', *Child Abuse Review*, 2, 1: 30–1.

Parton, H, (1985) *The Politics of Child Abuse*, London: Macmillan Education.

Peters, T. (1987) *Thriving on Chaos: A Handbook of Management Revolution*, London: Macmillan.

Pilisuk, M. and Parks, S. H. (1986) *The Healing Webb: Social Networks and Human Survival*, Hanover, NH: University Press of New England.

Pugh, D. (1986) 'Understanding and managing organizational change', in E. Maynor-White (ed.) *Planning and Managing Change*, London: Open University /Harper & Row.

Sgroi, H. S. (1984) *Handbook of Clinical Intervention in Child Sexual Abuse*, Lexington, Mass: Lexington Books.

Spring, J. (1987) *Cry Hard and Swim*, London: Virago.

Staw, B. M. (1982) 'Counterforces to change', in P. S. Goodman and associates, *Change in Organizations*, London: Jossey-Bass.

Stevenson, D. (1988) 'Multi-disciplinary work – Where next?' *Child Abuse Review*, 2, 1: 5–9.

Toffler, A. (1971) *Future Shock*, New York: Bantam.

Watzlawick, P., Weakland, J. and Fisch, R. (1974) *Change: Principles of Problem Formation and Problem Resolution*, New York: W. W. Norton.

10
Black youth clubs and black workers

Lincoln Williams

> As far as I'm concerned they should close every fucking
> youth club in the area, especially Carib.
>
> (Robert speaking)

This quotation is taken from a recent interview undertaken with a group of
young black males in west London. The answer was given in response to a
question as to what they thought about the youth clubs which they used
infrequently. I had expected a fairly intense rejection of clubs run by white
workers. What I did not expect was the intensity of the hatred towards the
Carib Youth club. It was a black club in the sense that it was set up by the
local Community Relations Council with the specific aim of catering for the
needs of Afro-Caribbean young people. At the time all the workers, full- and
part-time, were black. Encountering this hostility on the part of young black
males forced me to focus on what should be the role of black youth clubs and
black youth workers.

Before proceeding it is essential to define more specifically what is the
meaning of the term 'black', as no consensus exists. Some argue that the
term should be used only to those of African descent (Gueye 1988). They
contend that the positive image connoted by the term arises from the
struggle of the Black Consciousness movement started by Marcus Garvey
and picked up by the Black Power movement in the USA in the 1960s. The
fruits of this struggle, they argue, should not be usurped or bestowed on
other ethnic groups who were not active in that struggle. Others maintain
that it is vital that all who suffer from white discrimination should unite.
Such unity being assisted by the adoption of a universal term, 'black'
therefore signifies this potential. A major agency in the Youth Service, the
National Youth Bureau, has certainly adopted this perspective. Their literature largely defines the term 'black' to include all who are systematically
disadvantaged by white racism. This shift from a descriptive use of the term
'black' to an evaluative or aspirational one, has far-reaching political

implications, in particular for the Asian Community's struggles in this country:

> the aspirational use of this term black implies that while some persons or groups are more black than others, if being black is something to be encouraged, the more ambiguous blacks ought to aspire to be more like the 'true' blacks.
>
> (Modood 1988: 4)

In such a framework, he argues, Asians are ascribed a secondariness to the political leadership of the Afro-Caribbean. He accepts that this has had some beneficial spin-off for the Asian community; however the price to be paid in the explicit loss of identity entailed is too high. The use of the term forces Asians to subordinate their public identity to political concerns; many reject this because it has no meaning for them. The implied unity in this use of black is, therefore, purely illusionary because

> The choice is not between Asian ethnicity and the unity of the racially oppressed. It is between a political realism which accords dignity to ethnic groups on their own terms and a coercive ideological fantasy.
>
> (Modood 1988: 5)

I certainly would not wish to impose an Afro-Caribbean identity on to Asian young people and force them to accept the leadership of the former. However, politically both groups must benefit from some kind of alliance in their separate struggles against racial domination. In terms of young people, Gilroy reminds us that

> Youth culture has also created an important space for dialogue between black youth from the different communities. Asian youth movements have been inspired by the combativity of Afro-Caribbean young people which has received spectacular press coverage while their own equally tenacious defence of their communities remains concealed behind a stereotype of passivity.
>
> (Gilroy 1983: 295)

Thus both have a lot to learn from each other not only in terms of political and quasi-military defence strategies, but also regarding popular culture. An example here is the current popularity amongst young Asian people of Bhangra which fuses Black American soul with the music art form of the Asian subcontinent.

The conclusion of this debate, therefore, is that the use of the term black in this chapter refers exclusively to Afro-Caribbean. This does not mean however that the arguments used will not have validity if applied to Asian young people and youth workers.

Another theme which will be running through this chapter will be the clear rejection of the notion that black people should unite their struggle with the white Left. I do not believe that it is necessary to adduce Gorz's (1982) thesis to challenge the assertion that only the white working class is the continuous subject of history, and the only agent which can achieve the liberation of all.

History has shown that the white working class has consciously and continuously colluded with capital in the super exploitation of black labour both abroad and in Britain. They have shown a resistance to undertaking the struggle for racial justice. As Gilroy (1987) and Ramdin (1987) argue, the white working class has been constituted through racism and as such it is they who maintain this particular schism.

I am not questioning whether or not the division of humanity into social classes explains its history infinitely better than its division into races or peoples, or whether or not race is the modality in which class relations are experienced. I am merely arguing that in this particular historical conjuncture 'race' is a far more vital category around which black people are organizing the struggle in their communities. Class no longer, and probably never has had, a monopoly of the political stage. It is not a question of whether or not there should be black autonomous organizations; the fact is we have them.

This position is clearly applicable to the Youth Service. The Hunt Report (1967) attempted to stop the development of black youth clubs by arguing that the objective for the Youth Service should be for the development of racially integrated youth clubs. Separate provision should be only a temporary measure, usually because of language barriers, to assist integration. The last major report on the Service (Thompson 1982) categorically rejects this position, accepting the reality that there will be a demand for all black clubs, and that it is legitimate for the Youth Service to respond.

In talking about black youth clubs I have in mind those located in black districts and communities. Though I am of the opinion that many of the arguments used below may be transferable to multiracial youth clubs and to black workers working in predominantly white areas and white youth clubs, this has to be done with severe qualifications.

The arguments below must also be qualified when applied to black youth clubs with a mixture of male and female members. The sexism and machismo exhibited by the young men involved in my research was offensive in the extreme. This area of work has to be high on the agenda for all black male youth workers. Brown offers a tentative explanation for this sexism;

> If lack of power over their social, political and racial position is a fact of life for boys, then at least at the level of psychology and self-image they can compensate by expressing their power and control over girls and women.
> (Brown 1986: 23)

Suffice it to say that this explanation was used by many black men involved in the Black Power movement of the 1960s to marginalize the contribution of black women. It is the refusal of black men to deal with their sexism and their oppression of black women, and of the failure of the white feminist movement to deal with their racism, which has forced many black women to set up their own autonomous organizations (Hooks 1982). Part of the hostility of the young man towards the Carib Youth club, quoted at the head of this chapter, is explained by the fact that all the staff were women. Apart from their reaction to the police, the other issue which drew tremendous resentment was the men's exclusion one evening a week from the club, for the girls only evening.

Many may question the validity of black youth clubs. They would argue that the essential function of the Youth Service, as other similar state institutions, as outlined by Althusser (1971), is to contribute to the reproduction of capitalist social relations. That the Youth Service, both statutory and voluntary, is part of the local state and thereby contributes to the process of reproduction cannot be denied. What can be questioned however is that this is its only role and that it always fulfils this function effectively. The Youth Service is a site in the superstructure from which counter-hegemonic strategies can be developed. Space does not allow a detailed examination of the reproduction theories of Althusser (1971), Bowles and Gintis (1976), Bourdieu and Passeron (1977) and Bernstein (1977), except to say that they fail to recognize that ruling-class domination is not total. This failure has implications for theory and practice. Such theories spread a pessimism which disempowers activists, ruling out the possibility of any oppositional ideology leading to radical practices and pedagogy (Giroux 1983; Sumner 1979).

It is for this reason that I am attracted to the neo-Marxist theories of writers such as Willis (1983), Hebdige (1979) and Corrigan (1979). These theories make the concept of conflict and resistance the starting-point of their analysis. Willis in particular points out that in such sites, it is not only reproduction that takes place but also cultural production, which at times is capable of penetrating the hegemonic culture. This should not be taken to mean that every action taken by black young people can be deemed as oppositional. Willis's model and Giroux's (1983) theory of resistance remind us that such cultures are riddled with contradictions. Actions which stem from opposition not only may be accommodation to domination but also may be oppressive in their own right. For example, the 'macho-ness' which black young men display in their opposition to police harassment becomes oppressive when used to maintain sexist relationships. Actions which give the impression of being oppositional may often be no more than what Giroux calls 'outright self-indulgence' (1983: 106). One of the principal functions of black workers is to exploit these contradictions and gaps and use them to assist black young people and the local black community in their struggle for racial justice. In doing so they will constantly have to try and deduce which actions are authentically oppositional and/or just outright self-indulgent.

In looking at the role of black youth clubs and black workers, my starting-point will be the work of John (1981). His starting-point is that even black 'self-help' projects are merely more efficient ways of transmitting the hegemonic culture. Black projects, he concludes, are no less agents of cultural reproduction than projects run by the white power structure for black young people. This is an example of the type of reproduction thesis that was alluded to earlier. Central to John's argument is that in order to understand the role played by the Youth Service *vis-à-vis* black young people, it is necessary to locate the Service in the context of the general relationships between the black working class and capitalism.

Like Sivanandan (1982) and Hall *et al.* (1978), John argues that cheap black labour was imported into the UK in the 1950s and 1960s not only to maintain the rate of profit but also to break the power that the white working class had achieved during the post-war labour shortage. Thus the major burden of immigration was borne by labour in terms of increased competition for housing, jobs and welfare services. This only increased cost which capital had related to law and order, which had to be met by the state. This was due to the social unrest caused by racist attacks on the black communities which escalated during the mid-1960s, followed by the community's attempts to defend itself both against the attacks and against police harassment. Discussing the conflict between the black and white communities in general, and the Notting Hill disturbances in particular, Hall *et al.* make the point that

> Spearheaded by white youths, egged on in a carefully planned intervention by the organised facist movement, the riots represent a major break in the 'friendly relations', not simply between black people and the Teddy Boys, but between the black and white communities.
>
> (Hall *et al.* 1978: 348)

Thus by the 1960s, Hall *et al.* argue, the black communities had adopted a strategy of *acceptance* which *de facto* meant informal segregation within the culture of a subordinate class:

> What was principally at issue in this compromise solution was the differentiated incorporation of the black community into the white respectable working class.
>
> (Hall *et al.* 1978: 548)

The black communities attempted to make decent lives while keeping themselves to themselves. Hall *et al.* argue that the first generation of mass immigrants did not totally give up hope of some sort of integration because although the strategy of acceptance was hard,

> it could be endured in the belief that the experience of rejection and relative failure was not necessarily the systematic fate of race, and that 'the children' would have a chance of succeeding in ways in which their parents were destined to fail.
>
> (Hall *et al.* 1978: 350)

Unfortunately the evidence suggests that even this hope was misplaced. Their children now live in a society that not only rejects them socially but also does not even want their labour power.

John argues, like Hall *et al.* (1978), that black young people are at the sharp end of the conflict between the two communities. The black community, having retreated to their 'colonies', used the space created to preserve, reproduce and develop their own culture. It is in this context that the role of black youth clubs and workers must be analysed. Within these internal colonies, young people have 'captured' youth clubs as spaces in which they preserve elements of their Caribbean culture, to assist them in their struggle against racism in general and routine police harassment in particular. They are carrying on the strategy of *acceptance* which their parents were forced to adopt; Hall *et al.* make the point that this generation

> have grown up with racial segregation as a part of life . . . young blacks see no visual signs of social integration between races in the adult world they inhabit; they do not notice racially mixed groups of adults walking in the streets or leaving the pub; no white friends visit their families; the only whites with whom they have contact are people doing a job (postman, meter readers, etc) or welfare officers and social workers.
>
> (Hall *et al.* 1978: 354)

My research in a part of London would partially support this. After leaving school or earlier many of the group had had little day-to-day informal contact with the white community. During one week of my research, the only contact the group had with white people was with a youth worker, the owner of the amusement arcade where they met and spent the greater part of the day, the staff in the betting shop and the DHSS, and the police.

For these young people, racism has structured their lives to the point where its operation is seen as 'natural'. Many of them did not perceive it as something negative, severely limiting their opportunities. They know intuitively that British society works through race. They do not need a youth worker to tell them that it is racist. Further, they can no longer avail themselves of the optimism of their parents or their grandparents, namely that one day they will go home. For them, home is Brixton, Harlesden and Notting Hill Gate. The second and third generation knows that it is a black generation, knows that it is not going to be anything else but black. I shall be looking at the implications of this for black youth workers and black clubs below. The essential point to grasp is that a sizeable proportion of black young people are in no doubt that they were born black in a society which accords them second-class status. For these black young people

> The Youth Service is part of a series of local settings within which black young people attempt to respond to their conditions. Proportionately more black young people than their white peer group use the Youth Service provisions and many use it well beyond the upper statutory age limit. Black young people see youth clubs much less as clubs in the traditional sense, and much more as territory within which they could give expressions to cultural preferences and political options and establish an identity as young blacks and resist the repressive attempts of the state.
>
> (John 1981: 38)

Black young people therefore must be seen as an integral part of the black community, engaged like their elders in a struggle against the white working-class subculture which, in tandem with the middle-class hegemonic culture, seeks to neutralize and contain their struggle for racial justice. Black young people like their parents will resist those attempts to subordinate them. When black young people experience the effects of racism in 'caring' institutions they resist and the institutions (schools, clubs, intermediate treatment, and so on) interpret their behaviour as neatly fitting into their racist preconceptions about black people in general and black young people in particular. Traditionally their behaviour is viewed as, for example, rebellion for its own sake, the inability of blacks to exercise self-discipline or confirmation of the tendency towards criminal behaviour (Walvin 1982; Jordan 1982; Solomos *et al.* 1982). It is the 'caring' institutions which begin the process of labelling black young people as either pathological or criminal.

If black youth clubs are to assist young people in their general struggle (and I would say this is one of their principal functions), then they must identify themselves as an integral part of the black communities. From such a position, the clubs could not abstract themselves from the general political issues confronting the black community. By adopting a community development approach to youth work the present hegemony of the person-centred approach is diminished.

Black workers need to challenge the pathological view which underlies the work of white institutions with black young people. Many black workers unwittingly adopt this perspective in their work with black young people. First, because of the implicit assumptions underlying Youth and Community Work training courses. Students, by withdrawing from their communities into white institutions of higher education, develop skills and perceptions which are inherently Eurocentric and which disable many from challenging the dominant pathological perspective. Second, the perpetuation of this view of black young people has been a means by which black projects have been able to secure funding. How often do we hear funding criteria include the 'alienation' or 'identity crisis' of black young people?

If black workers are to undermine the pathological approach, they must be clear about their own ideology and the political context in which they work. If they are not, they are of little use to black young people. They will easily become co-opted by the state to undertake the 'cooling out' of black young people. As John notes, this means that as black workers, 'we cannot allow ourselves the luxury, like many of our white colleagues, of pretending that youth work takes place within a politically neutral context' (1984: 7).

Another struggle engaging black young people is against attempts by police and media to criminalize them as a group. This must be addressed in black youth clubs, not by 'turning a blind eye' to crime, but by being aware of the political context in which it is located. It is undoubtedly true that a proportion of black young people drift into crime. Given the objective situation of black young people this is hardly surprising. The majority do not take part in criminal activity, such as ganja dealing or personal robbery. Those who do tend to do so on a transitional basis either prior to a more conventional criminal career (like some of their white peers) or to dropping out altogether. It is reasonable to argue that with the discrimination against black young people in the labour market (Troyna and Smith 1983; Commission for Racial Equality 1980; Willis 1986; Troyna and Williams 1986) there will always be a faction who remain unemployed and who refuse to do 'shit work' (Pryce 1979). For these crime is an alternative.

What is the role for black young workers in this context? First, to defend black young people against police harassment, and to be aware that in doing so that we may appear to be 'defenders' of street criminals. We must be prepared to take on this label. Not to do so will mean the abandonment of this faction of black young people, who will systematically be driven further into the ranks of those who have been permanently criminalized, enabling the police and media more easily to label and criminalize the rest of the black community. We must recognize the no-win situation which confronts us. In such a situation we have to use the option which we believe to be in the best interests of the black community in general and black young people in particular.

There is a more positive role to play also with the black young people concerned. It is not enough to defend them, or to strive to reduce or prevent their involvement in crime. The additional task is to transform their rebellion and resistance into an effective strategy that can begin to be capable of challenging the material conditions of their oppression. Black youth clubs are strategically placed to help develop ways of working with black young people to transform their political consciousness and help to give them organization, both in the cultural sphere and in the political sphere. Youth workers and clubs are not only strategically placed to take on such a task given the quality and immediacy of their contact, but also because black people are unrepresented in the formal political structure and trade union movement. A lack of formal representation means that any effective strategy, such as that deployed by Black Power groups in the USA in the 1960s, must be located in the 'colonies', in youth clubs and community organizations, and in community politics. The adoption of the community development approach is based not only on a theoretical rationale but also on a practical and political imperative.

If black youth clubs do become an integral part of communities, and enlist the support and involvement of black people in their operation, then they will begin to perform another important function: that of maintaining and reinforcing links between black young people and their parents. The breakdown of the West Indian family is used to explain why young people are proportionately more likely to be placed in sin bin 'support' units, ESN schools, or suspended and expelled from schools, and thereafter placed in prisons and mental hospitals. The generational conflicts are no more marked than those in the indigenous cultures. Black young people had to, and continue to have to, make their own adjustments and accommodations to the white hegemonic culture. They will of course do so on different terms than their parents did. These adjustments do not signify a fundamental split between generations.

This was clearly illustrated for me in my research. Without exception, all members of the group were respectful and caring of their parents, in particular their mothers. Two factors reinforced the closeness between generations. First, unemployment, as parents, sons and daughters increasingly found themselves in the same position, and were forced to provide for each other. Second, the police, and the constant harassment of black young people, has been one of the most potent factors in uniting the generations. Initially police and media managed to isolate black young people, driving an ideological wedge between them and their parents, portraying the latter as law-abiding and the former as criminals. A process which originally divided them eventually united the generations. Black youth clubs can assist in this process of unification by offering facilities for cultural activities, advice and information.

It is within the cultural sphere that black youth clubs predominantly operate. Black youth workers must increasingly emphasize the political role of their clubs and projects. By this I do not mean that they should simply adopt a more radical rhetoric for it would not necessarily mean that there will be a qualitative change in practice. What is at issue is not rhetoric but methods and objectives in our work with black young people. In my experience, radical rhetoric has very little to do with the issues confronting black young people on a daily basis. To encourage black young people to riot for example merely plays into the hands of the law-and-order lobby. The police are now equipped to deal with any serious challenge to the state (Benyon 1984). Advocating a strategy based on open confrontation on the streets can only benefit the state as it is able to legitimize subsequent violence against black young people. I am aware of the frustration involved for radical youth workers wanting immediate change, who must satisfy themselves with a series of minor victories. Creating the conditions in which transformation in consciousness can take place and enabling black young people to begin to confront the economic, political and ideological issues in their lives cannot be achieved overnight.

Having argued for the 'war of positions' strategy it is important to examine now its implementation. Each club needs first to contruct a programme to meet the identified needs of its members. Whatever the content, this must be constructed and delivered in a way that involves a high degree of participation. Thompson (1982) reminds us just how dismal the attempts of the Youth Service have been to make participation a reality. First, if black youth clubs are going to begin to achieve their cultural and political functions, participation must become a reality. Black clubs and projects cannot afford to perpetuate dependence. This means that black workers like their white colleagues must be prepared to relinquish a high degree of their personal and institutional power. For black youth workers simply to open their clubs and hand out dominoes and pool cues, turning a blind eye to the smoking of dope, is a gross dereliction of duty. It is necessary to adopt not only a curriculum but also a methodology which encourages black young people to see the club as theirs and that they have a major role in ensuring that it meets both their cultural and political needs.

Second, black clubs must play a role in correcting the distortion in the relationship of black history to a racist and Eurocentric culture (Husband 1982). They must assist members to contextualize their socio-economic position, challenging the notion that black people are mere 'victims', objects rather than subjects in history. It is important to expose black young people to their history in a way that will enable them to go forward.

The third element is closely related. Many workers would hope that a principal objective of their organization must be to help black young people secure their 'black' identity. This proposition is not without contention. For example, as John (1981) argues, black young people are often more certain of their black identity than the black youth workers and project leaders. One problem that black young people do not have is an identity crisis. John's position finds support in the general framework sketched by Hall *et al.* (1978). They point out that the 'colonies' carved out by the first generation have provided the space in which the second generation could, and has, established an alternative identity to the one the white hegemonic culture has tried to impose on them. The importance of the Rastafarian movement in developing the counter-culture and identity of contemporary black youth needs to be stressed:

> It is the dress, beliefs, philosophy and language of this once marginal and despised group which has provided the basis for the generalisation and radicalisation of black consciousness amongst sectors of black youth in the cities, the source of an intense black cultural nationalism.
>
> (Hall *et al.* 1978: 357)

While agreeing with John (1981), Hall *et al.* (1978) and Stone (1981) that the Rastafarian movement has provided a section of black young people with a secure basis for their cultural identity, I think two points have to be made. First, the Rastafarian movement has failed to have any significant impact on the political configurations of this country. Cashmore (1983) argues that the failure of the Rasta movement to radicalize black young people is because it preached a philosophy of opting out of 'Babylon'. For Gilroy (1987) however, Cashmore misses the point. He argues that Cashmore ignores not only its potency as a conductor of political ideologies between the Caribbean and the overdeveloped world but also the important role that religion has played in the history of the liberation struggle in the Caribbean. The principal reason for the failure of Rastafarianism to speak to the conditions of living in contemporary Britain is that

> The organised sections of the movement could not translate the popularity of their language, style and vision into a single social or political initiative.
>
> (Gilroy 1987: 191)

Second, both Gilroy and my own research findings (Williams 1988) serve to update John's argument on this point. Though there is a sizeable proportion of black young people who are undoubtedly reaffirming their identity by drawing on the cultures of the black diaspora there is a growing number who are trying to come to terms with the fact that they are 'black British'. Many black young people who have never been to the Caribbean: they are reluctant to describe themselves as English, but they know that they are not Jamaicans or Trinidadians or West Indians. They inhabit a world which is neither English nor Caribbean. It is a distinctive culture which has not yet crystallized. Although it maintains the oppositional core of black youth culture, it is no longer permeated by a wholehearted rejection of Englishness. For example the black young people in my research switched with ease between a variant of Jamaican patois and a variant of London cockney (Sebba 1986). Thus though I would agree with John's critique of black workers whose work with black young people is informed by a pathological perspective (that is black young people have an identity crisis) and his criticism of the senior officers responsible for the various youth service provisions, for failing to come to grips with the concept of black Englishness; nowhere in his report does he pick up on this and tease out the implications of being black and British for black youth clubs and their workers. Having identified the failure of the white providers to recognize this, he quickly moves on to deal with those older black young people who already have a clear and positive black identity, principally those born in the Caribbean.

The black youth workers of today and tomorrow must constantly ask themselves what identity are those black young people born here trying to create. What does it mean to be black and British? We cannot say a priori what this black British identity will consist of, or even how it will be constructed. We do not yet know which parts of the culture inherited from the black diaspora or which parts of white working-class culture will be used in constructing this new identity. As it is a subordinate culture in relation to the hegemonic white middle-class culture, it will also depend on how the attitudes within British society towards its black citizens develop. In such a situation all we can say is that it is imperative that black youth workers in black clubs provide the space within which this identity can be developed.

These black young people, including those of mixed parentage, must be facilitated to explore and eventually feel secure in whatever meaning they choose to give to the concept of black-British. They must not be forced to have to accept a definition of blackness of which they have had no experience. If this is attempted they will vote with their feet, like the majority of their white peers, and abandon youth clubs. It may be that this facilitation role can effectively be carried out only by those young up-and-coming youth and community workers who were not born in the Caribbean. It may be that those of us born in the Caribbean cannot sufficiently escape our early socialization, memories and our politicization in the Black Power movement of the 1960s (Rodney 1969), to allow those born here the space to explore the new identity needed to feel rooted and a part of this society.

This generation cannot call the Caribbean home. They have to stay here and claim their birthright. It is they who have to bear the burden of forcing this society to concede racial justice. Black youth clubs and workers have a role to play in assisting these young people in the formulation and implementation of strategies to secure their birthright from a society structured along racial and class lines. It is vital that their attempt to develop this new identity is not interpreted by the Youth Service as yet another example of a pathological identity crisis.

Lastly, the fourth element in our work with black young people, and in particular black young men, must be to tackle the sexism alluded to in the earlier part of this chapter. If our work with black young people is about liberation then we must intervene positively to reduce the oppression of women by men in general, and of black women by black men in particular. Racial liberation cannot be achieved by the adoption of sexist ways of working and by colluding in practices which seek to subjugate women.

In summary, there is a need for black youth workers to distinguish between the acts of resistance of black young people which are authentic, containing elements of critical thinking, 'which have the possibility of stimulating collective political action which in some way undermines existing power relations' (Williams 1988), and those acts which are mere accommodation to racial domination, or downright self-indulgence (Giroux 1983).

The task is not easy. For workers seeking to evaluate work with black young people, there are two questions to ask:

first, has this piece of work brought about any real structural change in the way power is exercised in the club/project? Secondly, has the piece of work brought about any change in the ideological disposition of black young people?

(Brown 1986: 70)

To conclude on an even more realistic note, I am aware that those of us working with young people in general and black young people in particular, must be prepared to be let down, as Brown puts it:

with something of a bump from the dizzy heights of praxis and hegemony to the mundane depths of table tennis balls and canteen hygiene.

(Brown 1986: 63)

The real challenge is to ensure that this is not where we remain. To do so would only be fulfilling our reproductive and social control role of keeping them off the streets and amused. As black workers however we owe it to our young people not to give up. They will not.

References

Althusser, L. (1971) *Ideology and Ideological State Apparatuses in Lenin and Philosophy and Other Essays*, London: New Left Books.
Benyon, J. (ed.) (1984) *Scarman and After*, Oxford: Pergamon.
Bernstein, B. (1977) *Class, Codes and Control*, Vol. 3: *Towards a Theory of Educational Transmission*, London: Routledge & Kegan Paul.
Bourdieu, P. and Passeron, J. (1977) *Reproduction in Education, Society and Culture*, trans. R. Nice, London: Sage.
Bowles, S. and Gintis, H. (1976) *Schooling in Capitalist America*, London: Routledge & Kegan Paul.
Brown, S. (1986) *Critical Theory and Practice in a Black Youth Club*, occasional paper, Sunderland: Youth and Policy.
Cashmore, E. (1983) *Rastaman*, London: Counterpoint.
Coard, B. (1971) *How the West Indian Child is Made Educationally Subnormal in the British School System*, as quoted in A. Gueye (1988) *Supplementary Schools in the Black Community*, London: Dragon's Teeth, 29, Spring, National Committee for Racism in Children's Books.

Commission for Racial Equality (1980) *Ethnic Minority Youth Unemployment*, a paper presented to government, July, London: CRE.
Community Relations Commission (1976) *Self Help Report*, October, London: CRC.
Corrigan, P. (1979) *Schooling the Smash Street Kids*, London: Macmillan.
Gilroy, P. (1983) *Steppin' Out of Babylon – Race, Class and Autonomy*, in Centre for Contemporary Cultural Studies, *The Empire Strikes Back*, London: Hutchinson.
—— (1987) *There Ain't No Black in the Union Jack*, London: Hutchinson.
Giroux, H. A. (1983) *Theory and Resistance in Education: A Pedagogy for the Opposition*, London: Heinemann.
Gorz, A. (1982) *Farewell to the Working Class*, London: Pluto.
Gueye, A. (1988) *Supplementary Schools in the Black Community*, London: Dragon's Teeth, 29, Spring, National Committee for Racism in Children's Books.
Hall, S. (1985) 'Authoritarian populism: a reply to Jessop *et al.*, *New Left Review*, 151: 115–24
Hall, S., Chritcher, C., Jefferson, T., Clarke, J. and Roberts, B. (1978) *Policing the Crisis*, London: Macmillan.
Hebdige, D. (1979) *Subculture: The Meaning of Style*, London: Methuen.
Hooks, B. (1982) *Ain't I a Woman*, London: Pluto.
Hunt, Lord J. (1967) *Immigrants and the Youth Service*, London: HMSO.
Husband, C. (1982) 'Race: the continuity of a concept', in C. Husband (ed.) *'Race' in Britain*, London: Hutchinson.
John, G. (1981) *In the Service of Black Youth*, Leicester: National Association of Youth Clubs.
—— (1984) 'The power of racism', *Working with Black Youth. The Report of the Panel to Promote the Continuing Development of Training for Part-Time and Voluntary Youth and Community Workers*, Leicester: National Youth Bureau.
Jordan, W. D. (1982) 'First impressions: initial English confrontations with Africans' in C. Husband (ed.) *'Race' in Britain*, London: Hutchinson.
Modood, T. (1988) 'Who's defining who?', *New Society*, March: 4–5.
Pryce, K. (1979) *Endless Pressure*, Harmondsworth: Penguin.
Ramdin, R. (1987) *The Making of the Black Working Class in Britain*, Aldershot: Wildwood House.
Rodney, W. (1969) *Grounding with my Brothers*, London: Bogle L'Ouverture.
Scarman, Lord (1981) *The Scarman Report*, Harmondsworth: Penguin.
Sebba, M. (1986) 'London Jamaican and Black London English', in D. Sutcliffe and A. Wong (eds) *The Language of the Black Experience*, Oxford: Blackwell
Sivanandan, A. (1982) *A Different Hunger*, London: Pluto.
Solomos, J., Findlay, B., Jones, S. and Gilroy, P. (1982) 'The organic crisis of British capitalism and race: the experience of the 70s', in CCCS, *The Empire Strikes Back*, London: Hutchinson.
Stone, M. (1981) *Educating the Black Child*, Glasgow: Fontana.
Sumner, C. (1979) *Reading Ideologies*, London: Academic Press.
Thompson, A. (1982) *Experience and Participation. Report of the Review Group on the Youth Service in England*, Cmnd 8686, London: HMSO.
Troyna, B. and Smith, D. (1983) *Racism, School and the Labour Market*, Leicester: National Youth Bureau.
Troyna, B. and Williams, J. (1986) *Racism, Education and the State*, London: Croom Helm.
Walvin, J. (1982) 'Black caricature: The roots of racialism', in C. Husband (ed.) *'Race' in Britain*, London: Hutchinson.
Williams, L. (1988) *Partial Surrender: Race and Resistance in the Youth Service*, Lewes: Falmer Press.
Willis, P. (1980) *Learning to Labour*, Farnborough, Hants: Gower.

—— (1983) 'Cultural production and theories of reproduction', in S. Barton and L. Walker (eds) *Race, Class and Education*, London: Croom Helm.
—— (1986) 'Unemployment: the final inequality', *British Journal of Sociological Education*, 7, 2: 155–70.

11
Access to children in care: legal rights and social work practice in Scotland

Ruth Adler and Christopher Turner

The aim of this chapter is to apply a specific theory of children's rights, termed 'modified protectionism', to a particular area of child law and to examine the extent to which practice in this chosen sphere conforms to the principles implicit in that theory. It will be shown that these principles are also enshrined in the relevant statutory provisions. The area selected is that of access to children in care. Special attention is paid to some of the dilemmas surrounding permanency planning for such children. The focus is on children in care under sections 15, 16 and 44 of the Social Work (Scotland) Act 1968 with specific reference to the following legal rights:

1 the rights of children to contact with parents
2 the rights of natural or birth parent(s) to access to children in care
3 the rights of social workers to restrict or terminate access of natural or birth parent(s) to children in care.

Children's rights: A theoretical perspective

It is appropriate to begin by setting out the theoretical framework within which the discussion is to take place. This framework has been worked out much more fully elsewhere (Adler 1985). It is summarized here only to place what follows into a specific context and a particular theoretical perspective.

Many disputes in the area of children's legal rights are, at least in part, the results of confusion on issues of theory. At the most general level on competing conceptions of what it is to have a right and more specifically on the nature of children's rights in particular. With regard to the first, it is not possible to do more here than offer brief quotations to indicate the position adopted on the nature of rights. It seems clear that:

> To have a right is to have a claim against someone, whose recognition as valid is called for by some set of governing rules or moral principles.
>
> (Feinberg 1980: 155)

Moreover:

> A world with claim rights is one in which all persons, as actual or potential claimants, are dignified objects of respect, both in their own eyes and in the view of others. No amount of love and compassion, or obedience to higher authority, or *noblesse oblige*, can substitute for those values.
>
> (Feinberg 1973: 58–9)

These 'values' can be summed up in the Kantian concept of respect for persons as ends in themselves. Finally, 'a right is . . . a legally (or quasi-legally) protected or furthered interest' (Campbell 1983: 27).

To summarize, rights are viewed here as having a common normative element and as securing goods or interests within a normative order. What of the rights of children?

The view of rights presented above is consistent with any one of the three prevailing theories of children's rights which each represent different ways in which the law can deal with children. These orthodoxies can be captured under the headings: parentalist, child-libertarian and protectionist. Each approach is the outcome of a particular perspective on the status of childhood. All three are consistent with a common view of adults as rational, self-determining, autonomous agents. However they disagree fundamentally with respect to their perceptions of children and of the status of childhood.

Parentalists acknowledge that children have rights to care, protection and education in their own interests, but maintain that it is parents who can and should identify the relevant interests of children, provided there is no violation of what are usually called 'human rights' (that is the rights not to be tortured, enslaved or degraded, which do not depend in any way on merit, are unforfeitable, non-conflicting and, where recognized, are seen as belonging to human beings as such and hence to children too). Victoria Gillick clearly falls into the category of parentalist.

Child-libertarians, on the other hand, argue that children have no special rights arising from their perceived helplessness and dependency. On the contrary, children have or should have exactly the same rights as adults. No distinction should be made between the two groups.

Both views are problematic. The first assumes that children's interests are knowable. In addition, it largely ignores the fact that, from a very early age, they have their own distinct characters and viewpoints which cannot simply be ignored whenever they conflict with parental desires and opinions. The second view rejects as irrelevant the fact that children's capacities are not yet fully developed and fails to recognize that the right to develop these capacities may conflict irreconcilably with the rights it advocates, such as the right to choose whether or not to receive formal education. The confusions in both views raise several theoretical and empirical issues.

Protectionists, like parentalists, focus on the relative dependency of children. They insist that children may sometimes have to be protected against their own actions by intervention on the part of adults, not necessarily parents, 'for their own good'. The following paragraphs will attempt to highlight in brief some of the problems, arguing that 'modified protectionism' offers the best possibility of reconciling the positive aspects of each position.

The central question which parentalists and protectionists such as Mill avoid is 'What rights ('freedoms' for Mill), if any, belong to developing individuals?' Child-libertarians like Farson seem to regard this as almost irrelevant: 'The incapacity of the child in infancy should only mean that extra steps must be taken to guarantee the protection of his rights' (Farson 1978: 73).

According to child-libertarians, children have the same rights as adults and because of their limitations may need to have them protected in the same way as adults who fall ill or are in some way temporarily incapacitated. In other words, they do not regard children's limited abilities as in any way relevant in determining their rights or limiting their scope of action. In the realm of law, protectionists regard the 'immaturity' of juveniles as the key factor in determining how to deal with them. Libertarians claim that this is of no relevance at all and that measures taken should be based on the principle of 'equality before the law' which should be applicable to all, irrespective of age. Protectionists wish to define children's legal rights in terms of specific objective needs and interests. Child-libertarians claim that basing decisions on such dubious factors is a violation of generally acknowledged moral rights which are often systematically denied to children. By contrast, protectionists, and parentalists too, would argue that at least some rights, to liberty for example, are ascribed only to self-determining autonomous individuals. They are therefore inappropriate to the status of childhood, but the young have special rights to care and protection which are not accorded to independent adults and which should be enshrined in the law.

Reflections on day-to-day dealings with children seem to lend considerable support to the protectionist argument, but the central dilemma remains: if different rights are accorded to the dependent and the independent and if childhood is seen as a journey from dependency to independence, how can one decide which rights are to be ascribed to children? It must be acknowledged that 'dependency' is not only a vague term but also often used to support differential treatment in a manner that begs the whole question at issue. The Gillick case cited below provides an outstanding example. There is need to articulate a 'modified protectionism'. Indeed *Gillick* was ultimately decided on precisely such terms.

In the Gillick case, Lord Denning's views in *Hewer v. Bryant* ([1969] 3 All ER 578) were cited with approval by Lord Fraser: parents have a dwindling right which the courts will hesitate to enforce against the wishes of the child and the more so the older he is. It starts with the right of control and ends with little more than advice.

Lord Scarman stated further:

If the law should impose upon the process of growing up fixed limits where nature knew only a continuous process, the price would be artificiality and a lack of realism in an area where the law must be sensitive to human development and social change.

These are the principles which we believe should inform any decision concerning the legal rights of children and young people. There is a need for flexibility and any successful theory of children's rights must ultimately accommodate the concept of development and some kind of description of maturity as that towards which development is directed.

Having presented this brief outline of the theoretical issues it is now possible to turn to the question of some of the legal rights of children and young people in Scotland in relation to access and permanency planning.

Legal rights

The legal framework for taking decisions on access and permanency planning is extremely complex, in some respects unnecessarily so. This framework encompasses a number of practical dilemmas in relation to individual cases, all of which raise the issue of the rights of children and young people in an acute form. This section will take a more detailed look at the law, while the next section will examine social work practice in the area.

Children in voluntary care

Children and young people may be in voluntary care under section 15 of the Social Work (Scotland) Act 1968 which came into force in 1971. In such a situation there should, in theory, be no problems in relation to access since – *again in theory* – any lack of satisfaction with existing arrangements can be remedied by parents' removing the child from care, always remembering that if the child has been in care for longer than six months, they must give twenty-eight days' notice before taking such action. The reason for stressing that this is the *legal* position is that it may be in stark conflict with reality. Even where children are in voluntary care, it often requires social work intervention to facilitate access, that is to make the necessary arrangements and offer help with transport, etc. Where such support is not forthcoming and parents are not in a position to care for the children involved, then access may end *de facto* in exactly the same way as where children are in care under a compulsory order.

Children in compulsory care

There are two main categories of children in compulsory care, those under:

1 an order of *Assumption of Parental Rights* under *Section 16* of the *Social Work (Scotland) Act 1968*
2 an order from a Children's Hearing under *Section 44* of the *Social Work (Scotland) Act 1968*.

Assumption of parental rights under section 16 is carried out by processes internal to regional social work departments, although councillors and senior officials are involved as well as practitioners. The position of children is such that the assessment of their needs and interests tends to be paramount even with so-called 'good practice'. Parents have one month after formal notice has been given informing them of the local authority's resolution assuming parental rights, to object by submitting a counter-notice. If parents choose this course of action, the local authority then has to determine whether to take the issue to the Sheriff Court or to accept the parents' objections.

The law relating to access to children in care under section 16 is set out in an amendment to the Social Work (Scotland) Act in section 7 of the Health and Social Services and Social Security Adjudications Act 1983 (HASSASSAA), now known as sections 17(A), (B) and (C) of the Social Work (Scotland) Act. Natural parents' rights of access do not automatically end where a local authority has assumed parental rights. In order to terminate access, the local authority must give parents written notice of such termination and they, in their turn, have a right of appeal to the Sheriff Court. The Sheriff is empowered to grant an Access Order, granting access subject to the conditions set down in the Order. The Order itself may be subsequently amended or terminated on application of either the parents or the local authority. The Sheriff is, of course, also empowered to deny access.

Schaffer (1986) pointed out that the introduction of these procedures was the subject of much criticism. It had previously been thought that where a local authority assumed parental rights, it was automatically entitled to terminate access on the part of natural parents. This, however, is not the law as it stands today. It also seems very important to note that children have no independent rights in these new provisions either to ask for a termination or to request additional granting of access.

In December 1983 the secretary of state produced a Code of Practice setting out the responsibilities of local authorities in relation to children in care or under supervision. The interpretation initially given to this Code was that it was local authorities rather than Children's Hearings which had power to regulate access. As Schaffer (1986) points out, it seemed doubly wrong that parents should be granted no appeal where local authorities terminated access. It was both a breach of natural justice and an anomaly, since under the provisions outlined in the previous paragraph, parents whose rights had been assumed appeared to be in a stronger position that those who had not lost those rights. A number of unreported cases cited by Schaffer gave diverse rulings as to the powers of Children's Hearings in relation to access. However, the situation has been clarified by *Kennedy v. A & A* 1986 SLT 358, and by the Social Work Services Group circular on access (SW11/1986). Children's Hearings are empowered to place conditions in a supervision requirement. It is, therefore, lawful to attach a condition relating to access when making, continuing or varying such a requirement. This must include a condition to end access. Of course, these rulings apply only in the minority of cases where there is disagreement between parents and the social work department as to the nature and degree of access. These matters are usually regulated on a voluntary basis. What of children's rights in these two cases?

It is to be hoped that the views of children and young people are always taken into account in making any decisions on their behalf. Indeed, section 20 of the Social Work (Scotland) Act, amended by the Children Act 1975, requires the local authority 'so far as practicable to ascertain the wishes and feelings of the child'. However, this leaves a very great deal to 'good practice'. It is only in the context of a Children's Hearing that the statutory right to be heard is given a strong interpretation and indeed great weight will often be placed on the wishes of the child, particularly the older child in the context of a Hearing. However, it must be pointed out once again that the *de facto* situation and the legal rights of children and young people may stand in marked contrast to one another. Where parents do not wish access, talk of rights to such access is almost vacuous. The position of children and young people in these situations is like that of those who are the subject of a custody dispute and do not wish their parents to divorce at all. Their rights, in reality, consist of no more than the right to be heard. The situation is markedly different where children and young people want to terminate access against their parents' wishes. Here, where their views are deemed reasonable, they may well determine the outcome of any legal proceedings and in this area at least, they can therefore be said to hold *de facto* rights. Here, we see the principles enunciated in *Gillick* and advocated by us being put into practice.

Adoption and freeing for adoption

The legal rights of children are much stronger under the provisions of the Adoption (Scotland) Act 1968 which came into force in 1984. The principles formulated in *Gillick* are fully recognized in the sense that both a Freeing Order and an Adoption Order are covered by the following conditions set out in sections 12(8) and sections 18(8) of the Act. No such Orders can be made with respect to children

> unless with the consent of the minor, except that where the Court is satisfied that the minor is incapable of giving his consent to the making of the Order, it may dispense with that consent.

In light of the previous discussion of the provisions of the Social Work (Scotland) Act 1968, it seems very important to note here that even where the local authority assumes parental rights, consent of the natural or birth parent(s) as well as of the children remains mandatory for any subsequent Freeing or Adoption Orders. The only grounds on which a Court may dispense with parental consent to such Orders are clearly set out in section 16(2) of the Act.

It is extremely important to stress that Scottish Adoption Legislation is strongly geared to the termination of access. This is not because of any provisions inherent in the legislation, but is rather a reflection of social work practice. The next section will explain this more fully.

This brief summary of the legal principles respecting the access rights of children which are enshrined in the Social Work (Scotland) Act and the Adoption (Scotland) Act, make it quite clear that the principles put forward in *Gillick* and regarded here as the most appropriate approach to matters relating to the legal rights of children, always receive *implicit* and sometimes explicit recognition in the statutory provisions discussed. However, it is only by taking a more detailed look at the implementation of these provisions that it is possible to assess the degree to which children's rights are upheld in practice.

Social work practice

Child care policies and practices both reflect the law and develop in ways which lead to changes in the law. This is an ongoing process. The pace of change varies over time, but has been brisk during most of the 1970s and 1980s. The passage of the Social Work (Scotland) Act 1968 was a significant turning-point. It was clearly and unequivocally based on the premise that the central focus in child care should be upon assessing and meeting the needs of children. It also introduced the first of a major series of changes in the organization and management of social work with the creation of social work departments and the introduction of the Children's Hearing system.

Social work departments exercise considerable powers under the Act. Social workers are key agents in intervention which leads to the removal of children from the parental home. The power and influence of social workers have major implications for the rights of children, parents and relatives. Social workers are in a strong position either to encourage the exercise of rights or to take a more *laissez-faire* approach, always remembering that they have broad responsibilities for promoting the welfare of children in care and have a clear duty to ascertain their wishes and feelings and to give them due consideration.

Changes in social work policy and practice since the mid-1970s have led to a major debate about the values underpinning reception of children into care. 'Permanency' and 'permanency planning', to use the distinctively 1980s vernacular, have become key concepts in the rationale for social work intervention. The policy debate has been fuelled by a wide range of developments in both the USA and UK. Scottish policy and practice issues, while reflecting these broader concerns, have crystallized around supplementary support and care, including working actively and constructively towards rehabilitation when a child is away from the parental home. This has involved a major commitment to the development of community-based resources on the part of social work departments. Access of parents to children in care, and access of children to parents, relatives and friends have become key issues. Yet at the same time there is still a commitment to arranging long-term alternative care, primarily in 'new families' for those children who, for whatever reason, are excluded from living in a parental home.

The different Scottish regional social work managements have developed and articulated diverse child care policies. Strathclyde, for example, has indicated a clear hierarchy of preference (Edwards undated). First, the prevention strategy is aimed at keeping and supporting children and parents in their own homes. Second, the rehabilitative strategy is to work constructively with the families of children outwith the parental home in order to enable them to return as soon as is consistent with their general welfare. Third, the home-finding strategy depends upon the premises that all children have a right to family life and, if it is not possible or not consistent with their welfare to achieve a return to the parental home, a new family should be found for them. Finally, the residential care strategy is based upon a child-centred approach. It calls for the flexible use of residential facilities in order to allow children access to their own local social networks. It also emphasizes the essentially short-term character of residential care, whether as a backup for the rehabilitative strategy, or as a temporary base for the home-finding strategy. However, it does not preclude the use of appropriate forms of residential care for teenagers who clearly reject the home-finding strategy. The policies of other social work departments differ in emphasis and are expressed in different terms, but most appear to be moving in parallel directions. Fife Region has been somewhat more controversial in its formal statements of policy, and in the speed and determination with which social work management has moved towards the objective of reducing the use of residential care in all but the most exceptional cases. Tayside Region is now moving in similar directions. Grampian and Borders have been somewhat more conservative, but nevertheless are committed to developing family care.

The policy statements of social work management, whether written or verbal, tend to be expressed in a very generalized way. At a more pragmatic level, social workers with responsibility for translating policy into practice have a considerable influence. The meanings which policies have for children, their parents, relatives and friends and new families are, in practice, strongly mediated by the knowledge, skills and values of the particular social workers involved (including residential social workers).

The position with respect to current dilemmas relating to permanency and access can be traced in three major strands of social work thinking and practice. The first is a radical shift in thinking about the nature and use of adoption. The second is related to the critique of long-stay institutions, and the development of ideas about how to translate the concept of community care into practice in ways which enhance the quality of life for both children and their carers. The third stems from the emergence of new perspectives on cruelty and neglect, and new ways of thinking and acting in relation to non-accidental injury, sexual abuse, failure to thrive and emotional deprivation.

In the late 1960s major changes were set in motion which changed adoption practice by extending the range of children defined as fit for adoption, and, by implication, fit for long-term fostering (Raynor 1970). In both Britain and the USA adoption across ethnic boundaries began to be extended until it became routine. Prejudices about age at adoption were challenged and found wanting. 'Hard-to-place' children, including those with the most severe mental and/or physical handicaps, were found both foster homes and adoptive homes (Tizard 1977; Triseliotis and Russell 1984; Macaskill 1985). In addition, some ideas regarding the criteria for screening potential adoptive parents were abandoned. Restrictions according to class, creed and ethnicity became less obvious, and adoptive parents were drawn from more diverse social backgrounds. These changes had a gradual impact, though in Scotland ethnic aspects were less significant than in England. Hence the current controversy over cross-ethnic adoption has had little practical impact in Scotland. Nevertheless the potential for finding new families for a much wider range of children in residential care than had hitherto been thought possible was recognized and translated into practice. Changes in the law followed which facilitated adoption against parental wishes (Adoption (Scotland) Act 1978). The device of fostering with a view to adoption came to be used as an important option. Permanency planning for alternative care in new families became one of the tenets of sound child-care practice.

The reaction against residential care was particularly strong in Scotland in the late 1970s. The effects were clearly visible in the declining use of medium- to long-term residential care in the voluntary sector, and by the early 1980s a similar pattern could be observed in List D schools and in local authority residential accommodation. The fundamental criticism of long-term residential care was that it did not seem to provide the majority of children with sufficient opportunities for personal development or for the generation of a matrix of social relationships which would involve them in a mutually supportive local network during the transition to adulthood. The anti-residential trend was undoubtedly intensified by the changing terms and conditions of service in residential establishments which resulted in the introduction of systematic shift work, and decreasing continuity among primary adult carers. At the same time a 'right to family life' was being strongly advocated. Arguments about the costs of residential care surfaced in debates about inter-agency transfer of responsibilities, but never became a central feature of policy debate.

Short-term fostering, as well as long-term fostering and fostering with a view to adoption, were favoured. Changes in practice had major implications for access. Parents and relatives with an interest in maintaining contact with children in care tended to experience much greater difficulty in sustaining access to children in foster care than to children in residential care. There was also a major 'professional' debate over whether contact with parents and relatives was desirable or not for children in long-term foster care, and a varied pattern of practice emerged. Social workers at one end of the continuum did their utmost to encourage and facilitate meaningful contact with parents and relatives even when it became apparent that a child was not likely to return 'home' in the forseeable future. At the other end of the continuum there were social workers who believed that longer-term fostering would work effectively only if contact with parents and relatives was broken. The question of permanency also emerged as a controversial issue. Lack of adequate planning for children in care, and a tendency for short-term measures to drift into much longer-term haphazard arrangements, came under severe criticism.

During the 1980s the use of residential care has been increasingly short term, for example for crisis reception into care, respite care, residential assessment, a brief period of preparation for a new family or an emergency measure consequent upon the breakdown of new family care. The age structure of children in residential care has changed significantly. Teenagers tend to predominate. Even in the older age ranges, however, there has been an attempt to develop and use community carers and various forms of 'contract caring'. The concept of a new family may be less strongly emphasized, but the notion of living in a family context is retained.

The rediscovery and reconstruction of child abuse, which is still ongoing, is fuelled by a powerful combination of public and professional concern (Parton 1985). There is major government and general public backing for increased intervention by health and welfare specialists to limit and, if possible, eliminate child abuse. The initial social work response following the death of Maria Colwell and the succession of inquiries into child abuse cases was heavily biased towards receiving children with non-accidental injuries into residential care. This led to a professional backlash, using ideas pioneered in the USA by Goldstein, Freud and Solnit (1973). They questioned the extent to which public authorities were entitled to interpose themselves between parent and child, and advocated a policy of minimum intervention and supplementary support to parents and children. The swing towards returning children home was justified in terms of the basic philosophy that children had a need to live with parent figures in an ordinary home. The dramatic rise in the number of suspected non-accidental injury cases coming to the attention of social workers may also have had an influence on practice because of the increased demand for resources.

The management of non-accidental injury cases continues to pose a fundamental dilemma for social workers, and has attracted a considerable amount of adverse publicity. If they judge that they should attempt to work with parents and children in the home to change circumstances in such a way as to reduce the level of risk to children, they find that they are likely to be pilloried in the media if a child suffers death or serious injury. If they judge that the parents are unfit to bring up children and take appropriate measures to remove them from the parental home, they are likely to be publicly criticized for excessive interference and infringing parental rights. This has undoubtedly led to the systematic development of new ways of working with parents and children which make flexible use of residential and day facilities for support and care to birth families. It has also stimulated some social workers to look outwards towards the network of close relatives and friends as a supplementary care resource. The help derived ranges from casual informal support to custody. Similar dilemmas and ways of working are currently being developed in cases of sexual abuse, failure to thrive and emotional deprivation.

Permanency planning and access

Social workers involved in permanency planning are concerned with several different strands of 'permanency':

1 a sense of being part of an enduring network of relatives and friends;
2 a feeling of security through having a home and a knowledge of belonging there;
3 a sense of belonging to a wider community, expressed and reinforced through a range of social activities as well as by familiarity with the immediate environment;
4 a long-term commitment by the major parties involved to shared values and activities.

The emphasis is on continuity against a backcloth of change. The major objective of permanency planning is to ensure that children should have a home base that is as stable and secure as possible in order to facilitate their personal development through to adulthood (Thoburn, Murdoch and O'Brien 1986; Maluccio, Fein and Olmstead 1986).

The major policy issue and practice decision with respect to permanency planning concerns the transition from supplementary care to alternative care. As long as the primary aim of intervention is to support the child in the parental home, or to return a child to the parental home as soon as 'the crisis' which led to removal can be resolved, the permanency objective is clear and unequivocal. By contrast, the means of achieving that objective may be extremely complex. The social work task is to encourage, facilitate and support, by whatever practical means available, the maintenance of a permanent home with parents throughout childhood. The nature, timing, places of access and range of relatives and friends involved are vitally important in such circumstances. There is still a tendency to accept, as adequate, limited access by parents in surroundings which are hardly conducive to reinforcing or developing parent–child relations. Even when it is not possible to keep siblings in care together under the same roof, regular contact is not difficult to engineer. On a much broader basis, it takes far more planning co-ordination, and calls for the expenditure of greater social work resources to sustain constructive contact between children away from home and their relatives and friends. Yet it can be and is being achieved in at least a few instances.

When it is equally clear that there is no possibility of a child's having a permanent home with parents, the social work task is to find an alternative long-term arrangement which is satisfactory to children and their carers. In Scotland there has been a tendency to assume that family-based alternative long-term care with strangers is facilitated by allowing previous bonds to lapse or by deliberately terminating them. This is especially so with adoption. Instances of open adoption (where the child remains in contact with birth parent(s) or relatives) are relatively rare even in comparison with England and Wales. Even with planned long-term fostering, an effective veto on contact between foster-child and birth-parent or relatives has tended to operate. In the policy climate of the late 1980s, in which fostering with contact is formally recognized as a possible option by certain local authorities, severe practical difficulties have been encountered in some cases.

It is likely that major difficulties will arise when one of the primary parties involved (a child or a parent) is in open dissent with a permanency proposal. Similarly there are problems when a social worker's permanency intention is guarded or conditional. Accurate assessment, possibly involving a wide range of professionals, is particularly important in such cases. Parents who desperately want a child to be returned home are likely to achieve their wishes, despite resistance by the child, unless it is assessed that the child will be at substantial risk or in danger. Access is a key issue in such situations, and can be extremely difficult to manage, especially if the child resorts to what is euphemistically labelled 'acting out' after contacts. Conversely parents who reject a child in care away from home, and are not prepared to sustain contact or to offer a return home, are likely to see the child drift into permanent alternative care.

The outcome in situations in which the uncertainty rests with social workers and their professional colleagues in health, education and welfare tends to be more varied. Nevertheless the onus tends to be upon the parent(s). A social worker who genuinely believes that a child may be at risk from parents is likely to restrict and control access. In practice, the minimal standards of parenting required for returning the child home are likely to be higher than those used to justify removing a child from the parental home in the first place. Furthermore restrictions on access can limit parents' opportunities to demonstrate their fitness to resume direct responsibility for parenting.

The freeing for adoption legislation is in principle well attuned to the needs of permanency planning. By permitting a court hearing at an early stage in social work planning for long-term alternative care it offers opportunities to

1 allow a child of sufficient age and understanding to determine whether to give formal consent to adoption;
2 allow parents who wish to place their child for adoption to give final consent to adoption at an early stage;
3 resolve conflicts between parents and social work departments over the long-term future of children in care;
4 give greater security to children and potential new families during what can often be a difficult transition process.

However, in practice social workers have experienced considerable difficulties with freeing procedures. The major problem is one of timing. Social workers, especially when working with very young children and new carers, are firmly committed to the view that rapid decisions are essential if damage to a child is to be limited. Once a freeing application is made, the swifter the decision the better. Even recognizing the need for due process, their expectations are in terms of weeks rather than months. The courts, by contrast, have crowded schedules and relatively slow processes of deliberation. The priorities are very different from those of social workers and the gap between application and decision tends to be in months or even years. Since the freeing legislation came into operation only in 1984, these may be only 'teething problems'. Nevertheless, the effects of delays with respect to freeing appear to be leading many social workers to use the other available routes for arranging long-term alternative care.

The rights of children in care away from the parental home are subject to interpretation and mediation by birth parents and relatives, by the local authority as parent and by alternative carers. Children's Hearings and the Courts also have a major influence. These various parties usually claim to represent the interests of the child in their distinctive ways. However, the classic dilemma remains. The welfare of children is dependent upon the actions and personal commitment of others. It is within the power of Hearings and the Courts to determine how a child's needs should be met. It is exceedingly difficult for such bodies to ensure high-quality support and care which leads to positive personal development and a genuine sense of belonging to a local culture and local social networks. All too often the rights of children and young people at the centre of such decisions become subsumed under considerations of needs and interests, in ways which may involve a violation of those very rights themselves. There is often a failure to recognize that the actual identification of needs and interests requires a process of continuing communication to ascertain fully the opinions and wishes of the children involved. Both the Social Work (Scotland) Act and the Adoption (Scotland) Act give children the legal right to be consulted on all decisions affecting their future. In practice, the exercise of that right often takes second place to the rights of the parents and of the local authorities involved. It therefore seems appropriate to conclude by asking what changes in the law might serve to give these rights the primacy they deserve.

Conclusions: proposals for changes in the law

We should like to suggest several legislative reforms to ensure that the rights of children and young people and those of their parents are always fully guaranteed by law and not merely (as is sometimes the case at present), by good practice.

First, we should like to recommend the abolition of section 16 of the Social Work (Scotland) Act 1968. It seems quite inappropriate that social work departments should have the power to assume parental rights without recourse to any outside forum. Such an over-concentration of power can lead, among other things, to a serious violation of the rights of children and families to be fully appraised *in advance* of any potential decisions respecting their future. These rights have been given some recognition in Statute (see the fourth point below) but need to be strengthened further by establishing an independent decision-making process at all stages, be it through the Courts or the Hearings

System or, as sometimes suggested, a further independent tribunal such as a Family Court. Furthermore, given the provisions of the 'freeing' legislation and the rulings on access described above, section 16 is now something of an anomaly.

Second, we should like to recommend measures which would ensure that the provisions of section 18 of the Adoption (Scotland) Act 1978, which were brought into force in 1984, become effective and really do speed up the process of permanency planning as had originally been envisaged. Both uncontested and contested freeing applications have been subject to long delays, of a year or more. There is an urgent need to introduce strict time-tabling. We recommend statutory measures to ensure a preliminary hearing within twenty-eight days of the original application and further amendments which would guarantee that the whole process be completed within six months.

Third, there is a need to ensure that children and their parents are kept informed about and, as far as possible, are involved in any discussions and decisions relating to the future of the young people, whether these occur in the context of the Hearings System, in a Court setting or within the social work department. It is particularly in the latter case that there appear to be insufficient legal safeguards. The provision of child representatives, recommended next, would go *some* way towards achieving this.

Fourth, there is a need to enforce more fully the provisions of section 20 of the Social Work (Scotland) Act which were introduced by amendments to the original Act in 1975 and 1983. These laid down that in reaching any decision relating to the child, local authorities and voluntary organizations

shall so far as practicable ascertain the wishes and feelings of the child regarding the decision and give due consideration to them.

The child's right to be heard has received similar recognition within the Children's Hearings system and in the Courts with respect to cases of disputed custody, as well as in section 6 of the Adoption (Scotland) Act 1978. However, we would wish to argue that at the present time the child's right to be heard is often interpreted as what is sometimes termed 'a right of non-interference' and that it would be more appropriate to interpret it at all times as 'a right of performance'. In other words, it is wrong simply to understand the right to be heard as involving no more than perhaps asking children their views and not interfering when they express them. The right to be heard should rather be interpreted as implying an obligation to help children to exercise this right. We suggest that this could be most effectively enforced by the provision of representatives for children, representatives who would be readily available for all children and young people coming before any Court, tribunal, hearing or internal child care review. Their sole remit would be *to represent the children*, rather than, in the manner of safeguarders, introduced in section 34A of the Social Work (Scotland) Act, to represent what they may *perceive* to be their interests. Of course, such a distinction makes no sense at all with respect to the very young. It is also true that children and young people might feel fully able to articulate their views, either without additional support, or with the help of their key workers when they are in residential care, of their parents when involved in disputes with the education authority for example, or of their social workers when appearing at a children's hearing. The point we wish to emphasize is that all children and young people should be given the *option* of consulting individuals who are prepared to act for them and for them alone and who would be available on request. They could be consulted in total confidence and anything said could be reported only on the specific instructions of the children or young people involved. Such representatives might be lawyers, social workers, teachers, former panel members or just interested members of the public, all specifically trained for the task. The newly created Scottish Child Law Centre might be the forum for the development and implementation of such a scheme which would give new impetus to the principles enunciated in *Gillick* and advocated here. We feel that it is only in this way that full recognition would be given to the rights of those children and young people who find themselves in the midst of disputes about access, or are confronted with potential decisions about their entire future which are often extremely painful. At present, almost everyone involved in the system which may ultimately interfere with the liberty of such young people, is trained for the role; everyone that is except the young people themselves. We submit that it is time to redress the balance.

Acknowledgements

The authors would like to thank Michael Adler for casting an eagle eye over the first draft of the chapter and Eileen Turner for her critical reading of the final version. Both have ensured that it is considerably better than it might otherwise have been. The errors remain our own.

References

Adler, R. M. (1985) *Taking Juvenile Justice Seriously*, Edinburgh: Scottish Academic Press.
Campbell, T. D. (1983) *The Left and Rights*, London: Routledge & Kegan Paul.
Farson, R. (1978) *Birthright*, New York: Penguin.
Feinberg, J. (1973) *Social Philosophy*, Englewood Cliffs, NJ: Prentice-Hall.
—— (1980) 'The nature and value of rights', in J. Feinberg (eds) *Rights, Justice and the Bounds of Liberty*, Princeton, NJ: Princeton University Press.
Goldstein, J., Freud, A. and Solnit, A. J. (1973) *Beyond the Best Interests of the Child*, New York: Free Press.
Macaskill, C. (1985) *Against the Odds*, London: BAAF.
McNeill, P. G. B. (1986) *Adoption of Children in Scotland*, 2nd edn, Edinburgh: W. Green.
Maluccio, A. N., Fein, E. and Olmstead, K. (1986) *Permanency Planning for Children*, London: Tavistock.
Millham, S., Bullock, R., Hosie, K. and Haak, M. (1986) *Lost in Care*, Aldershot: Gower.
Parton, N. (1985) *The Politics of Child Abuse*, London: Macmillan.
Raynor, L. (1970) *Adoption of Non-White Children*, London: Allen & Unwin.

Schaffer, M. (1986) 'Parental access to children in care – current law', *Scottish Child*, 13: 25–32.
Thoburn, J., Murdoch, A. and O'Brien, A. (1986) *Permanence in Child Care*, Oxford: Blackwell.
Tizard, B. (1977) *Adoption: A Second Chance*, London: Open Books.
Triseliotis, J. and Russell, J. (1984) *Hard to Place*, London: Heinemann.

Statutes

Adoption (Scotland) Act 1978.
Children Act 1975.
Health and Social Services and Social Security Adjudications Act 1983.
Social Work (Scotland) Act 1968.

Cases

Hewer v. Bryant [1969] 3 All ER 578.
Gillick v. West Norfolk and Wisbech Area Health Authority [1985] 3 All ER 402.
Kennedy v. A & A 1986 SLT 358.
A v. Children's Hearing for the Tayside Region 1987 SLT 126.

Social Work Services Group Circulars

Supervision Requirements under Section 44 of the Social Work (Scotland) Act 1968 – Access by Parents or Other Relatives to Children in Care, SW11/1986.

Unpublished work

The authors acknowledge use of a draft discussion paper by A. Black, Divisional Director, Lothian Regional Council Department of Social Work, *Adoption and Freeing for Adoption: Some Points for Discussion*, dated 8 February 1988.
Edwards, F. E. (undated) 'Residential child care strategy for the eighties. Home or away?', Strathclyde Region Council Social Work Department.

12
Radical social work: lessons for the 1990s

Mike Simpkin

For many perfectly legitimate reasons social work lacks much of a sense of history. Even at the individual level there is no satisfactory and agreed model of relating past to present. Predominantly reactive, social work lurches from one universal solution to another as the pendulum swings between justice and welfare, residential care and fostering, specialism and patchwork, and a host of other concepts which are often complementary rather than contradictory, but which scarcity presents in competitive poses.

While the attempt to establish a radical and challenging social work did not avoid this error, the mistake should not be repeated by applying ahistorical criteria in evaluating its effect. It is misleading to blame the over-inclusive ambitiousness of radicalism for some of social work's difficulties today (see for example C. Brown 1986) without taking account of the conditions and opportunities which predominated at that time and which shaped the radical response. Brown is right, however, to assert that present conditions need something different. In this essay I shall try to put 1970s radicalism into some perspective and to indicate some of the ways in which the influence of radical social work has persisted during the long period of re-evaluation on the left ushered in by the Thatcher years.

During the 1970s the most public expression of radical social work was *Case Con*, which existed as a magazine and an organization between 1970 and 1978. Although by no means representing all those who regarded themselves as radicals, the lack of anything similar today is one reason why some regard radicalism as having shot its bolt. As the authors of a brief and slightly puzzled history of *Case Con* remark, the issues of poverty, housing, health and unemployment, which were the major concerns at the birth of radical social work, are all still with us but there is now no coherent voice on the left to take them up (Brown and Hanvey 1987). Indeed much of the radical rhetoric which remains is at present experienced as being imposed from above, whether by progressive Labour councils or by senior managers. Ideas which may be innovative and politically catalytic are discredited both by the style in which they are advanced and by their inevitable linking with tortuous justifications for cut-backs. Radical careerism (Hearn 1982) and ingenuous political opportunism (cf. Weinstein 1986; Thomas 1987) are inherent sources of division whose reality must in some way be accommodated.

Meanwhile social workers, whose professional progressives have been lumped by Thatcher rather incongruously together with those among Labour councils and broadcasters as creating 'a fog of excuses in which mugger and burglar operate', funnel away from the trident of public expectation, media surveillance and political demand by retreating into protective procedures. These may be practice controls if devised by management, barriers of expertise if created by aspiring professionals, or negative sanctions if agreed through trade unions. Alternatively there are personal strategies which include routinization, perpetual crisis, and escape through promotion or departure. Nowhere is this more apparent than in the field of child abuse, where there are few signs of any broadly based strategies for reducing the risks; only reactive tactics which begin to look increasingly like the old 'rescue motive' in disguise.

This retreat into individualism contrasts strongly with the overtly political context in which *Case Con* sought to locate social work activity. Yet social workers are probably now in the position of having every day to confront the effects of political decisions based on a hostility both to themselves and to those they work with. In discussing the elements which combined to make *Case Con* possible, and which determined both its strengths and weaknesses, I hope to suggest some of the differences which would be required in a radical movement for the present.

The emergence of social work radicalism in Britain cannot be understood without reference first to 1968, the year which saw the spectacular plunge of an intellectual generation into the attempt to dictate its own history, and then to the political transition as students began to grapple with the very different organization and demands of paid labour.

The events of 1968 released an energy which manifested itself in a variety of social and cultural forms, one of which was a political activism which became more and more independent of the traditional parties. This consciousness was fed by a generalized sense of injustice which sought both inspiration and justification from the now burgeoning academic industry of social analysis. A growing acquaintance with the hypocrisy, injustice and repression which characterized the machinery of state created a wider and more receptive audience for class-based doctrines of revolt. The libertarian ethos of protest politics gave way to a concern for organization. The working class had become culturally fashionable during the 'Swinging Sixties'; now was the time to translate this into political status. For some this meant an entry into left politics either around a traditional working-class base, or adopting an approach which emphasized the revolutionary potential of the Third World, and of groups which had hitherto been regarded as marginal by the British labour movement. Others preferred more direct action; the community activism of Claimants Unions and the squatters' movement was the most influential; the most extreme were the Angry Brigade.

For those who did not remain students, the most seductive route towards reconciling and implementing sets of often very contradictory principles became participation in public service organizations, joining a state apparatus which was being newly expanded in the optimistic belief that economic growth would finance a philosophy of welfare which could satisfy an increasing clamour over poverty and injustice on the one hand, and delinquency on the other.

Many people with influence in politics and in social work hoped, even believed, that the construction of social services departments in local authorities would make a key contribution to this process; others predicted that they were set up to fail. But one thing was certain; the massive expectations engendered by political aspirations, new legislation and re-organization were matched neither by resources nor by a professional outlook within social work which could muster the experience, the spirit and even the language to engage in any realistic way with the agenda it had helped to set for itself. Radicalism was shaped by this contradiction and in turn attempted to transform it.

At that time British social work had seized upon unification as the route towards overcoming its perennial identification crisis. Given present trends, it is worth remembering how gross before 1970 were the divisions of ethos and standing between the children's departments, welfare departments (including mental welfare), psychiatric social work, medical social work, educational welfare and probation. Welfare departments were run by a chief medical officer and it was from the medical yoke that analytic caseworkers and social reformers were most anxious to escape.

Each department had strengths on which it prided itself and weaknesses which the others often regarded as glaringly obvious. Children's departments probably were, as they claimed, the most socially progressive as they began to grapple with the increased concern about poverty and stigma. Work sections were relatively small and managers tended to be closer to practice. There was little union organization and the work was still regarded as vocational. Contacts between the branches of field social work were relatively sporadic; residential workers were even more isolated.

Many social workers agreed with the principles behind the creation of a unified and effective family service. These included the argument that the relatively low status of social workers, both in the health service and in local authorities, led to corresponding lack of muscle on behalf of their clients. The untiring efforts of figures such as Kenneth Brill to lay the foundations for professional unity were intended not just to ease the pains of integration but to achieve the advantages of higher status for both workers and clients.

But there were also a number of sceptics, of whom Barbara Wootton was only the best known. Forder remarked how 'the concentration on developing skills has sometimes resulted in a tendency to define problems in terms of those skills rather than considering the problem more broadly and objectively'; individualization, stigmatization and a new, if often defensive professional elitism, were set against 'a renewed interest in social groupwork and community development . . . support of such associations as the Child Poverty Action Group . . . an increasing recognition of the value of voluntary workers' and the challenge of 'learning to share responsibility with workers from other professions in the same field' (Forder 1969: 204–5). More searching critiques were published by the Fabian Society, expressing serious doubts about either the effectiveness or the relevance of conventional social work to the social problems it was intended to tackle. Even the *Sunday Times* ran a piece as the Social Services Act was passed, classifying social workers as agents of social control whose purpose was at best to make poverty tolerable. The first edition of *Case Con* appeared shortly afterwards, in June 1970.

The lack of clear consensus was masked by considerable political indifference. The Social Services Act became a predominantly administrative instrument with a financial memorandum attached, stating that no significant increase in public manpower or expenditure was to be expected. This equivocal reception by the Labour Government of the Seebohm Report was teasingly picked out by the Conservative spokesman Lord Balniel:

> Something more than machinery, however well intentioned, is needed if we are to solve the social problems in our midst. I refer to resources, action, drive, training, manpower and money. Instinctively I feel that something over and above these material things is needed. It is something psychological. . . . The Seebohm Report was really asking society to recognise the social work profession as having come of age. Social worker morale needs a boost. . . . The Bill lacks a quality of political leadership.
>
> (*Hansard* 26.2.70)

The issue of status was becoming central.

While the BASW professionals prepared to take their seats alongside doctors and lawyers in public estimation, they were also jockeying for jobs in a new hierarchy which would remove them from front-line work. This careerism was largely male dominated; many women were either unwilling or unable to seek promotion. It was a pattern which would be self-perpetuating (Popplestone 1980; Howe 1986). Fieldwork vacancies were filled by the newly qualified, trained in specialisms and forms of social casework which could not match the reality they were to face. They were supplemented by unqualified staff who inevitably had to take on a good deal of statutory work. Nobody at any level had proven competence in the new generic social work.

The new departments were heralded as universal and non-stigmatizing sources of welfare, and it fell to the field workers who had been flung together to bear the immediate and often overwhelming burden of assessing need and making provision. They were also the best-placed group to organize. Rejecting professional status, the new radicals looked to the very size of social services departments as offering the opportunity to organize for mass action and hence a much more effective promotion of the interests of those they were set up to serve. There was considerable support for the enterprise of building foundations for mutual support which offered the chance of relating to clients and public without the exclusivity of professionalism, or the impersonality of the bureaucracies, with which social services were quick to surround themselves.

Such an agenda had more credibility than might now seem apparent, given the premise that social work neither could nor should be seen in isolation from the increasingly active response of working people, both nationally and internationally, to new forms of capitalist development. The period of Heath's Conservative government from 1970 to 1974 saw large-scale trade union mobilization against the Industrial Relations Act, the Housing Finance Act and unemployment. Setbacks such as the failure to secure the release of the Shrewsbury building pickets lay in the future and it was not as unrealistic then as it may appear now to believe that social work could make an active contribution towards major social change.

In such a context, social workers' reactions to the conditions in which they found themselves were not exceptional. There were no more honeyed words from the Conservatives. While property boomed, cuts in social expenditure were the order of the day. Social workers were sandwiched between growing pressure from local authorities and the public, and an addled occupational tradition within which not a single section of theory or practice could be taken for granted. There was considerable support for developing principled stands at least on particular issues and while radicalism was predictably dismissed in official circles, it offered an energy and sense of direction which the professionals lacked. The isolation and powerlessness implied by those on both right and left who began to assert the marginality of social work were unacceptable.

Two further influences fed this process among social workers. One was trade unionism; among white-collar workers as a whole both organization and militancy were increasing. Members' pressure was beginning to transform NALGO from a 'gentleman's association' (Bolger 1981 *et al.*; Joyce, Corrigan and Hayes 1988), and social workers were themselves coming to realize the need for individual and group protection. The second influence was the attempt by staff and students in some social work courses to devise rationales on which to deal realistically with the changes around them. Here the virtues of a united profession were not quite so self-evident. Some of the tension between sociologists and caseworkers was expressed in fierce resentment of students who were analysed as having 'authority problems' for daring to challenge cherished assumptions. It was clear that both students on courses and workers in the services needed to organize to protect themselves. Nor was it difficult to understand the similarities between what was being done to them and what they were being expected to do to clients; perhaps this could be the base for effective alliances.

There was thus a ready response to *Case Con*'s call in 1970 on all those who were disaffected to unite both in critique and in action. Within a few months a conference was held to agree a manifesto and elect a collective. The appeal of

Case Con lay in four factors; it addressed issues which were publicly recognized but to which the social work establishment had no answer; it spoke out of the immediate experiences of front-line workers; it acted as a forum to express a wide range of disaffection; and it developed a supportive organization which also had the potential to act as a pressure group at both local and national levels. While the magazine attempted both to develop a framework and to share news, its contents were sometimes less important than the fact that it existed. It was the embodiment of a belief that alternative approaches could be developed; it encouraged social workers all over the country to find support by forming groups to focus on the possibilities of radical action. Some of these were large enough to produce their own regular newsletters although not all of them organized under the *Case Con* banner; for example West Midlands social workers produced a broadsheet called *Treaclestick*.

Supporters of *Case Con* had immediately to face up to two fundamental contradictions which underlie any attempt at radical practice and were highlighted at the end of the decade by the publication of *In and Against the State* (London Edinburgh Weekend Return Group 1980). The first, and most obvious, was already flagged up through community action; how far could radicals actually go against their employers on behalf of client interests? How great was the risk of being forced into compromise and betrayal? This led on to the second set of issues which revolved around the questioning of the role of social work in society: did it even have any right to exist? Could it have a sufficient impact on economic redistribution and social awareness to negate its control functions and to compensate for the benefits which any welfare bureaucracy confers upon its members?

These questions were sidestepped rather than resolved. Indeed the bedrock of the radical case was and still is that the issues cannot properly be addressed without moving outside and beyond the boundaries of social work thought; recognizing a political agenda; and developing forms of organization and alliances which would move towards the achievement of structural change. One way to do this was to develop an understanding of the ways in which social workers at all levels were being exploited by appeals to their individual consciences. Large area offices, the 'Seebohm factories', gave the opportunity to build up solidarity through a much broader exchange of ideas and by collective action. The aim was not simply to remedy particular wrongs but to force managers and politicians to shoulder their due responsibilities instead of sloughing them off.

Case Con groups would never have the power either to pursue this struggle on their own or to provide the protection against victimization and scapegoating for which individuals were increasingly feeling the need. Therefore from the outset *Case Con* set itself the task of winning the case for social work trade unionism. The way was left open by BASW's agreement not to take on issues relating to pay and conditions of service. Initially there was considerable debate about which union was most appropriate for those employed by local authorities; union membership in the children's departments was lower than among welfare officers where it was divided. NALGO was unpopular for its elitism and non-political stance and there was some attempt to organize in COHSE and NUPE. But trade union consciousness could not really be spread on a supposedly altruistic political vision. Like any other group social workers needed the consideration of service conditions to be galvanized into action.

As it happened, the first issue to present itself was that of stand-by duty for mental welfare officers (MWOs). After several years of negotiation the National Joint Council had in 1970 agreed a small allowance but the scheme was not implemented, at least partly, because it was both paltry and unworkable. It was not only MWOs who would be affected but all social workers; the differential payment was soon to be swallowed up by the reorganization. Anxiety about generic work was magnified by the fear of being left alone and vulnerable at night in territory which would be unfamiliar both in work content and in geography.

It was NALGO which took on the organization of this dispute and won a partial victory; for many this was the first contact with trade unionism in practice. As other disputes developed radicals began to establish links with other departments, although their challenge to the union establishment and a political agenda which was often interpreted as critical of other workers was a hindrance which contributed to their isolation later. None the less they were able to make a significant contribution towards reshaping NALGO which has remained the dominant union despite frequent dissatisfaction over its conduct of various disputes.

The politicization both of trade unions and of social work was central to *Case Con*, which was characterized as a 'revolutionary magazine for social workers'. The input of left groups, in particular the International Socialists (IS – later SWP), was crucial to its success, its limitations, and its eventual disappearance. IS at the time represented a (relatively) non-doctrinaire and pragmatic strand of Trotskyite tradition which underwent rapid expansion between 1968 and 1974. It attracted support from many of the 1968 generation who had joined the public sector and wished to pursue activist politics outside the Labour party. The essence of IS was an emphasis on rank-and-file activism which appealed to those social workers who were concerned with encouraging democracy and participation in their union, their departments and their work with clients. Members of IS were instrumental in creating *Case Con* and though rarely a majority on the collective, contributed both hard graft and the foundation of a political analysis which enabled social workers and others to make common issue across boundaries set either by professional convention or the traditional structure of the Labour movement. Furthermore the political network of IS was invaluable in expanding support for *Case Con* across the country.

But there was a price to be paid for this political involvement. Many social workers who were in sympathy with *Case Con* baulked at the revolutionary rhetoric which was judged necessary to keep radicalism on the correct line (Tasker and Wunnam 1977). Some *Case Con* meetings were filled with sectarian wrangling between members of the different left groups. Rank-and-file politics produced enemies in the labour movement as well as allies. Most seriously of all the fortunes of *Case Con* were tied in part to changing priorities within IS and to the momentum of that type of activism.

In 1974 IS determined to reorient itself to the new working-class militancy which had helped to bring Labour to power but would soon be betrayed. As Leninist politics took a firmer hold, with their stress on the centrality of the industrial working class in any revolutionary struggle, the role of white-collar workers, however 'proletarianized', became downgraded. IS demanded a much more organized commitment to rank-and-file trade unionism and began to shed its libertarian wing. Women's issues, gay rights and personal politics were regarded as *petit bourgeois* as IS defied the arguments of feminists and gay socialists by refusing for several years to take any line on sexism; sexual politics had to be related directly to the class struggle (Weeks 1977: 234–6; Rowbotham 1983: I, 8; II, 7). This deliberate disregard of the personal did not preclude the raising of lively and successful campaigns such as the Right to Work Campaign, the Anti-Nazi League and later Rock against Racism, all of which were highly relevant to social workers. But trade union work was paramount and priority was to be given to NALGO Action rather than *Case Con*.

The activists grouped in *Case Con* had not been reluctant to grapple with personal issues. In spring 1974 an all-woman group produced a Women's Issue whose coherence and success led to all future issues becoming topic based, often raising concerns which were to be crucial to social work debate in subsequent years. Nevertheless the increasing concentration on trade unions was not unwelcome to social work radicals. It fitted the reality of their situation as workers and bestowed a more positive sense of struggle and achievement. *Case Con* had from the beginning recognized the need to focus on practice in greater depth without being quite sure how to do it. Social workers were demanding answers without yet being at all sure of the questions. The powerful critique of casework and successful mobilization around single issues had not yet resulted in a strategy which could be implemented consistently. *Case Con* supporters remained a relatively small minority.

Politics aside, one reason for this was that it was hard enough just to keep going in social work, let alone to provide workable models of practice in departments which in many instances still regarded ordinary groupwork as either a waste of time or inherently subversive. Direct action techniques which got the adrenalin flowing both in community work and trade unionism depended for their success on particular conjunctures of circumstances which could not be created at whim; furthermore the political, trade union and management bureaucracies were developing more sophisticated strategies for dealing with them. Indeed radicals were beginning to regard their previous efforts to gain acceptance for community action and advocacy with far more scepticism. Goldup expressed this general pessimism in arguing that both advocacy and 'consciousness raising' activities by social workers were inherently corrupted by the inequalities which were endemic in their relationship with clients; the social and economic pressures which trapped most clients in isolation, depression, apathy or frustration were paralleled by a tightly controlled training ideology. Drawing on Garrett's analysis that challenge to authoritarian structures was the integral key to change, he concluded that 'the challenge radicals in social work present is not primarily on the job. It is in confronting their own status as low level bureaucrats' (Goldup 1977; cf. Garrett 1980).

Another area of difficulty was the resentment elsewhere in local government at the rapid expansion of social services. When this was allied with a new political militancy at basic grade level, often expressed by women, radicals ran up against a hostility which began to isolate them and drive them into sectional actions which were often self-defeating (Joyce, Corrigan and Hayes 1988). The formation of national and local NALGO Action Groups (NAG) was not in itself a solution, given NAG's reliance in many branches on social services workers. Nevertheless NAG did succeed in drawing a much wider support, and activism linked explicitly with *Case Con* began to be diluted. As the *Case Con* supporters' network was weakened, both by frustration and by a rapidly changing membership, the special interest groups which were producing each new issue of the magazine were less and less able to reflect the organization as a whole; union developments were covered in part by the expanding *NALGO Action News*. One significant reason for *Case Con* cessation in 1978 was that there was no longer any dynamic relationship between the collective and its readership.

However the end of *Case Con* was also the result of a strategic decision based on the fact that the context for *Case Con* had also changed. In the harsher political and economic climate of the late 1970s the public sector unions began grinding up towards a series of confrontations which ended with the Pyrrhic victories of 1979. There were already the seeds of the field workers' strikes of 1978/9 but radicals were also looking to replace *Case Con* with a magazine which would express the need for a public sector alliance, centred initially around the first wave of hospital closures. Questions of individual practice seemed less important than the fight to preserve resources. The fact that this enterprise never really got off the ground was a reflection of the inherent difficulties of that particular struggle, of political differences, of the practicalities of reconciling the variety of different interests involved, and of sheer overload.

While radicalism in social services departments was becoming dominated by a politicized trade unionism, social work education was developing a different emphasis. Sympathetic academics had been faced with the need to develop a more sophisticated analysis of the limitations and possibilities of radical practice; apart from the demands of radicals and non-radicals among their students, they were required to engage with the proponents of an orthodoxy which was itself beginning to admit the need for change and to explore fresh theoretical formats.

At one remove from the departments it was not too difficult to see how easily the new activism could be transformed into the self-protectiveness which radicals had previously scorned if the gap between workers and clients could not be bridged. A unidimensional class-based theory was too rigid in its categories to allow for the fierce insights of feminism, and an embryonic awareness of racism in social work. Nor did the complete mistrust of state machinery permit much development of policy outside a crudely economistic struggle to increase benefit rates. Instead it was argued that the state should be regarded as an arena of class struggle, thus conferring a greater legitimacy on socialist activity within the state (Corrigan and Leonard 1978). For revolutionary socialists this smacked of a sell-out, especially given its roots in broad left reformism and Eurocommunism. The state might not always be directly engaged in control, but it would generally attempt to cover for the inherent inability of capitalism to meet working-class demands. To become drawn in would render socialists unable to confront and expose this fallibility. Some of these differences were expressed in a trenchant essay by Clarke, who drew attention to the gulf between the theoreticism of some radical sociology with its misleading slip into Marxist functionalism and an arbitrary practice in which novelty or an anti-authoritarian stance were often enough to attract a radical label (Clarke 1979).

Although these theoretical stances reflected political differences between the broad left and revolutionary socialism, radical practitioners remained largely united in trade union organization around cuts, pay and conditions of service as the dominant activity. But 1979 and 1980 saw the turn of a tide with which we are all now familiar. The social work and other public sector strikes, the fragmenting of left orthodoxy and Thatcher's determination to pursue her own agenda began to make the presentation of impossible demands seem rather more like head-banging. Development of the critical awareness required to secure and legitimate radical activity became much more crucial; subsequent writing has begun to build up a more sophisticated integration of theory with practice but without yet being able to make a consistent inroad into orthodoxy.

Within social work the field workers' strikes of 1978/9 (Bolger *et al.* 1981; Jones 1983; Simpkin 1983) were crucial in changing the parameters of a possibility for radicalism. In the first place the widespread sympathy among field workers for the action could not conceal that only a minority of departments were directly affected. Second, the relatively spontaneous nature of the action was reflected both in the confusion of its demands and in the fact that it was co-ordinated at rank-and-file level by *ad hoc* bodies in which the influence of pre-existing groups like NAG was not dominant. Third, the unsatisfactory conduct of the strikes at the official level and the drawn-out procedure of the imposed settlement had a draining effect on participants and observers alike, not least in those authorities like Newcastle and Tower Hamlets where final agreement took years rather than months. Fourth, the return of the strikers to work was generally met with management attempts to reassert authority; this was not just a response to the strikes but part of the wider trend towards control procedures in welfare (Jones 1983) and the 'coercive tilt' in penal policy (Walker and Beaumont 1981). Fifth, there was a new concern with practice issues as social workers attempted to relate their experience back to the job. Sixth, there was a new (and often painful) perspective of the position of field workers in relationship to other social service workers. The sum effect was to enforce a realization that rhetoric was no longer enough; radicals, and indeed all social workers, had to re-establish their feet on the ground.

This process paralleled a wider metamorphosis in socialism generally as it attempted to free itself from outmoded analyses and stale forms of organization, corrupted not just by a lack of internal democracy but by patriarchy and racism. Such healthy self-questioning and 'letting go' have inevitably made socialist thought and organization more vulnerable both to accusations of feebleness in opposition and to developments such as 'new realism', in which a reorientation to perceived demand is inevitably tangled with a real or apparent surrender to hostile values. The search for ways to legitimize a new base has led to the adoption of democratization and accountability as slogans in place of the old organizational rallying calls. Even more significant is the advance of more personalist politics prompted by the challenges first of feminism and then, in a different way, of anti-racism to the macho and white-dominated assumptions (presumptions), strategies and activism of the past. For some on the left this tendency is a retreat into narcissistic individualism. Such a danger is all the more real in social work which by its nature contains the temptation of new forms of psychologism, the reduction of structural issues to individual personality problems. But whereas 'new realism' appears to be more of an erosion than a renewal, both feminism and anti-racism are central to the dialectic of individual and collective, giving an essential depth of awareness to any possible renewal of radicalism (cf. Sivanandan 1988).

It is impossible to give a comprehensive account of radical social work since 1980, because, for all the reasons I have listed, it has not developed in any co-ordinated way, and, for reasons which I shall try to suggest, some of the progress has been hidden. However the ferocity of the assault against the welfare state means that radicals will now probably have to use this experience to raise their profile if the term is to retain any practical meaning.

Perhaps surprisingly after the bitterness of the strikes, social work's trade union base is probably stronger than it has ever been. Despite a period of quiescence, social services militancy was not crushed by the difficulties of the return to work, though it may have taken different forms. There was a steady *rapprochement* between social workers and NALGO, based on a recognition of mutual need in the increasingly hostile political climate. At branch level local activists began a more effective representation of social services workers who had hitherto been under-represented; some also began to play a more central role not just in branches but in NALGO as a whole. Meanwhile NALGO itself made some effort to integrate social workers into its policy-making, both on general issues, and by developing specific consultation machinery, for example over the new Approved Social Worker proposals of the 1983 Mental Health Act. The subsequent boycott of the examinations, against heavy professional opposition, proved that action could be successful. The mere existence of the residential workers' strike of 1984, despite being bedevilled by some of the same problems as those which field workers had faced, was proof that militancy was far from extinct.

At local level, both in urban areas and in counties, there has been a succession of actions over conditions and gradings, cuts, and not covering for vacancies. The tension within departments is illustrated by the two short strikes in Manchester and Brent against the effective dismissals of their directors; within statutory organizations at least, union membership is generally seen as the most effective form of self-defence. This continuing solidarity is at least partly due to the failure of social work professionalism to develop an ethos which commands general acceptance. The contradictions of BASW's situation are illustrated by the fact that although its policy of non-cooperation with the social fund was one of the most determined of any organization, its conference attendance suggests that its interests are more representative of middle management than of social workers as a whole.

However some of the limitations of both NALGO and BASW have led to more autonomous organization. In the early 1980s Women in Social Work set up a conference and network. Its formal existence appears to have been shortlived but the current debate over men and child abuse may revive something similar. This period also saw the beginning of black workers' groups. Racism and the specific problems of black people had been virtually ignored before except in so far as racism was linked with the fight against fascism. The fact that there were virtually no black workers in qualified social work escaped the notice of radicals and establishment alike. The subsequent process of stripping these racist blinkers and the refusal of black people to accept that they should become acculturated to white assumptions and practice are potent challenges to social work. Like the feminist analysis of child abuse, they raise the whole question of 'Who is doing what to whom?' in a form which cannot be sidestepped. This struggle has had to overcome major resistance in social work organizations, in courses, and in unions where the Black Workers Trade Union Solidarity Movement, founded in 1983, acted as a spur. NALGO held its own conference of black workers in 1986 and there is also a more radical caucus. Black social workers too are beginning to organize nationally, based on the autonomous groups which departments have reluctantly begun to recognize. Recognition of white workers' anti-racist groups has been even slower.

Social work trainers in all settings have also been stopped in their tracks by the demands of black students, whose first task, still far from complete, has been to get them to hear. Although the black agenda is not necessarily the same as that of white radicalism, it poses fundamental questions with a great degree of overlap and in so doing it has also challenged the distancing and marginalization through which training has sought to undermine the coherence of the radical stance. The integration of sociological understanding into training, the recognition of a repertoire other than casework method, a renewed emphasis on standards, a disillusion with rhetoric, and frequent misunderstandings of the dynamics of social work activism, have all combined to sideline radicalism either as one possible style among others or as a limited concept offering a few useful insights (cf. Davis 1987: 87). Black students have returned to the central issue, that of power.

Marginalization in training has, as some of us feared at the time, been complemented by the incorporation into mainline social services of those aspects of radicalism which have gained professional or even political respectability. Managers have succeeded at least partly in absorbing some of the energy and 'acceptable' face of radicalism, while colluding with the diversion of organized activism into trade union channels which can then be attacked in a more orthodox manner. Many progressive measures and methods initiated by radicals and others fifteen years ago in the face of considerable opposition are now accepted elements of good practice. There has been a far greater willingness to legitimize clients' rights and to introduce projects such as self-advocacy and credit unions, plus the serious and successful efforts to keep young people out of custody. Participation and choice have been all the rage in theory. But practice and commitment have lagged behind, particularly where choice goes against the local political credo, whether right or left. Sympathy with the plight of Labour councils in the context of continual cuts has to be separated from collusion with their often dictatorial tactics (Weinstein 1986).

The pressures upon generic workers have inevitably meant that some of the most challenging developments have taken place on the fringes of the statutory sector, often in municipally funded projects which may well need the support of radical workers in statutory agencies. The process of incorporation on the one hand and hiving off on the other has been encouraged first by a general retreat from the old universalism and second, by the introduction of the market.

Social work may have a key contribution towards the demarginalization and empowerment of the poor but it is only one sector of social services departments which in turn are only one part of social welfare as a whole (Davis 1987). The left academic version of the former political agenda of radicalism has been to place social work firmly in the context of wider social policy. The reaction of the *Critical Social Policy* journal to the Barclay Report (NISW 1982) was to publish a commentary commending many of the arguments of Pinker's minority essay on 'slimline social work' and defending specialism from a socialist view (Pearson 1983). Practitioners are equally repelled by any new purist universalism (Brown 1986).

Meanwhile Thatcherism is offering the seductions of a consumer-led market to groups which may be affected by the current round of cuts and the end of the Community Programme. Whatever the added strain to mainstream services, the range of problems and possibilities for left radicals will change dramatically if Barclay's concept of 'social care planning' is transmuted into any version of the designing and managing of care packages envisaged in the Griffiths Report (Griffiths 1988). It is a criticism of the statutory sector that organizations such as the Afro-Caribbean Mental Health Association are considering that they and their users would get a much better deal elsewhere, but the gains and sacrifices need to be weighed up much more carefully than they have been on the left hitherto.

What all these trends appear to indicate is that while radical practice has in some ways become more integrated, radicalism itself has become diluted and fragmented. Although this is in part a reflection of social work as a whole, does it mean that the project has lost any pretence at coherence? If so, does it matter?

In these days of rampant pluralism, coherence is not in itself seen as a virtue; some would argue that the growing body of critical theory and the diversity of practice are in fact sources of strength and a protection against the presumption of earlier days. New contributions no longer have to be burdened with the obligation to reveal some mystical essence to radical social work; coherence and organizational unity are not the same. Nevertheless, without organization radicals lack the opportunities both for mutual support and development and for an oppositional rallying point. Clarke's call in 1979 for a systematic and principled set of criteria by which to distinguish progressive and oppressive elements of welfare still lacks any broadly agreed response. Radicals need to find some way of pulling together what is happening both at different levels in social work and outside, remembering the fundamental proposition that social work cannot be understood in its own terms. That radicalism in social work is also relative; it is within social work, not anti-social work (Hearn 1982), but must consciously subject itself to influences outside such as the community activism of Beresford and Croft (1986).

Case Con prospered while it was asking questions and as long as the political energy with which it was infused was able to expand its audience but it was unable to create a tradition and culture strong enough to sustain it when that energy diffused. Over the last ten years the base has been laid for a much more informed debate on the context and content of social work as the prelude to a renewed commitment to change. But whereas the organizing philosophy of *Case Con* was founded on the shared experience of front-line workers in the new Seebohm departments, now division is the order of the day. To the rifts between interest groups are added the pressures of competition for scarce resources, the separative effect of specialisms and the potential isolation resulting from decentralization. The only equivalent to Seebohm is the new stress on multidisciplinary working. In some instances this may prove a source of fresh and potentially exciting alliances; in others it may deter.

Trade unionism should continue to provide the underpinning of efforts to preserve the fundamental collectivity of radicalism. Unions, however great their new interest in policy, cannot be flexible enough either to give adequate weight to the concerns of those ineligible for membership, to root out archaic practice, or to debate issues such as the feminist analysis of child abuse, the consequences of community treatment orders, the desirability of social work specialisms, the effects of accredited practice teaching, the status and significance of professional skills, relationships with Labour councils, or the role of competitive welfare provision. Radicals also need to confront more personalist concerns in an occupation whose most immediate tool is the use of the self.

The relentless advance of Thatcherite individualism demands that radicals find some way of building a leadership which is based not on opportunism, nor on discredited macho principles of vanguard organization, nor on a competitive hierarchy of oppression but on a respect, which has to be earned, for the courage of attempting to integrate the struggle for change into the different aspects of living. If lack of confidence and an increasingly coercive state prevent organization around major political issues like the poll tax or the social fund, a forum is still needed within which the radical initiatives which exist both within and outside the statutory services can step beyond their specialist networks and explore the scope for a common agenda. Radicalism may have to be limited to irregular and guerrilla activity for some time to come, but there is no intrinsic reason why a more unified strategy cannot be developed to secure an increasing degree of legitimation without sacrificing the pressure for change.

References

Beresford, P. and Croft, S. (1986) *Whose Welfare?*, Brighton: Lewis Cohen Urban Studies.
Bolger, S., Corrigan, P., Docking, J. and Frost, N. (1981) *Towards Socialist Welfare Work*, London: Macmillan.
Brown, C. (1986) 'Response to Lena Dominelli', *Critical Social Policy*, 6, 2: 105–6.
Brown, T. and Hanvey, C. (1987) 'A spirit of the times', *Community Care*, 9 July; 18–19.
Clarke, J. (1979) 'Critical sociology and radical practice', in N. Parry, M. Rustin and C. Satyamurti (eds) *Social Work, Welfare and the State*, London: Edward Arnold.
Corrigan, P. and Leonard, P. (1978) *Social Work Practice under Capitalism: A Marxist Approach*, London: Macmillan.
Davis, A. (1987) 'Hazardous lives: social work in the 1980s – a view from the Left', in M. Loney (ed.) *The State or the Market?*, London: Sage.
Forder, A. (1969) *Social Services in England and Wales*, London: Routledge & Kegan Paul.
Garrett, M. (1980) 'The problem with authority', in M. Brake and R. Bailey (eds) *Radical Social Work and Practice*, London: Edward Arnold.
Goldup, J. (1977) 'How the radicals are kept in check', *Community Care*, 14 September: 23–5.
Griffiths, R. (1988) *Community Care: An Agenda for Action*, Griffiths Report, London: HMSO.
Hearn, J. (1982) 'Radical social work', *Critical Social Policy*, 2, 1: 19–38.
Howe, D. (1986) 'The segregation of women and their work in the personal social services', *Critical Social Policy*, 5, 3: 21–35.
Jones, C. (1983) *The State, Social Work and the Working Class*, London: Macmillan.
Joyce, P., Corrigan, P. and Hayes, M. (1988) *Striking Out*, London: Macmillan.
London Edinburgh Weekend Return Group (1980) *In and Against the State*, London: LEWRG.
NISW (National Institute of Social Work) (1982) *Social Workers: Their Roles and Tasks*, Barclay Report, London: Bedford Square Press.
Pearson, G. (1983) 'The Barclay Report and community social work', *Critical Social Policy*, 2, 3: 78–85.
Popplestone, R. (1980) 'Top jobs for women?', *Social Work Today*, 23 September: 12–14.
Rowbotham, S. (1983) *Dreams and Dilemmas*, London: Virago.
Simpkin, M. (1983) *Trapped Within Welfare*, 2nd edn, London: Macmillan.
Sivanandan, A. (1988) 'No such thing as anti-racist ideology', *New Statesman*, 27 May: 14–17.

Tasker, L. and Wunnam, A. (1977) 'The ethos of radical social workers and community workers', *Social Work Today*, 15 March: 11–14.

Thomas, H. (1987) 'Labour councils and white collar unionism', *Critical Social Policy*, 7, 2: 86–7.

Walker, H. and Beaumont, B. (1981) *Probation Work, Critical Theory and Socialist Practice*, Oxford: Blackwell.

Weeks, J. (1977) *Coming Out*, London: Quartet.

Weinstein, J. (1986) 'Left Labour councils and white collar trade unionism', *Critical Social Policy*, 6, 2: 41–60.

13
Economic perspectives on foster care

Martin Knapp and
Andrew Fenyo

Foster care has long been preferred to residential care for the majority of children in the care of local authorities who, for whatever reasons, cannot be accommodated by or with their birth parent(s). That preference has been couched overwhelmingly in 'welfare' terms: a child's development, it is argued, will be better enhanced in a foster placement as compared to a residential home. This simplistic summary of a wealth of argument obviously does not do justice to the body of theory and empirical evidence which rests beneath, and continues to bolster, this policy and practice preference. Nor does it do more than hint at the existence of persuasive counter-arguments for the continued availability of residential care for a sizeable minority of present and future child-care populations (cf. Parker 1988). However, this chapter is not directly concerned with these 'welfare' arguments, although we most certainly do not mean to suggest they be ignored. Instead we shall focus on the encouragement given to these arguments by claims that foster care is a cheap alternative to residential. In the vernacular of the new managerialism of today's public services foster care is claimed, frequently and loudly, to offer greater value for money.

While the terminology may have altered, the financial case for encouraging foster care is much the same today as it was over a hundred years ago. Then, some Boards of Poor Law Guardians adopted the relative cost argument with alacrity, though constrained by legislation and the symbolic value of institutional edifices from making sweeping changes. In the early post-war years the Home Office lent strong support to the recommendations of the Curtis Committee (1946) – which, without evidence, had whole-heartedly preferred boarding out to 'institutional care' – by appealing for economy.

Expansion of boarding-out should relieve pressure on accommodation in children's homes and residential nurseries, at a time when restrictions on capital investment limit severely the improvement of existing premises. . . . Boarding-out is the least expensive method of child care both in money and manpower, and in the present financial condition of the country it is imperative to exercise the strictest economy consistent with a proper regard for the interests of the children.

(Home Office 1952: para 2)

The same sentiments are voiced today, perhaps less baldly stated, by the Audit Commission and taken up by auditors when examining the activities and spending patterns of local authority child care services. 'The potential for improving value for money by further increasing the percentage of children placed with foster parents continues to exist for most authorities' (Audit Commission 1985: 2). This view is given further credence by the cost statistics produced by the Department of Health and Social Security (DHSS) and laid before Parliament annually as a requirement of the Child Care Act 1980. The most recent figures (for 1984–5) suggest that foster placements cost an average of £42 per child week in England, compared with £304 for local authority residential accommodation.

The aim of this chapter is to examine this oft-assumed relative cost or value-for-money difference. We will not, in fact, overturn it; the new empirical evidence assembled here confirms that the costs of foster placements are lower than the costs of residential placements. But they are not as low as some commentators suggest; the putative cost savings to be reaped from expanding the fostering proportion have generally been exaggerated. Related to this exaggeration are various dangers in propelling foster care proportions upward at too fast a rate. It should also be pointed out now, although this is something to which we shall be returning later in the chapter, that the case for expanding foster care and the fragility of some of the arguments which comprise that case exactly parallel the debates about, for example, de-hospitalization, community care for elderly people or intermediate treatment for young offenders. In each case a cost advantage is posited and employed to bolster a preference formed on the basis of 'welfare' or outcome considerations. In each case the cost argument has some validity but is often over-played (cf. Knapp 1988a; 1988b; Robertson and Knapp 1988).

Comprehensive costs

The DHSS cost figures quoted above are no worse than the figures compiled annually by the Chartered Institute for Public Finance and Accountancy (CIPFA), nor likely to be inferior than those monitoring statistics produced by many local authorities. With one or two exceptions, each of these sets of statistics fails to measure the *full* costs of a child-care package. The available figures on foster care costs refer only to the boarding-out payments – the regular weekly fees to foster parents plus any enhanced payments – and miss a whole lot else. *Inter alia*, they ignore:

1 the costs of recruiting, assessing, selecting and matching foster families
2 field social worker and 'fostering officer' support costs
3 other services received by children in foster placements and by their birth and foster families
4 administrative overhead costs
5 the hidden costs of foster care borne by foster families but not met by boarding out payments.

We discuss the first of these (the recruitment costs) and the last (the uncompensated costs to foster families) later in the chapter. How important are the others? Evidence comes from two studies: a one-year longitudinal study of children admitted into the care of Suffolk County Council and a cross-section study (with one year follow-up) of all children in family placements in the care of an outer London borough. Both studies are based on data gathered in 1982–3, and costs are expressed in prices for that same year. The Suffolk study took the cohort of all admissions to care during October–December 1982 and followed them until the end of their care period or for one year, whichever was the shorter. Costs are calculated from information gathered during interviews with case holders at four points during the year. The London study looked at all children in family placements on one particular day in November 1982 and followed them until their placement changed

Table 13.1   Towards the comprehensive costs of foster care

Study and length of period/placement	Boarding-out payments (£)	Social worker costs (£)	Other service costs (£)	Total service costs[a] (£)
Suffolk Cohort (care period length)				
0–7 days	30	88	20	138
8–30 days	31	29	16	76
31–91 days	27	12	8	48
92–365 days	27	12	7	47
All children	29	37	14	80
London Cohort (placement length)				
Less than 6 months	45	18	5	68
6 months to 1 year	38	25	6	69
1 year to 3 years	40	11	9	60
3 years to 5 years	32	17	12	61
5 years or more	40	7	2	49
All children	39	14	6	59

Note: [a] These total costs *exclude* recruitment and uncompensated foster family costs, and include administrative and senior management overheads only when these are directly associated with identified individual children. All costs are expressed in 1982–3 prices; they should be inflated by about 40 per cent to bring them to 1987–8 price levels.

(including discharge from care) or for one year, again whichever was the shorter.

For those Suffolk children entering care and spending the whole of their care periods (or the whole of the first year) in foster placements, the 'hidden costs' range from a very small proportion of the boarding out payments to a large multiple (see Table 13.1). Hidden costs average 176 per cent of the directly recorded boarding-out rates, but can be as much as 360 per cent for those children in care for only a few days. These costs are averaged over the full care period or full first year. The London study does not focus specifically on admissions to care, and some children in the sample had been in the care of the authority, and often also in the same placement, for six years. The costs are based on services received over a four-month period. Except in a few cases this did not include the start of a care period or placement, so the results are not strictly comparable with those for Suffolk. In the longer term as the London results demonstrate, the hidden costs can still be substantial when compared with the boarding-out payments. It is well known from other studies that social worker inputs to all placement types decline over time (Millham *et al.* 1986). This can be seen from the Suffolk results and – less dramatically – from those for the London borough.

The first caveat to enter about the most commonly quoted costs of foster care, then, is that the directly provided 'support' costs – field social worker and fostering officer time, other social care services, health and education inputs where associated with child-care needs and so on – can cost far more than the boarding-out payments themselves for short care periods, and certainly remain high for the longest of periods. A conservative estimate would put these particular 'hidden' costs at more than 50 per cent of the average boarding-out payment for a typical cross-section of children in foster placements, to which must be added others (see below). The lion's share of these costs is claimed by social worker and fostering officer time and proponents of an expanded foster care proportion should not overlook these 'burdens', nor their implications for placement supervision and quality assurance, particularly during the early days of a new placement.

Residential and foster care costs

The hidden costs revealed by the Suffolk and London studies have their equivalents for residential child-care placements. Almost every child in a residential home – whether local authority, voluntary or private – will be on the caseload of a field social worker, and many will receive special health and education services not provided within the budget of the residential facility. Thus the currently reported costs of residential care must be supplemented with data on the non-residential elements of care packages if we are to take a consistent line with foster care. Evidence on these hidden costs comes from two studies – the Suffolk cohort cited earlier and a special collection in Mid-Glamorgan in 1983 (Knapp 1986a; Knapp and Baines 1987) – and is summarized in Table 13.2. The costs of residential care packages are tabulated

Table 13.2   Towards the comprehensive costs of residential care

Study and type of residential home	Placement length	Direct costs of home[a]	Field social worker and other service costs	Total service costs
Suffolk				
All homes[b]	≥ 91 days	272	27	299
Mid-Glamorgan				
Community homes	< 91 days	155	46	201
	≥ 91 days	155	20	175
	All	155	26	181
CHEs[c]	< 91 days	301	22	303
	≥ 91 days	301	17	318
	All	301	18	319
Assessment centres	< 91 days	296	35	331
	≥ 91 days	296	21	317
	All	296	31	327
Other specialist[d]	≥ 91 days	234	13	247
	All	234	12	246
All homes	< 91 days	190	34	224
	≥ 91 days	190	20	210
	All	190	24	214

All costs are expressed in 1982–3 prices; they should be inflated by about 40 per cent to bring them to 1987–8 price levels.

Notes [a] These are the costs of residential care as recorded in the accounts of local authorities (and the charges levied to local authorities by voluntary or private organizations), *less* the recorded depreciation or debt charge element, but *plus* a capital cost element based on more suitable calculations (see, for example, Knapp 1984; ch. 4).
[b] Only fifteen care periods in the Suffolk cohort study comprised *only* residential placements, this total being too small to produce reliable costings by *type* of residential home.
[c] Community homes with education on the premises.
[d] These are, in fact, homes for children with a physical handicap or a learning difficulty (mental handicap). There were insufficient children in these homes for less than ninety-one days to allow reliable estimation of costs for this subcategory.

by type of residential home and duration of placement (to date), both of which prove to be important in predicting variations in the hidden costs element. Again there are much higher field social worker and other costs in the early months of a placement.

If we can compare the costs reported in Tables 13.1 and 13.2 – and we will be arguing in the next section that they may not be strictly comparable, but we leave this to one side for the moment – then we see that in absolute terms the hidden costs of foster and residential care are not greatly different for placements lasting more than three months. The biggest difference comes in short-term placements. Here the average hidden costs of foster care were approximately £60 per week in Suffolk in 1982–3, considerably larger than the equivalent figures for the Mid-Glamorgan residential sample. The major element of hidden cost, field social worker time (including fostering officer time if authorities have separately designated posts), also differs significantly between foster and residential care. This finding contradicts the assumption of equivalence of the field social work inputs into these two varieties made by, for example, Hazel (1981) and derived by the Audit Commission (1985: Appendix 13) from data collected in three areas.

These cost comparisons between foster and residential care are regrettably not straightforward (though nothing better is yet available) but two conclusions emerge. First, adding in the hidden costs of equivalent services for the two types of child care, the cost advantage enjoyed by foster care narrows slightly but does not disappear. Note, however, that we have not yet taken into account the fact that children in residential care are likely to present more 'difficult' or 'challenging' patterns of behaviour so that we are probably not comparing like with like. Second, we would urge caution in assuming that the ratio of the number of children in foster care to the number in residential care can be raised without any impact on the needs for field social work resources. A high proportion of all child care periods last for less than three months. If a local authority substituted foster placements for residential for these children, field social work needs could increase by 4 per cent of a whole time equivalent level 3 social worker for each child thus 'relocated'. This is not a huge amount but it is significantly larger than the zero implications posited by the Audit Commission, and cumulatively it could have a marked effect on a social work team's operational activities. The costs of providing additional social work support could easily be met from the savings that accrue from closing children's homes, but a number of authorities prefer to divert any such savings to improve services for people with learning difficulties or age-related needs.

Like-with-like comparisons

The characteristics of children accommodated in residential homes are different from the characteristics of children boarded out. Children in residential care are typically more 'difficult' than children boarded out. The meaning of the term 'more difficult' is not easy to specify exactly, but it is clear that children with physical and mental handicaps, with delinquent tendencies or backgrounds, older children and those with emotional or behavioural characteristics such as aggression, hyperactivity or propensity to self-mutilation are much less likely to be boarded out than to be in residential care. The relevance of these differences between the two child-care populations stems from the cost correlates of 'difficulty'.

In the residential setting evidence of a cost-difficulty association has been found in the public, voluntary and private sectors (Knapp 1986b; Knapp and Smith 1985), but has not previously been revealed for foster placements. We were able to explore the sources of cost variations with the data collected in the London borough study. Consider, for example, the boarding-out payment and the costs of social worker and fostering officer time. Taking cost per week as the variable to be explained, we examined the influences of a range of factors describing *child characteristics* (age, gender, legal status, health status, emotional and behavioural characteristics, educational needs, previous placement and time in care), *placements* (duration to date, location, the composition and previous fostering experience of the family, objectives and plans, housing size and tenure), *birth families* (parents alive, visiting frequency, their own long-term care experience, siblings) and some aspects of the supervising *social worker*. The intention of the multivariate analyses was to 'explain' variations in the two cost measures. We can briefly summarize the results here. (For more details see Knapp *et al.* forthcoming). The multiple regression analyses 'explained' 76 per cent of the observed variation in weekly boarding-out payments (basic plus special allowances) and 65 per cent of the average weekly costs of field social worker and fostering officer time. Among the cost-raising factors were physical and mental disability or illness, hyperactivity, speech/communication problems and disruptive behaviour at school. Similar associations between costs and child characteristics were found in a New York study by Young and Finch (1977: ch. 6). As a DHSS report described:

> Children with special needs, such as those who are handicapped or very disturbed make great demands on foster parents and may, for instance, necessitate their employing domestic help in order to free themselves for the children's care. In addition, the wear and tear on clothes, furniture and fittings is likely to be greater than with a less handicapped child. . . . Occasionally a local authority may be able to offer special housing facilities that would enable foster parents to meet a particular need.
>
> (DHSS 1976: para 373)

In projecting the savings to be reaped from a switch from residential to foster care, the Audit Commission (1985: Appendix 18) assumed that the costs of the latter are invariant with respect to numbers of children fostered and their characteristics. This would not appear to be the case, so that their model exaggerates the savings to local authorities. The need for like-with-like comparisons of costs is paramount. If, as we have just shown, the costs of both foster and residential placements increase with 'difficulty', and if today's foster care population is less difficult on average than the residential population (Melotte 1979; Millham *et al.* 1986; Parker 1988; Vernon and Fruin 1986), then comparisons of today's cost averages will exaggerate the difference between the two services. This can be seen with the aid of Figure 13.1. Residential care costs (ACR) and foster care costs (ACF) increase with 'difficulty' (taken to be some composite indicator of child characteristics). For simplicity it has been assumed that the cost of residential care always exceeds the cost of foster care, a reasonable supposition on the basis of available evidence. The average degree of difficulty for the children currently accommodated in residential and foster homes is DR and DF respectively. Associated with them will be two average cost figures (CR and CF). If a child of difficulty DR currently in a residential home is successfully boarded out, the cost to the authority will not be the present average boarding out cost (CF) but the larger amount CM. The extent of the exaggeration in costs that follows if *today's*

Figure 13.1   Cost-difficulty relationship for residential care and boarding out

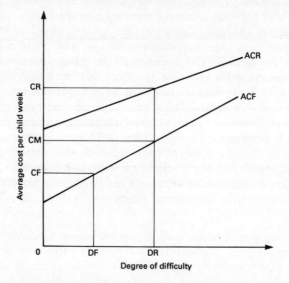

averages are employed to justify savings, and to justify a changing balance of care, is not possible to estimate with present data sets, but the sensitivity of costs to child characteristics suggests it could be considerable.

Changing the balance of care

There are two important corollaries to this analysis of like-with-like comparisons. We must remember that the cost difference between residential and foster care is only one rationale for altering the balance of care. This changed balance is effected most commonly by trying to place in foster families children whose characteristics are 'more difficult' than the average for the foster care group (DF in Figure 13.1) but 'less difficult' than the average residential child (DR). The effect is to raise the average difficulty in *both* settings. The first implication of this, following our previous arguments, is obviously to push up average costs in both settings. This may look like a perverse consequence of a policy which has cost savings as one of its aims, but in fact the *total* costs of the child-care system will fall.

This may explain the real cost inflation experienced by both residential and boarding-out services in the last few years. The proportion of children boarded out has risen from 33 per cent in 1976/7 to more than 50 per cent today and over the same period the real costs of both placement types have inflated by more than 30 per cent. Further changes in the balance of care must mean higher direct and hidden costs for foster care. But residential care is left with the more difficult children, raising its own average cost. It will become yet more conspicuous to elected members in budget-conscious authorities at the same time as residential staff are facing a harder residential task. Under-funding of foster care expansion programmes will most likely result in the 'cream-skimming' of *only* the 'easiest' children from residential homes, widening the differences between the sectors further.

The second corollary concerns placement breakdowns. The Audit Commission (1985) concluded from its examination of eight authorities that higher fostering percentages were not associated with higher breakdown rates. The authors of this report conceded that breakdown had not necessarily been consistently measured between authorities (and probably not *within* authorities either). More useful, then, are the interim findings of work by Rowe and colleagues based on more reliable and consistent definitions of placement 'success'. In a six-authority study of over 25,000 placement beginnings or endings over a two-year period, Rowe (1988) has found that authorities fostering a relatively low proportion of children in their care have higher rates of successful placement endings (fewer breakdowns) in both the foster care and residential care populations. This, of course, exactly parallels the cost implications. Placement breakdown is by no means the only indicator of outcome and the higher breakdown rates apparently associated with higher levels of fostering activity may well be acceptable. What we do *not* know is whether these higher breakdown rates result from the under-resourcing of services or whether they are simply an intrinsic facet of care for some groups of more difficult children.

Supply response

A number of London boroughs have recently found that they cannot recruit any more families within their boundaries. Contrary to the 'localization' recommendation of the Child Care Act 1980 they are boarding children out with families some miles from their home areas and birth parents. They may pay high boarding-out rates in order to attract foster parents away from other authorities. In these circumstances, simplistic criticisms of local authorities for not boarding out 'enough' children or for paying 'excessive' boarding out rates are dangerous. They simply face a supply constraint. This should be noted in the calculation of grant-related expenditure assessments and in discussions of the appropriate and the feasible balance of care.

The expansion of foster care as an alternative to (some) residential care is crucially dependent on an adequate supply of foster families. As authorities endeavour to raise their foster care proportions they are going to have to find placements for children with special and demanding needs. Higher boarding-out rates will have to be paid, as already revealed in the London borough results described earlier and as witnessed by the rapid development around the country of 'special' family placement services for 'hard-to-place' children following the successes of Hazel's (1981) pioneering efforts. These higher payments are intended to compensate for what the DHSS called the 'wear and tear' of fostering but they raise the question of whether 'rewards' should be paid (they were abhored by the Curtis Committee) and still stimulates fears of baby-farming and criticisms of inequity (cf. Hill 1987).

Traditionally, and as a protection against baby farming, boarding-out allowances have not contained any element of reward. Foster parents themselves have often said that they find distasteful any element of profit motive in association with fostering. However, this attitude is changing as more foster parents see fostering as a professional task and as more women work; they need to earn if they stay at home to care for foster children.

(Rowe 1983: 23)

There are four issues to be resolved. What are the costs to families of providing foster care services? What is the relationship between these costs and the boarding-out payment needed to stimulate an offer of a foster care placement? What, in these circumstances, constitutes a 'reward' or 'profit' element? And finally, will the scandals of nineteenth-century 'baby-farming' reappear?

The costs to foster families can be broken into three categories, following the framework suggested by Culley, Settles and Van Name (1976):

1 *Direct costs* which are the out-of-pocket expenses incurred in raising a foster child. These are likely to be higher than the costs of raising a child in their 'birth' family because of the felt need to compensate for deprivation or to continue a material standard of living enjoyed in a residential home. These direct costs are calculated annually by the National Foster Care Association.

2 *Indirect costs* which are the opportunity costs to families of forgoing work (and its income) or leisure (and its implicit value). Implicit in many policy approaches (local and central, and stretching back many decades) is the assumed female caring role creating what some might see as an exploitable pool of labour recruitable at low cost for fostering. Low wage rates in many labour markets, particularly for women, reduce the opportunity cost of paid work outside the home. Homeworking, including fostering, therefore imposes low indirect costs on families and (as we shall see in a moment) lowers the supply price. Of course, indirect costs of this kind arise for *all* children, fostered or not, although different children will make different demands on parents.

3 *Non-economic costs* defined by Culley, Settles and Van Name (1976: 3) as including 'the time and effort the family members put into raising children that does not compete with the family's money making activities'. The psychic costs of fostering would be included here. These non-economic costs are likely to be higher for children with special needs or characteristics (hyperactivity, delinquency, enuresis and so on) and for 'inclusive fostering', which encourages the involvement of the foster child's birth parents to the full.

There are direct, indirect and non-economic costs associated with each and every foster placement, but the important policy datum is the amount needed to compensate a family for such costs. Generally the latter will be rather smaller than the former because of the joy associated with bringing up children. These benefits will be greater for some families than for others and

Figure 13.2   Supply of foster placements

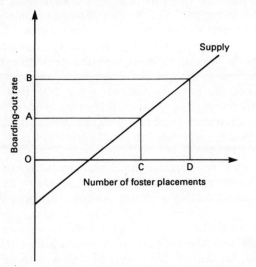

may also be related to the characteristics of the children fostered. This is one reason why some families currently foster and the majority do not. What we have, in effect, is a supply of foster families dependent upon a number of factors, one of which is the boarding-out rate (see Figure 13.2). At a rate of £A per week a local authority will be able to recruit C foster placements. If the authority is actually looking for rather more – say D placements – then it will need to raise the rate to an amount £B. This is highly simplified analysis which glosses over a host of other determinants of the supply of foster family care. But it is an analysis which has received empirical verification in two US studies (Simon 1975; Campbell and Downs 1987) and which has face validity in the UK context.

That some families currently offering foster homes are prepared to accept boarding-out payments which are below full costs should not be an excuse for complacency nor a reason to maintain boarding-out rates at their present level. There can be few local authorities which have a more than sufficient supply of potential foster families or which would not benefit from having a wider choice of families to match with the needs of children in care. Berridge and Cleaver (1987), for example, have identified foster child and foster family characteristics correlated with a high breakdown propensity – as did Parker (1966) in his seminal study – which local authorities and voluntary agencies would do well to note when matching children with families. Might it be the case, perhaps, that a marginally higher boarding-out payment would have reduced the breakdown rate among certain families? And surely a higher payment level would encourage a larger supply from which to make more effective matches. In circumstances where the only way to secure a greater supply of foster families is to offer higher boarding-out payments, and where those payments anyway are unlikely to compensate for the full direct, indirect and non-economic costs of fostering, it is disingenuous to talk of profits, rewards or remuneration as if they are unearned pecuniary gains. Payments above the direct costs of fostering are a compensation – and usually only a partial compensation – for what can be very heavy indirect and non-economic costs. They are the price of the skills, time and commitment of very dedicated foster families. Such characteristics command higher wages in most employments; it would be unreasonable to argue that they do not warrant compensation in foster care, and it would be plainly unrealistic to assume that the best foster parents are those accepting the lowest boarding-out payments. 'Inadequate remuneration is no safeguard against inadequate or unscupulous service' (Prosser 1973: 33).

Of course, once we recognize that higher boarding-out rates stimulate a supply response the spectre of baby-farming looms over us. Boarding out, in the form of apprenticeship and wet-nursing, had been formalized in the seventeenth century. Gilbert's Act of 1782 had encouraged boarding-out of 'all infant children of tender years, and who, from accident or misfortune, shall become chargeable to the parish or place to which they belong'. Contrary to the spirit of the Act some children were placed 'with those persons who will take them at the cheapest rate' (Wordsworth 1808; quoted by Heywood 1978). Neglect and abuse were often the outcome. Competitive tendering of this kind effectively disappeared after the Poor Law Act of 1834, as did the discredited practice of parish apprenticeship, but baby-farming continued with the sale of largely illegitimate children to 'professional' foster parents. A series of scandals followed, perhaps the most notorious being the case of Margaret Waters who was hanged for murder in 1870 (Heywood 1978: ch. 6; Horsburgh 1983). In her house were found nine small children, none with names and five in an emaciated, saturated, filthy condition. Others were discovered by the investigating police sergeant to be 'in better condition' because, according to Waters, she received a rather higher payment for them.

No one has yet suggested that scandals of this kind will reappear in the last decade of the twentieth century, but placement agencies will have to continue to exercise vigilance in the recruitment and supervision of foster families to ensure that they do not. This will be increasingly difficult as the numbers of children in foster placements grow, if placements become more geographically dispersed (despite the localization policies of local authorities) and as payment levels increase. The need to increase field social work resources should be clear.

Recruitment costs

The tasks of recruitment, selection, training and 'matching' foster families with foster children will generally be time-consuming, but particularly so when seeking placements for children with special or 'difficult' needs. Again two issues arise: what is the resource cost of this service and how is that cost likely to change as local authorities board out higher proportions of children?

The Audit Commission report (1985: Appendix 13) includes a hypothetical costing of these overhead and associated costs based on assumptions about what they call the 'man-days' required for publicity, fielding inquiries, assessment, visiting and placement. The assumptions (and terminology!) may require alteration but the basic structure would produce useful figures. At today's prices the Audit Commission's illustrative costs amount to £14 per child week, averaged across all fostered children. Other evidence has concentrated on the costs of finding placements for identified children, that is estimating the 'lump sum' costs of placement. London Borough of Wandsworth (1977) costed the placement of eight adolescents with foster parents at £2,400 (today's prices), rather smaller than the estimated £8,500 for finding permanent placements for 'special needs' children in The Child Wants a Home project run by the Children's Society (Thoburn, Murdoch and O'Brien 1986) and the £10,000 for Essex County Council's three home-finding units, again making permanent placements (Wedge 1986). If we take these last two figures and assume the average duration of placement to be four years, these lump sum costs are equivalent to about £50 per child per week *over and above* the boarding-out payments and any other hidden costs. This figure refers to the 'harder-to-place' children, and a cost rather closer to £20 per week will be more accurate for the 'typical' fostered child. But even this magnitude is enough to encourage caution when looking to foster care expansion to generate expenditure savings in local authorities and other child care agencies. If it is added to the foster care costs for the London borough reported in Table 13.1, for example, it would increase the total costs for the average child by 25 per cent.

Indeed foster care expansion programmes which depend on finding placements for increasingly 'hard-to-place' children will likely face increasingly high placement finding costs. If at the same time the expansion of foster care brings with it an increase in breakdown rates, as Rowe's data suggest, then these costs will be higher still because they will be averaged over a shorter placement duration.

Proceed with caution

In common with a number of today's social care policy emphases, the encouragement of foster care as an alternative to residential care is based primarily on assumptions (and some evidence) about comparative effectiveness gauged in terms of client welfare, and reinforced by assumptions (but usually *no* evidence) about comparative costs. We can see these arguments rehearsed by advocates of the closure of hospitals caring mainly for long-stay psychiatric, elderly or learning difficulty patients. They are employed to support a case for domiciliary rather than residential care for frail elderly people, or to substitute intermediate treatment for custodial sentences. In each of these cases the sophistication of the policy debate has undergone marked changes in just the last few years. Simplistic cost comparisons are now much less common and financial data tend only to be employed when hedged with caveats. But even the more cultivated of today's cost arguments fall short of the adequate. Comparisons are made between care alternatives which are not really comparable, major resource implications of care decisions tend to be overlooked, wide variations around averages remain unexplained (and unexploited) and future projections generally ignore the system effects of changes in the balance of provision.

As we move closer to an adequately costed child care system the policy relevance of the information obviously improves. At the same time we are also afforded new insights into the organization and management of care services. We begin to move beyond the reliance on averages and to examine the individual, familial and organizational circumstances in which one care mode is not merely 'cheaper' than another but more *cost-effective* carefully balancing expenditure and opportunity cost savings against differences in client and carer outcomes.

The research evidence that has been gathered to date for foster care and its principal alternative, residential care, still leaves us some distance short of an adequately costed system of services. It is, for example, not yet possible to plot costs by child characteristics by fostering proportion, or to link the financial information into any system producing reliable measures of outcome. But the evidence we have gathered here – and we are not aware of any other findings which would yet improve it – has cumulative force. It does *not* imply that recommendations to expand the proportion of children in care placed in foster homes rather than residential settings are inappropriate. What the evidence implies is that the commonly employed cost argument for this expansion seriously under-estimates the future costs of foster care and dangerously exaggerates the savings that will flow from changes in the balance of care. If the funding base for social care services is as fragile as some local authorities maintain, these *real* future costs could have unfortunate implications for the development of this service and for its effectiveness.

References

Audit Commission (1985) *Child Care Report*, London: Audit Commission.

Berridge, D. and Cleaver, H. (1987) *Foster Home Breakdown*, Oxford: Blackwell.

Campbell, C. and Downs, S. W. (1987) 'The impact of economic incentives on foster parents', *Social Service Review*, 61: 599–609.

Culley, J. D., Settles, B. H. and Van Name, J. B. (1976) *Understanding and Measuring the Costs of Foster Family Care*, Newark, Del: Bureau of Economic and Business Research, University of Delaware.

Curtis Committee (1946) *Care of Children: Interdepartment Committee Report*, Curtis Report, Cmd 6922, London: HMSO.

DHSS (1976) *Foster Care: A Guide to Practice*, London: HMSO.

Hazel, N. (1981) *A Bridge to Independence*, Oxford: Blackwell.

Heywood, J. S. (1978) *Children in Care*, 3rd edn, London: Routledge & Kegan Paul.

Hill, M. (1987) 'Payments for adopted children – right or wrong?', *Journal of Social Policy*, 16, 4: 461–88.

Home Office (1952) Circular 258/52, November, London: Home Office.

Horsburgh, M. (1983) '"No sufficient security": the reaction of the poor law authorities to boarding out', *Journal of Social Policy*, 12, 1: 51–73.

Knapp, M. R. J. (1984) *The Economics of Social Care*, London: Macmillan.

—— (1986a) 'The field social work implications of residential child care', *British Journal of Social Work*, 16, 1: 25–48.

—— (1986b) 'The relative cost-effectiveness of public, voluntary and private providers of residential child care', in A. J. Culyer and B. Jonsson (eds) *Public and Private Health Services*, Oxford: Blackwell.

—— (1988a) 'Searching for efficiency in long-term care: deinstitutionalisation and privatisation', *British Journal of Social Work*, 18, supplement: 149–71.

—— (1988b) 'Economic barriers to innovation in mental health care: community care in the UK', in I. Marks and R. Scott (eds) *Barriers to Innovation in Mental Health Care*, forthcoming.

Knapp, M. R. J. and Baines, B. (1987) 'Hidden cost multipliers for residential child care', *Local Government Studies*, 13, 4: 53–73.

Knapp, M. R. J. and Smith, J. (1985) 'The costs of residential child care: explaining variations in the public sector', *Policy and Politics*, 13, 2: 127–54.

Knapp, M. R. J., Baines, B. and Fenyo, A. J. (1988) 'Consistencies and inconsistencies in child care placements', *British Journal of Social Work*, 18, supplement: 107–30.

Knapp, M. R. J., Baines, B., Fenyo, A. J. and Robertson, E. (forthcoming) *The Costs of Child Care*, Aldershot: Gower.

Melotte, C. (1979) 'The placement decision', *Adoption and Fostering*, 95: 56–62.

Millham, S., Bullock, R., Hosie, K. and Haak, M. (1986) *Lost in Care*, Aldershot: Gower.

Parker, R. A. (1966) *Decision in Child Care*, London: Allen & Unwin.

—— (1988) 'Residential care for children', in I. Sinclair (ed.) *Residential Care: The Research Reviewed*, vol. 2 of the Wagner Committee Report, London: HMSO.

Prosser, H. (1973) *Perspectives on Foster Care*, London: NFER.

Robertson, E. and Knapp, M. R. J. (1988) 'Promoting intermediate treatment: a problem of excess demand or excess supply?', *British Journal of Social Work*, 18, supplement: 131–47.

Rowe, J. (1983) *Fostering in the Eighties*, London: British Agencies for Adoption and Fostering.

—— (1988) Presentation at Dartington Social Research Unit (Bristol University) seminar, April.

Simon, J. L. (1975) 'The effect of foster-care payment levels on the number of foster children given homes', *Social Service Review*, 49: 405–11.

Thoburn, J., Murdoch, A. and O'Brien, A. (1986) *Permanence in Child Care*, Oxford: Blackwell.

Vernon, J. and Fruin, D. (1986) *In Care: A Study of Social Work Decision Making*, London: National Children's Bureau.

Wandsworth, London Borough (1977) 'Adolescent boarding-out project: an evaluation report', mimeograph, London: Borough of Wandsworth.

Wedge, P. (1986) 'Family finding in Essex', in P. Wedge and J. Thoburn (eds) *The Hard to Place Experience*, London: British Agencies for Adoption and Fostering.

Wordsworth, D. (1808) *Narrative Concerning George and Sarah Green of the Parish of Grasmere* (later edited and published by the Clarendon Press, Oxford).

Young, D. R. and Finch, S. J. (1977) *Foster Care and Nonprofit Agencies*, Lexington, Mass: D. C. Heath.

14
The social model of disability: current reflections

Mike Oliver

It is now some five years since the social model of disability began to be more widely disseminated among social workers in an attempt to provide a framework for practice that was both more professionally rewarding and personally enhancing for disabled people (Oliver 1983). The time is now right, therefore, for consideration to be given to the impact that this has had on both social work and the lives of disabled people. It will of course be necessary to discuss this in the context of a number of other wider changes that have occurred over the past five years, some positive and some negative. On the positive side, the disabled people's movement has gone from strength to strength and become more coherent. On the negative side, economic constraints have further eroded the range of statutory services available, moves towards privatization have raised uncertainties about future services and changes in the social security system pose a threat to the wishes of disabled people to live in the community. Finally, the Disabled Person's (Services, Consultation and Representation) Act 1986 may alter the legal context within which services are provided, as may further statutory changes resulting from the Wagner Report (NISW 1988) and Griffiths Report (DHSS 1988a).

The changing context

My goal in introducing social workers to the social model of disability was to

> provide a framework against which to provide more effective services for and with disabled people and offer the possibility of making the relationships between disabled people and social workers more effective and fruitful for all concerned than they have been up to now.

> (Oliver 1983: 137)

While there have been some attempts by social services departments to develop new initiatives with disabled people or to provide existing services in more appropriate and acceptable ways, and some individual social workers have attempted to reconstruct their practice in line with disabled people's own definition of their needs, it is perhaps true that the goal I had then is even further away. In fact, the goalposts may have been removed altogether.

My three main criticisms of social work at the time were first, that it was for, rather than with, disabled people; second, that practice was based upon an individual rather than a social model of disability; and third, that social service departments failed to give any priority to the needs of disabled people. These criticisms still apply with equal, if not greater force, and this situation has been exacerbated by the further financial constraints that have been forced upon social service departments; increased moral panics about child abuse; pressures arising from the ageing of the population; the rise of AIDS and the current uncertainties and anxieties which exist over training.

However, throughout the 1970s and 1980s the disabled people's movement has arisen and gone from strength to strength (Oliver 1984). The movement has had three central dimensions to it. First, it has provided a critique of existing welfare services. Second, it has redefined the problem of disability away from the functional and psychological limitations of individuals and argued that disability is caused by social restrictions and therefore is a particular form of social oppression. Third, it has begun to organize its own services on the basis of disabled people's own definitions of their needs, sometimes in collaboration with, and sometimes in isolation from other agencies (Oliver 1986).

As has already been suggested, there have been some attempts to incorporate the social model of disability into practice. Two further initiatives need to be mentioned here; first, the British Council of Organizations of Disabled People (BCODP) and the British Association of Social Workers (BASW) organized a joint study day in 1986 to examine the implications of the social model for social work practice. Unfortunately the conference papers have not been made widely available. Second, the Social Services Research Group (SSRG) and BCODP organized a similar study day to consider the implications of the social model for research in social services departments (Oliver 1987). Third, a DHSS Report on visual impairment has endorsed the social model.

> This view is important in any consideration of visual disability: it should influence what service providers actually do in response to their client's request for help.
>
> (DHSS 1988b: 3)

One final issue relevant to the changing context has been the rise of the carers' movement in the last five years. Some traditional voluntary organizations such as the Royal Society for Mentally Handicapped Children and Adults (Mencap), the Spastics Society and the Association for Spina Bifida and Hydrocephalus (ASBAH) were set up by parents to improve provision for their disabled children, and in 1964 the National Council for Single Women and their Dependants, was established. However it was not until 1981 that the first organization of, rather than for, carers was set up with the formation of the Association of Carers to articulate their own needs, independent of the needs of their disabled relatives. Since then there has been an upsurge in research on the numbers and needs of carers, legislative acknowledgement of their needs in the Disabled Person's Act 1986, and a legal victory in the European Court for the right of married women to claim the Invalid Care Allowance. However, for the purposes of this chapter, the key issue it raises is that carers have needs independent of, and possibly in conflict with, those of disabled people. The implications of this for the social model of disability will be considered later.

The individual model of disability

Historically the individual model of disability has been the dominant one providing a framework for social work intervention. Underpinned by the personal tragedy theory of disability and reinforced by the medicalization of disability (Oliver 1989), it sees the problems of disability as arising from the functional or psychological limitations of impaired individuals. Accordingly social work intervention is to be geared towards helping individuals to adjust to, or come to terms with, their limitations. Within this model, loss is the metaphor through which all the behaviour of disabled people is interpreted.

The growth of the disabled people's movement and, especially, its redefinition of the problem as social oppression has given rise to the concept of disablism which is inherent within the individual model of disability. Within social work there has been an increasing willingness to combat the other 'isms' in recent years, notably racism and sexism but disablism within the individual model is more deeply ingrained. A recent analysis of disability within the American social work literature shows how this remains:

> we continued to use the Erik Erikson (1959) model of human development that emphasised bladder and bowel continency as a precursor to the development of a sense of competency. There was no contradiction because we had no knowledge of those disabled adults who would never have control over these functions, but who were obtaining an impressive level of personal competency and positive self image. Their new self confidence was propelling them toward a confrontation with society's negative evaluation of their abilities and rights.
>
> (Owen 1985: 397–8)

The individual model is not dead in British social work literature either. For example a recently published article in a leading social work journal claiming to be 'a comprehensive review of the diverse literature on human response to traumatic loss and disability' (Berger 1988) can be utilized to show exactly why the individual model offers an inappropriate and even disablist approach. Before proceeding to criticize this approach, it needs to be pointed out that the above review is neither comprehensive nor does it cover the diverse literature. It is a sympathetic account of the literature favourable to this loss model and fails to mention any literature critical of it (Finkelstein 1980; Oliver 1983) or which utilizes alternative models (Sutherland 1981; Silver and Wortman 1980; Creek *et al.*1987).

The first criticism that can be made of the individual model based on loss is its claim to universality. There are two dimensions to this: first, that all disabled people experience their disability as loss; second, this loss is experienced by other groups such as 'burn victims, the deformed, man made and natural disaster victims, concentration camp survivors, the severely and terminally ill, etc' (Berger 1988). The plain fact is that not all disabled people experience their disability as loss (Campling 1981; Oliver *et al.* 1988). If universality cannot be established within groups, its claims across groups are unsubstantiable. It is also worth pointing out that those advocating the social model do not seek to deny that some disabled people experience their disability as loss, but rather to challenge its universality and the usefulness of any guidelines for intervention based upon such explanations.

The second criticism that can be made is the tautological nature of the explanation accorded to all responses – 'initial denial is a ubiquitous psychological defence in the face of massive acquired losses' (Berger 1988). But disabled people who deny they experience their disabilities as loss are manifesting the pathological response of denial which is, in itself, evidence of how deep rooted their adjustment problems really are. Small wonder many disabled people feel victimized by able-bodied researchers whose writings on disability 'are more than based on theory than fact' (Trieschman 1981).

The third criticism concerns the positing of developmental stages of emotional reactions that disabled individuals, and even their families, must go through before they are 'able to gradually integrate the reality of the situation' (Berger 1988). Apart from presenting a totally mechanistic view of human nature (Oliver 1981), other reviews of the literature have found evidence to support the existence of these stages as far as individuals (Trieschman 1981) or families (Vargo and Stewin 1984) are concerned.

A fourth criticism concerns the retrospective reinterpretation of subsequent events within the loss metaphor; paralysed veterans from the Vietnam war suffer from 'delayed traumatic stress syndrome'; talking to other disabled people is 'bearing witness . . . to give meaning to their pain by sharing it with others'; engaging in self-help activities is individual therapy as is lecturing to social workers (Berger 1988). This retrospective reinterpretation reinforces the stereotypes of disabled people as 'supercripples' or 'pathetic victims', always struggling to overcome traumatic loss and sometimes succeeding, sometimes failing. Encapsulated within this metaphor, disabled people can never be ordinary people, doing ordinary things and pursuing ordinary goals. Fortunately most disabled people are ordinary, which is fortunate, for who wants to work with a group of people who are only superheroes or pathetic victims?

The final criticism of this approach centres on the way it de-politicizes the whole issue of disability, and inevitably, therefore, provides a very limited role for social work with disabled people and their families.

Much of social work is devoted to serving individuals and families when they experience these losses and disabilities. In fact, it can be said that a major purpose of social work is to facilitate the coping process for those who experience loss of one kind or another.

(Berger 1988: 14)

This view of social work practice flies in the face of the Barclay Report's endorsement of community social work (NISW 1982) and BASW's (1988) acceptance of the social model of disability as a basis for professional practice. As well as fitting neatly with the combination of Thatcherite ideology and the views of a minority of academics (Pinker 1982), seeking to limit the roles and tasks of social workers. In the following section the nature of this social work task, based upon the social model of disability, will be discussed more fully.

The social model of disability

At the BASW–BCODP Conference in 1986 current professional and inter-professional practice was criticized and the social model of disability endorsed as the basis for future developments (Phelan 1986). In addition the changing legal context that will follow from the Disabled Person's Act 1986 has prompted BASW to issue its own document which also endorses the social model of disability as the basis for social work practice and spells out its implications (BASW 1988). Within this approach, what now needs to be considered is the application of this model in respect of work with individuals, with families and with local groups, as well as its relevance to the changes that are occurring at the national level.

Working with individuals

Because the social model argues that disability is caused by society and social organization and not by individual pathology, that does not mean that there is not a social work role in working with individual disabled people. Disabled people may choose, individually or collectively, the ways in which they seek to overcome the problems imposed on them by society. However specific guidelines on how this individual work should be carried out cannot be produced in advance of, or isolated from the wishes of the disabled individual, for this would negate the right to self-determination.

All of this implies a willingness to work with, not for, the disabled individual, and this change in terminology is not a matter of semantics but of a fundamental reorientation of practice. But rather than produce a 'tips for social workers in how to do the social model', what is needed is a collection of case studies which show how the social model operates in practice, which can then become a learning resource for both social workers and disabled people. Examples of this kind of practice are beginning to emerge as the following case study, reported in *Community Care*, shows.

Steve, a tetraplegic, became disabled as the result of a PT accident in 1982, and after a lengthy spell in hospital he was discharged to live with his girlfriend.

When this relationship broke down, he reluctantly chose to go into residential care because there were no other options available. However he wished to live alone and independently in the community and the task of the workers involved was to help him to achieve that. In Steve's case he had 'an enormous number of personal care needs, needing almost 24-hour, seven-days-a-week cover'.

Some of the colleagues of the workers involved spoke of 'unrealistic demands' and 'unreasonable expectations'. Despite this the workers incorporated three elements of the social model of disability into their practice:

1 they worked within Steve's own definition of his needs;
2 they identified the disabling barriers to the achievement of his wishes – inflexible existing services, finance, low expectations of other professionals;
3 they built on expertise in the 'disability community' through liaison with organizations like the Hampshire Centre for Integrated Living, the Spinal Injuries Association and Community Service Volunteers.

By devising a care plan and involving other agencies, Steve moved into his own home in July 1987. The workers involved conclude

> that with a bit of flexibility, backed by specialist knowledge, it is possible to cater for individual need by using existing resources. In addition, by diffusing the cost of these care packages between agencies, they were more attractive to the individual agencies involved, and it is more likely that we may be able to build similar packages in the future.
>
> (Chaplin and Lawson 1988: 30)

However there are limits to the application of the social model to individual cases, and while the building of similar individual packages in the future may well be easier, this incremental approach cannot meet the existing and changing needs of all disabled people. Ford, who himself underwent a similar struggle to Steve, and also eventually achieved his wish to live independently, graphically demonstrates the need for a comprehensive infrastructure of flexible care provision.

> My personal living circumstances do not take into account future needs, changes and choices. The care support I have available to me is an exception, not the rule. What happens if I want to move on somewhere else? Social mobility is an option to most people even if they choose not to exercise it. Would it mean starting from scratch all over again? Probably so. What are the implications with regard to continuing support if I wish to live with a partner? Must they accept the role as unpaid carer as the price for a relationship? How do we make such normal living choices part of normal provision?
>
> (Ford 1986: 7)

Before considering wider issues of a comprehensive infrastructure, it is necessary to consider the question of what price partners may have to pay for sharing such a relationship.

Working with families

The individual model has also dominated the social work approach to working with families, though a recent article by two Canadian social workers represents a genuine attempt to analyse the implications of the social model for family work. It should be noted, however, that they do not talk about individual and social models but about the 'social pathology' and 'social action' paradigms. This is merely a semantic difference; the ideas underpinning them are the same.

The social pathology paradigm incorporates various assumptions into its approach:

1 over-protection and idealization are used by parents to avoid the reality of the disability;
2 insistence on obtaining full information and services is 'shopping around' for an alternate diagnosis in order to deny the reality of the handicap;
3 parental depression is the result of incomplete grief over the loss of the idealized child;
4 guilt, rage and hostility are frequent dynamics in the family with a disabled member;
5 parents who cope successfully and remain optimistic are over-compensating to diminish their sense of guilt;
6 family dysfunction results from inadequate emotional adjustment to bearing an eternal child.

The authors go on to point out that parents of normal children are more prone to idealization; that shopping around is a response to negative professional views and the withholding of information; that feelings of guilt, rage and hostility do not occur naturally but in the context of prejudice, discrimination and the existence of social barriers. They further suggest that a social action paradigm can provide a clearer understanding of the social effects of disability on the family; it can create alliances between families and professionals working on external causes of problems and help families to resist stigmatization and engage in social action on their own behalf.

The adoption of a social action perspective will, hence, involve professionals and families working together redefining the problem and arguing for better services; examining the family's belief system; introducing appropriate information, including the socio-historical context; and developing a future perspective. Finally, they point to both the dangers and the promises in adopting this social action perspective in the current climate.

Disabled persons may find themselves once again segregated from the mainstream of educational, economic and social life. On the other hand, this period of economic crisis may break down the old divisions between parents and professionals. In British Columbia for example, where cutbacks have been severe, the social workers' association has adopted a social action perspective in opposing the government and has allied itself with the disabled and other minority groups. Such parent-professional-disabled person coalitions may lead to further changes in societal attitudes, and may secure support services for the future.

(MacKinnon and Marlett 1985: 119)

While this article is a genuine attempt to apply the social model of disability to working with families, it does concentrate on those with disabled children. In addition, it also assumes that the family will adopt a unitary perspective over the definition and resolution of the problem. And finally it neglects the rise of the carers' movement in recent years which suggests that there may be two perspectives, at least, within any one family.

The issue of caring, and the demands of carers that they have their own separate needs, have come to the fore in recent years, prompted largely by the formation of the Association of Carers, but buttressed by a number of feminist analyses of community care (Finch and Groves 1983; Ungerson 1987; Dalley 1988). This is not the place to review the history and development of this movement, but rather to consider what implications it has for the social model of disability, or perhaps alternatively, whether a social model of caring needs to be developed.

The crucial question that this issue raises is whether, if a social model of disability was fully integrated into social work practice, would not only the self-defined needs of disabled people be fully met, but those of carers also? There is no doubt that, at present, there are conflicts between the wishes of some disabled people and their primary carers. The conflict often centres around the needs of carers to have a break from the physical burdens and emotional responsibilities of caring, and the wishes of disabled people to remain in their own homes. The individual model would suggest that this conflict is tied in with the psychologies of the individuals and the dynamics of the caring relationship. The social model, on the other hand, would suggest that this conflict has to be seen in the context of the support services available, adequate or otherwise, to the family as a whole.

Given the inadequacy or non-existence of many community-based services and the inappropriateness of most residential care facilities, it is not surprising that this conflict remains. Many carers carry on until the point of exhaustion and some disabled people may be forced to accept inappropriate and sometimes dangerous services in order to provide relief for their carers. However, if we imagine that flexible care attendant services were available within the community on demand, and that going into residential care for a break was no different from going to a hotel for a holiday, then in the vast majority of cases, this conflict would not occur.

It is not possible to say with certainty that, if these kinds of services were provided, then all the conflicts between disabled people and their carers would disappear but they would be substantially reduced. But within the social model of disability, the social work task in mediating this conflict is one of providing mutually acceptable support services, rather than simply dealing with the emotions surrounding it. This analysis only scratches the surface and points the direction, and there is an urgent need for representatives from disability groups, carers' organizations and professional bodies to collaborate together to develop social models of practice which are oppressive neither to disabled people nor to their carers.

Working with disability organizations

The last few years have seen the start of a revolution whereby at local, national and international levels organizations controlled and run by disabled people have gone from strength to strength. While there has been some initial analysis of this, the history of the movement has yet to be written. It is important, however, for social workers working within the social model of disability to recognize that there is a fundamental distinction between organizations for the disabled and organizations of disabled people (Oliver 1984). At the local level these organizations are likely to be of two kinds; centres for integrated living (CILs) or coalitions of disabled people, eschewing traditional attempts to divide up disabled people on the basis of clinical condition.

At the local level such developments have undoubtedly gone farthest in Derbyshire, where there is both a CIL and a coalition of disabled people involved in service provision with the local authority (Crosby and Davis 1986). Derbyshire has thus worked out its own strategy for collaboration (Davis 1986), but the issue here is, whether there are any general principles on which such collaboration might be based in other localities. The Chronically Sick and Disabled Persons Act 1970 made specific provision for disabled people to be involved in the planning of services to meet their needs but this has been largely ignored. The Disabled Persons (Services, Consultation and Representation) Act 1986 has reinforced this and goes further, suggesting that it is organizations of disabled people who must be involved. These developments mean that social services departments can no longer ignore the demands of disabled people for participation and representation in the design, planning and delivery of services.

There are at least three ways in which disabled people can participate in this process. First, on any committees, working parties or interest groups where disability is discussed. Second, as salaried professionals involved in the planning and delivery of services. Third, as consumers of services, devising plans and setting goals in equal partnership with the professionals concerned. The formulation of and commitment to equal opportunities policies, within which disability has a central place and is not relegated to the margins, can have a crucial role in facilitating this process.

To make this participation meaningful, it is not enough to simply involve individual disabled people or to ask the local organization for the disabled to nominate someone. The principle of representation has to be taken seriously and only organizations controlled and run by disabled people themselves can nominate a representative disabled person. As yet, such organizations do not exist in all localities, and if they do not, ways and means must be sought to establish them through the formation of a local forum on disability, a user group, the organization of open meetings and such developments as can be facilitated through the judicious application of community social work methods. It is also important to note that where such groups do exist, they should not be denigrated if they do not represent all disabled people in the area. That is to disable further through unrealistic expectations for we do not expect the Conservative party to represent all conservatives, the TUC to represent all trade unionists, nor indeed BASW to represent all social workers.

Finally, disabled people cannot be expected to participate fully or represent themselves in and to statutory authorities unless they are provided with the same level of resources available to professionals who work in these organizations. These resources available to professionals include secretarial assistance, financial remuneration, management and supervisory support and subsidized transport. In addition meetings take place in accessible buildings and all of the information provided, both written and verbal, must be accessible to people with sensory impairment. Only then can full participation be achieved, but this, by itself, will not be enough, for broader issues relating to national policies also need to be considered.

Social policies and the political dimension

Since the mid-1970s there has been a world economic recession, one result of which has been to call into question the nature and future of welfare states in the industrialized world. This questioning has usually been raised within the language of crisis, of which there are at least three dimensions:

1 a crisis in the welfare state in that it was not meeting social needs;
2 a crisis of the welfare state in that it was creating needs that could not be met;
3 a crisis by the welfare state in that the rising cost of welfare was creating a crisis of capitalism itself.

Further,

> The crisis definition is now being used as an ideological basis for reducing social expenditure, changing redistributive patterns in disfavour of marginal groups and reducing government responsibility in social policy.
> (Oyen 1986: 6)

As far as disabled people are concerned, their experiences of the welfare state have coincided with both the 'crisis in' and 'crisis of' dimensions. In other words, they have not received all the services they need, or indeed are entitled to, and in many cases, those services they have received have created further needs by locking them into dependency-creating relationships (Oliver 1988). In what follows, political strategies and policy implications for overcoming this crisis will be considered both from the perspective of the right and the left. So far, the right have been making the running and their main strategy has been to resolve the 'crisis of' the welfare state through the reduction in public expenditure and the privatization of state services.

The strategy of privatization is underpinned by the rhetoric of targeting, dependency reduction, consumer choice and control; and such rhetoric is not absent in either the Disabled Persons (Services, Consultation and Representation) Act 1986 nor the Griffiths Report (DHSS 1988a) or Wagner Report (NISW 1988). While these do not deny the state a central role in the provision of services for disabled people, all are relatively weak in advocating mechanisms whereby genuine choice and control can be given to users of services, rather than merely reproducing the dominant professional and administrative approaches to social problems in general and disability in particular. As Sir Roy Griffiths has recently put it, 'One only goes for structural change after being satisfied that existing structures won't and can't work' (*Social Work Today* 1988: 9).

There is ample evidence that the existing structure of services for disabled people won't and can't work. The Chronically Sick and Disabled Person's Act 1970 is both unimplementable and unenforceable (Cook and Mitchell 1982) and likely to remain so despite modifications in subsequent legislation. So too with the structure of health and rehabilitation services which fail to meet the real needs of disabled people as they define them (Royal College of Physicians 1986; Beardshaw 1988). The real question the social model of disability poses is, what structural changes are needed to ensure that disability is recognized, and responded to, as a human rights issue, and not simply a medical or social problem for individuals?

The political right, responding to the crisis of the welfare state, see structural changes as occurring through privatization. It is, perhaps, ironic that the model for providing these privatized services is that of the supermarket; the argument being that packages of care can be purchased just as customers purchase products from the supermarket shelves. Ironic because many disabled people find shopping in supermarkets difficult, if not impossible. For many disabled people the supermarket model of provision is unlikely to offer anything substantially different from existing state services; that is to say, little choice over what is provided and little control over how it is provided.

The political left, responding to the crisis of the welfare state, have made some acknowledgement of disability as a human rights issue (Meacher, Beckett and Morris 1986) though without offering a radical challenge to existing welfare state infrastructures. It has become clear that if disabled people are to have legal and social rights to services, then the legislative framework must do more than list these services or provide professional and administrative approaches to their provision. This inevitably implies the need for anti-discrimination legislation which would provide not only public affirmation of the unacceptability of discrimination against disabled people (Oliver 1985), but also, if properly drafted, a framework for the enforcement of service delivery and a mechanism for professional accountability.

By itself it would not be enough, of course, as the experience in the areas of race and gender show (Gregory 1987). Therefore an essential adjunct would be legislation facilitating complete freedom of information which goes beyond current attempts to provide access to information held on computers and in local authority files. The locked medical cabinets would need to be opened and the unofficial information that is kept as ways of avoiding disclosure (as with current practices which require information to be provided to parents under the statementing regulations of the Education Act 1981) would need to be made available.

Finally, a mechanism whereby the needs of groups and communities can be articulated must be developed. This can be accomplished only through the adequate funding and resourcing of organizations controlled and run by disabled people themselves. Significantly there is some evidence to suggest that organizations of disabled people find it easier to flourish in the Third World. This is due not only to the resistance to change of bureaucratic and professional structures in this country, but also to the existence of a large and powerful sector of traditional organizations for the disabled who also have vested interests in maintaining the status quo.

None of these developments by themselves, or an incremental approach to them, are likely to prove successful. Anti-discrimination legislation, without freedom of information and a supportive network of disabled people will simply mean that the lawyers will get rich; freedom of information by itself will mean that individual disabled people will be subjected to professional mystification and sleight of hand; and support for the disabled people's movement without a legal framework which guarantees basic human rights will leave the movement politically weakened. But an integrated programme along these lines could begin to resolve both – the crisis in and of the welfare state – at least as far as disabled people are concerned.

It could, of course, be argued that this political dimension to the social model of disability has nothing to do with social work, but as it presents a holistic approach to the issue of disability in society, this dimension has to be incorporated into social work consciousness. That is not to argue that all social workers must become political agitators at national or even local levels but rather that social workers must recognize all the dimensions of living in a disabling and disablist society and develop strategies for combating disabling services and disablist practices wherever they occur.

Conclusions

In advocating the adoption of the social model of disability as a basis for social work practice with disabled people, it has to be recognized that the social work profession and individual social workers are as much trapped within disabling structures as are disabled people themselves. Economic structures determine their roles as gatekeepers of scarce resources; legal structures determine their controlling functions as administrators of services; career structures determine their decisions about whose side they are actually on; and cognitive structures determine their practice with individual disabled people who need help – otherwise why would they be employed to help them (Finkelstein 1981)? The only way out of this trap is for both social workers and disabled people to work together within the social model of disability. A start along this road has already been made and this chapter offers further signposts towards the ultimate goal of living in an enabling rather than a disabling society.

References

Beardshaw, V. (1988) *Last on the List: Community Care and Physically Disabled People*, London: Kings Fund Centre.

Berger, R. (1988) 'Helping clients survive a loss' *Social Work Today*, 19, 34:14–17.

BASW (1988) *Meeting Needs*, Birmingham: British Association of Social Workers.

Campling, J. (1981) *Images of Ourselves*, London: Routledge & Kegan Paul.

Chaplin, A. and Lawson V. (1988) 'An achievement to be proud of' *Community Care*, 25 February: 30–1

Cook, J, and Mitchell, P. (1982) *Putting Teeth in the Act*, London: RADAR.

Creek, G., Moore, M., Oliver, M., Salisbury, V., Silver, J., and Zarb, G. (1987) 'Personal and social implications of spinal cord injury: a retrospective study', London: Thames Polytechnic.

Crosby, N. and Davis, K. (1986) 'Future trends: centres for integrated living', Paper presented at BASW/BCODP Conference, Birmingham.

Dalley, G. (1988) *Ideologies of Caring: Re-thinking Community and Collectivism*, Basingstoke: Macmillan.

Davis, K. (1986) 'Notes on the development of the Derbyshire Centre for Integrated Living', Paper presented at the BASW/BCODP Conference, Birmingham.

DHSS (1988a) *Community Care: Agenda for Action*, Griffiths Report, London: HMSO.

—— (1988b) *A Wider Vision*, London: HMSO.

Erikson, E. (1959) *Identity and the Life Cycle*, New York: International Universities Press.

Finch, J. and Groves, D. (eds) (1983) *A Labour of Love: Work and Caring*, London: Routledge & Kegan Paul.

Finkelstein, V. (1980) *Attitudes and Disabled People*, New York: World Rehabilitation Fund.

—— (1981) 'Disability and the helper/helped relationship: a historical view, in A. Brechin, P. Liddiard and J. Swain (eds) (1981) *Handicap in a Social World*, Sevenoaks: Hodder & Stoughton.

Ford, C. (1986) 'Collaboration: A personal experience in application', Paper presented at BASW/BCODP Conference, Birmingham.

Gregory, J. (1987) *Sex, Race and the Law: Legislating for Equality*, London: Sage.

MacKinnon, L. and Marlett, N. (1985) 'A social action perspective: the disabled and their families in context', in J. Hansen and E. Coppersmith (eds) (1985) *Families with Handicapped Members*, Tunbridge Wells: Aspen.

Meacher, M. Beckett, M. and Morris, A. (1986) 'As of right', London: House of Commons.

NISW (1982) *Social Workers: Their Roles and Tasks*, Barclay Report, London: Bedford Square Press.

—— (1988) *A Positive Choice*, Wagner Report, London: HMSO.

Oliver, M. (1981) 'Disability, adjustment and family life', in A. Brechin, P. Liddiard and J. Swain (eds) (1981) *Handicap in a Social World*, Sevenoaks: Hodder & Stoughton.

—— (1983) *Social Work with Disabled People*, Basingstoke: Macmillan.

—— (1984) 'The politics of disablement', *Critical Social Policy*, 11: 21–32.

—— (1985) 'Disability, discrimination and social policy', in C. Jones and M. Brenton (eds) (1985) *Yearbook of Social Policy*, London: Routledge & Kegan Paul.

—— (1986) 'Mixing the messages: disabled people and the community', *Journal of the Royal Society of Health*, 107, 2: 46–8.

—— (1987) 'Re-defining disability: some implications for research', *Research. Policy and Planning*, Spring: 9–13.

—— (1988) 'Disability and social policy: the creation of dependency', Paper given at OECD Conference, Sigtuna, Sweden.

—— (1989) *The Politics of Disablement*, Basingstoke: Macmillan.

Oliver, M, Zarb, G., Moore, M., Silver, J. and Salisbury, V. (1988) *Walking into Darkness: The Experience of Spinal Injury*, Basingstoke: Macmillan.

Owen, M. (1985) 'A view of disability in current social work literature', *American Behavioural Scientist*, 28, 3: 394–412.

Oyen, O. (ed.) (1986) *Comparing Welfare States and Their Futures*, Aldershot: Gower.

Phelan, P. (1986) 'The social model of disability: ways and means for practice', Paper presented at the BASW/BCODP Conference, Birmingham.

Pinker, R. (1982) 'An alternative view', in NISW (1982) *Social Workers: Their Roles and Tasks*, Barclay Report, London: Bedford Square Press.

Royal College of Physicians (1986) *Physical Disability: 1986 and Beyond* London: RCP.

Silver, R. and Wortman, C. (1980) 'Coping with undesirable life events' in J. Gerber and M. Seligman (eds) (1980) *Human Helplessness: Theory and Applications*, London: Academic Press.

Social Work Today (1988) 'An optimist rethinks care in the community', *Social Work Today*, 19, 37: 8–9.

Sutherland, A. (1981) *Disabled We Stand*, London: Souvenir Press.

Trieschman, R. (1981) *Spinal Cord Injuries*, Oxford: Pergamon.

Ungerson, C. (1987) *Policy is Personal*, London; Longman.

Vargo, F. and Stewin, L. (1984) 'Spousal adaptation to disability: ramifications and implications for counselling', *International Journal for the Advancement of Counselling*, 7: 253–60.

15
The end of the road? Issues in social work education

Chris Jones

All the shortcomings of social work practice can be blamed upon its teaching. This, at least, represents one simplistic view of a profession under siege desperately seeking scapegoats.
(*Community Care* editorial, 5.11.87: 9)

The case for reforming social work education as set out by the Central Council for Education and Training in Social Work (CCETSW) in *Care for Tomorrow* was inevitably partial given that this document was intended to persuade a Conservative government to invest an extra £40 million a year in social work training. So rather than address the internal debates within social work, CCETSW informed the government that, in its view, what was currently on offer in the form of the Certificate in Social Service (CSS) and the Certificate of Qualification in Social Work (CQSW) was now largely inadequate and failing to meet current needs:

> Neither programme [CSS and CQSW] provides adequate education and training in length and depth for the increasingly complex demands imposed on social workers. Indeed, some of those holding existing qualifications who are given professional and statutory responsibility to protect the vulnerable have demonstrably lacked the knowledge and skills to do so.
>
> (CCETSW 1987: 10)

This strategy of 'bad mouthing' current efforts in social work education led to considerable resentment amongst social work teachers, many of whom felt that they managed to sustain relevant courses in increasingly hard-pressed circumstances (see Carter's letter to *Community Care* 19.5.88). However, for CCETSW's purposes it was a well-grounded strategy. From the Colwell inquiry onwards, 'inadequate' basic professional social work education had been identified as a principal explanation for failures in social work practice (see Rossetti 1987). By 1988 social work education had been accused of being inadequate so many time that it required no further explanation. Similarly the great expansion in the statutory responsibilities and duties of social workers since 1971, identified by CCETSW as a further reason for reform, had also become part of the common-sense understanding of the limitations of social work education.

In publicly using these criticisms of social work education as a means to gain government support CCETSW played a dangerous game. There are, as we shall discuss, some profound problems with professional social work education. But to offer them openly to a government, which is well known for its antagonism to state welfare in general and to professional social work in particular, has made professional social work education extremely vulnerable. *Care for Tomorrow* could undoubtedly be used destructively to undermine social work education rather than to improve it as CCETSW intended.

A further flaw in *Care for Tomorrow* lay in its failure to confront the unrealistic expectations, which had taken root concerning what could be achieved in the basic CQSW courses. As Cypher, then BASW's (British Association of Social Workers) general secretary, noted in 1982, the 'handicap from which CQSW courses have suffered is that too many agency settings have expected more of CQSW courses than they can provide' (*Social Work Today* 21.9.82). The expectations that a basic professional course could provide all the skills and knowledge necessary for a constantly changing and expanding activity remained totally unrealistic throughout the debates about the future of social work education.

CCETSW not only failed to challenge these expectations, but also manipulated them in order to make its case for extending training courses from two to three years. Yet perhaps the most persistent weakness of the structure of British social work education over the past fifteen years has been not so much the inadequacies of its basic training (inadequate though this often is), but the lack of a well-structured system of post-professional education and training (see Bailey 1988: 206). In virtually all the established professions, post-professional education provides the crucial function of up-dating and refreshing. By utilizing the practice experience of the participants, good post-professional education can also greatly extend the practice wisdom of the profession. Yet only 475 students a year (CCETSW 1987) undertake CCETSW-approved post-qualifying courses.

With such a low level of post-professional course provision there has been no chance to create a culture of continuing education and educational progression which, for example, is a feature of professional social work in the USA. In its absence too much will continue to be expected of CQSW and CSS courses. That there was virtually no discussion about the overall needs of social work education in Britain in general, or post-professional education in particular, is indicative of the partial and focused character of the debate. From within social work, the principal target was the CQSW (and not the CSS as is discussed below), much vilified by many employers, and a terrain the government too was content to see fought over.

Pressure from employers

Employers of social workers were among the first to draw attention to the need for a more consistent output from qualifying courses, and to criticise the basic social work skills training on CQSW courses.

(CCETSW 1987: 15)

CCETSW's decision to review social work education and the proposals that were eventually arrived at were in large measure a response to employer pressure, particularly that expressed through the Association of Directors of Social Services (ADSS). While it is important to note that there are some significant political differences between individual directors of local authority social services departments (SSDs), the ADSS has tended in its public pronouncements on training to be consistent in its demands for wishing to exert greater control over CQSW courses.

Employer dissatisfaction with CQSW can be traced back to at least 1975 (Jones 1983). In its second Annual Report CCETSW (1975) commented that employers had a tendency to undervalue the academic inputs to CQSW and 'even to suspect that the education they receive makes them difficult employees more concerned to change the "system" than to get on with the job' (1975: 39). Throughout the 1970s directors persisted in this attack, arguing that the academics who controlled CQSW courses were failing in their task to turn out practitioners who were able to meet agency requirements. Amongst those most desired included familiarity with the key legislation and an ability and willingness to recognize and respect agency procedure. These criticisms of CQSW courses did have some purchase. No professional course has been able to keep pace with all the legislative changes, let alone the countless practice procedures which have been introduced in recent years. And on a generic course of limited duration in which half of the time is spent in practice, there are inevitable gaps in course content. Even so, it is clear that despite these limitations some of the crucial inputs on CQSW courses are inadequate. The review of law teaching undertaken for CCETSW presented a bleak picture revealing some stark failings in crucial areas such as child care and family law (Ball *et al.* 1988).

The developments within the welfare system and political climate as a whole from the mid-1970s onwards deepened and exacerbated these criticisms. Unfortunately the lack of response by social work educators not only did nothing to shift the focus of the attacks, but also in many instances worsened the situation. Ironically the long review of social work education, by effectively blighting developments for six years did not help. Few courses were prepared to restructure radically to come to terms with the changing practice context when it seemed likely that all would have to be redeveloped by the early 1990s. As a consequence CQSW courses became an ever more convenient scapegoat for the problems and tensions which have been acutely felt over the past decade by local authority social service departments.

Social work practice and education: a deepening divide

The cuts in state social expenditure have created chaos and confusion amongst SSDs especially as they have simultaneously had to confront unparalleled levels of social stress brought about by recession, global economic restructuring and government policy (Novak 1988). By 1983 one-third of the British population were living in or on the margins of poverty, an increase of 42 per cent since 1979 (Walker and Walker 1987: 24). In inner city areas, in regions such as Northern Ireland and parts of Wales, and amongst particularly marginal sections of the population such as ethnic minority groups and elderly working-class women, the degree of social stress and deprivation has become acute (Oppenheim 1987).

The plight of the poor (and therefore the predominant client population of social work) has been further worsened by a series of government policies such as cuts in benefit levels and a severe toughening up of the administration of social security. These policies have simultaneously penalized those already on the margins of society and impeded the capacity and scope of the SSDs to respond (Jordan 1988). Irrespective of local political complexion, nearly all social service departments have been compelled to shed non-urgent preventive work. Statutory emergency work has become the main feature of state social work practice in the 1980s. Increasingly departments have returned to special-ist teams of workers (for example, children and families; elderly; mental illness and handicap) as a means of rationing and targeting scarce resources.

Within professional social work education the same period has not been so tumultuous. There have been undoubted strains and considerable problems with some closure of courses, but there has not been a corresponding trans-formation of practice which has occurred in SSDs over the past ten years. It could be argued that social work education is not experiencing the kinds of internal debate and turmoil that was a feature of professional courses during the early 1970s. During those years the students themselves were at the forefront criticizing and rejecting the predominantly psycho-analytical base and professional aspirations of CQSW courses. A variety of critical groups including *Case Con*, a social work student group within the National Union of Students, and a range of NALGO (National Association of Local Government Officers) Action Groups came into existence at this time. Many of these sustained critical pressure on courses and in so doing assisted change within many social work courses. This radicalism was certainly one of the influences in shifting social work education from its psycho-analytic base towards a more pluralistic perspective during the early 1970s.

The situation is very different today. Currently, in common with other humanities and social science disciplines, there is not the student activism and concern within social work about the intellectual and political content and structures of their courses. There are exceptions, but it would seem today and in the most recent past that the majority of social work students have been far more passive and instrumentalist with respect to their courses, intent upon gaining the 'piece of paper' with the minimum of involvement and often effort.

A generous interpretation of student instrumentalism would be that it reflects, in part, the deepening divide between social work practice and education rather than just a utilitarian attitude towards the course. Instrumentalism might than be interpreted as a student strategy for dealing with an educational experience that is seen as irrelevant to practice. Why bother to become involved in a course if the staff show no interest in what is happening in practice? Which is how one might interpret the behaviour of a social work tutor who teaches the timeless material on interviewing and 'relationships' without any reference to the poverty, desperation and social characteristics of so many so-called individual problems (see Becker and MacPherson 1988). Similarly courses which have adopted a radical curriculum, organized around themes of oppression and discrimination, have also experienced problems in engaging their students who have found understandable difficulties in translating some of the structural analyses of contemporary social problems into effective practice strategies.

Whatever the interpretation, student passivity and instrumentalism has removed an important source of challenge and creativity in social work education. Similarly the demise of radical activity, as against radical ideas, in recent years – no *Case Con*, few active NALGO action groups, etc – has weakened both practice and education. The mainstream professional body, BASW, has been and remains a largely ineffectual and marginal organization. Little has come from that quarter and little is expected. Undoubtedly the absence of an influential professional body has contributed to the difficulties in social work education. The lack of a developed post-qualification structure is in part a measure of social work's professional weakness. Similarly CQSW courses have not been able to create links with a viable professional body that could have assisted and stimulated developments and applied pressure on raising standards.

Social work education in crisis

The problems of social work education are not however rooted in the failure or inadequacy of individual tutors or students. Rather the problem is that social work and social work education is an activity which was predominantly a product of the confident social democratic era that followed the end of the Second World War. After a decade of Thatcherism, such a legacy has left social work education high and dry.

Although rooted in the post-1945 expansion of state welfare, modern social work's attachment to social democracy was both weak and at times ambiguous. Thus, while social work opportunistically benefited from social democratic reformism which led to the creation of SSDs, and the expansion of social work as a state activity, its prevalent individualistic and psychologistic versions of human welfare rested uncomfortably at times with the more dominant sociological perspectives of social democracy as represented by groups like the Fabian Society. Indeed the Fabian Society published a telling critique of the 1968 Seebohm Report arguing (as did the New Right fifteen years later) that the major beneficiaries of a reorganized and bureaucratized social work service were the social workers themselves rather than the clients (Townsend 1970).

The person-centred orientation of social work theory and education has proved to be a major weakness. Certainly over the past fifteen years when unemployment, the enormous expansion of low-paid work and more recently government policy have clearly condemned many clients to a life of poverty and stress, the individualistic theories of social work have come to look increasingly inadequate. Similarly this orientation led much social work to overlook the impact and character of discrimination, especially racism and sexism in the determination of an individual's life chances. The colour and gender blind approach of most post-war social work is largely related to a narrow, depoliticized view of individuals masked with the liberal sentiment that all human beings are the same.

Within social work education the individualism of social work tutors who co-ordinate and lead courses has often led to a fragmentary course experience for students. Lack of integration on a CQSW course is almost taken as a given, and does not simply refer to the weak linkages between the college-based course content ('theory') and the placements ('practice'). Few courses are organized around any integrative core – those which are tend to be at different ends of the structural–individualistic continuum. The majority appear to be situated in the rather confused middle ground with social work tutors offering their individualistic material in social work methods, theories and values, while the social science inputs often offer a more structural analysis of poverty or discrimination at variance with social work's individualism. Moreover as employers or the Central Council have asked that courses address some new concern, so it is dropped into the cocktail: squeezed in. This in turn places further pressure on an already over-loaded curriculum with the result that few courses allow any space for student-centred and directed learning. Thus one of the great potential strengths of courses, the students, many of whom have had a wide range of relevant work and personal experience, is rarely utilized or even encouraged.

In many respects Thatcherism has highlighted the various long-standing inadequacies of social work education; it deepened the gulf between practice and theory. SSDs have been compelled by both political and economic pressure to develop forms of practice that are hardly recognizable as social work. Consequently the world of social work as defined on many CQSW courses, with its commitment to the contribution of the semi-autonomous professional and a much-lauded value base is quite different, and even oppositional, to the new social work that is emerging in state agencies.

It must be remembered that the great weight of criticism was being directed at CQSW education and not CSS courses. Indeed, the latter were created in 1975 in part as a response to employers' criticisms of CQSW professionalism (Jones 1983: 118–19). Unlike the CQSW courses, CSS are jointly managed by the participating colleges located mainly, but not exclusively, in further as against higher education. Employers enjoy substantial control over the courses, particularly with respect to recruitment, as the 'students' are their employees who are released to attend part-time. Unlike the CQSW courses and related higher education traditions, the employers have a structural role in designing the course content, ethos and assessment. Throughout the review period, employers, through the ADSS, have been pressing to extend the rights they enjoy over CSS to be expanded to cover all future forms of professional social work education. In many respects this campaign was successful in that *Care for Tomorrow* agreed that the CSS and CQSW should be given parity of status and united to form the QDSW. Above all this new qualification should be based upon a partnership of education and employment with employment-led competencies determining the essential content of the courses (CCETSW 1987: 18). In other words the right to define the crucial course content of the QDSW was taken out of the hands of education and placed with employers.

Since 1975 social work education has been internally divided between CQSW and CSS interests. Throughout the review period both groups were often more attentive about which side appeared to be gaining rather than uniting together to press for more resources and securing the future of social work education. The competition between the two sectors took many forms. Accusations of academic elitism were commonly levelled at the CQSW interests, while charges of anti-intellectualism and crude technicism were thrown at the CSS supporters. These internal divisions remain, despite CSS's 'victory' in winning parity of status with CQSW, and as with many divisions, it has weakened social work education at a crucial point in its history.

Signs of resistance?

Within this depressed area there are some interesting signs of development. The extended period of review between 1982 and 1988 saw the emergence of the Standing Conference of Heads of CQSW courses (SHOC). SHOC has developed into a lively and creative force which seized upon the opportunity to influence the plans and ideas for the new generation of professional courses which were being discussed. The informal and creative coalition within SHOC contrasted sharply with the more august and traditional Social Work Education Committee of the Joint University Council (JUC SWEC) where the professors of social work have tended to dominate proceedings. In some senses SHOC represented the new, whereas JUC SWEC represented the old, despite considerable overlap in the membership of the two groups.

Some of the political analysis pursued by SHOC and others, particularly with respect to anti-racism and sexism, have already found their way on to existing CQSW courses. CCETSW, to its credit, has insisted that all professional social work courses (CSS and CQSW) must henceforth contain an anti-racist perspective and contribute to ethnically sensitive social work practice. The Central Council's statements in this area suggest, at the time of writing, that it intends to take a firm line in insisting upon this requirement. This commitment places CCETSW in clear opposition to the New Right which views anti-racism as a form of totalitarianism to be rooted out (Gilroy 1987; Lewis 1988).

An arena of struggle

The confusing plight of social work education – on the one hand stagnation, division, blight and confusion and, on the other, signs of resistance and creativity – give some indication of its current status as one of the arenas of struggle in a wider debate concerning the role of the state, the place of professionals and the purpose of education.

That the Conservative government turned down CCETSW's proposals was massively disappointing to those involved in the long review period. A favourable government decision would have lifted the planning blight on courses and ended a period of demoralizing stagnation. Nevertheless, the government's decision ought to have come as no surprise.

The New Right has since the mid-1970s developed a powerful critique of and opposition to welfare professionalism. CCETSW never seemed to appreciate this development which should have informed a low profile rather than an all-out review and demand for fundamental change. This major political misjudgement was shared by many within social work education, who, for a variety of reasons, were happy to go along with CCETSW. There were relatively few voices expressing disquiet at the process. CCETSW itself is not an homogeneous body and, one suspects, that the Central Council relented to employer pressure in launching its review in 1982 at such an unpropitious moment for social welfare in general.

Government ministers and its New Right supporters had never shifted from their opposition to welfare professionalism. The dependency culture which they claimed to be one of the root causes of Britain's weakness prior to 1979 was attributed largely to the consequences of state welfare policies and the activities of welfare professionals in particular (Benton 1987). The leaked minutes of the Cabinet subcommittee, the Family Policy Group warned in its appendix H 'Professionals and the individual', that the growing numbers of state welfare professionals enjoyed 'a substantial degree of monopoly power' and tended to

> undermine the individual's self-reliance and self respect. He or she may have no effective choice about what services he will receive (even refusal may be difficult!), and even less about the form in which they will be delivered. . . . The result is that he makes little input to the decisions affecting him and hence feels little responsibility for the outcome.
>
> (Guardian, 18.2.83: 11)

Alongside the generalized critique of the influence of welfare professionals termed by New Right ideologues such as Irving Kristol as the new class (see Steinfels 1979: ch. 5), the Conservative party leadership has expressed on many occasions a marked contempt for social workers. Just prior to the government's formal rejection of CCETSW's proposals, the Prime Minister in a speech to party supporters in Buxton (March 1988) stated that the crime rate was due, after the criminals themselves, to the irresponsible behaviour of social workers who pandered to the deviants and undermined family life.

Ironically the government continues to need social workers. It has never proposed abolishing them for they are too valuable in controlling and managing some of the consequences of poverty and social stress. But what the government has no intention of promoting, or strengthening, is professionalized social work. For while professionalism has its own conservative and reactionary history, its stress on professional autonomy and judgement makes it both potentially and increasingly in practice an obstacle to a restructured and more minimalistic welfare system. Furthermore, the Conservative government and its New Right advisers have come to regard welfare professionals as being one of the powerful vested interest groups who benefit from an active interventionist welfare state. It's not simply, therefore, that the New Right accuses social workers of being responsible for undermining crucial family values and social duties amongst the poor, but that as members of a 'new class' they subscribe to values and beliefs oppositional to the government's project.

Of all elements within the new class, those professional groups such as social workers who emerge from courses within higher education and the social sciences are those deemed to be most pernicious in terms of standing against the central beliefs of the New Right. They are considered to be anti-market, anti-capitalist and business, anti-enterprise, even anti-family. They are also condemned for being pro-welfare state and for their arrogance in believing that they 'can do a better job of running our society' than the market itself (see Steinfels 1979: 92–5).

Little wonder then that the government should have rejected CCETSW's plans. *Care for Tomorrow*, despite containing many elements close to the government's heart, including an extended and significant role for employers in the control and design of courses, was essentially a proposal that would have deepened welfare professionalism. This was apparent in the central proposal to go for three years training at degree level. In my view this proposal was the crucial factor in the government's rejection. It would have been contrary to all of Thatcher's instincts and beliefs to have provided support which would have reinforced and strengthened both applied social studies in higher education and social work professionalism. And that it was only through a last-minute prompting by the then minister Newton that CCETSW even considered the training needs of 85 per cent of the work-force within the personal social services (such as day care and residential workers); this would have reinforced the Prime Minister's resolve to dismiss the proposal.

Non-professionalized social work

The government's current initiatives with respect to changing social work education are all consistent with its concern to weaken welfare professionalization and its base within higher education. For example between 1987 and 1989 the government is redirecting £20 million into social work training, but not through CCETSW and not through higher education and existing professional courses whether CSS or CQSW. Rather the training cash, which is being targeted at training needs with respect to care for the elderly and child abuse, is being distributed to SSDs. Employment-based and employer-controlled training is what the government appears prepared to support.

This strategy is most evident with respect to its encouragement and promotion of the National Council for Vocational Qualifications: NCVQ is a fine example of a New Right state agency. It is, in the language of Thatcherist education, a 'fast track development' with government ministries 'driving it' onwards. No six-year review periods here. The government clearly expects most of the new initiatives in social work training to take place within the framework and philosophy laid down by the NCVQ. The National Council was formed in 1986 following the publication of the De Ville committee's recommendations on vocational qualifications of the same year (De Ville Report 1986). The NCVQ is a standard-setting authority with respect to vocational qualifications and anticipates being on full stream by 1991. In setting these standards the key criteria are those of technical competency, measured by the skills to carry out a particular job. Even if NCVQ is forced to acknowledge in some small way the value base of social welfare work it is unlikely that there will be any scope for critical analysis and understanding.

For courses to gain the NCVQ seal of approval they will have to conform to certain principles. The most important of these is that qualifications should measure outcomes in the form of competencies related to the performance of prescribed relevant tasks in employment (NCVQ Information Leaflet no 2, January 1988: 4). As Hall (1987) noted, the driving test is a useful means for grasping this key feature of NCVQ. The test measures competency to drive. If one satisfies the assessor the licence is given. The assessor is not concerned with the means by which the person learnt to drive. There are considerable implications for the traditional educational sector, especially further education which currently provides the majority of vocational courses, in these developments:

> In an atmosphere of deregulation, privatisation and hostility to the public sector, the worries about a new system operating along the lines of the driving test have obvious analogies – many private instructors competing for the training and only the test being regulated and administered by a public sector agency.
>
> (Hall 1987: 298–9)

The government's intent to undermine and reduce the role of higher education looks set to be realized should NCVQ be successful for the emphasis on, and definition of practice competency means that,

> Trainers and supervisors in the workplace will frequently be the only people with the opportunity to observe demonstrations of performance required for assessment. It is therefore anticipated that employers will

increasingly become approved centres for assessment leading to the award of qualifications.

(NCVQ Information Leaflet no 2, January 1988: 2)

The influence of employers, however, is scheduled to be extended given that they form the largest bloc on the 'industrial lead bodies' (ILB) responsible for determining the various levels of qualifications within each area. The social care consortium, which is the ILB responsible for social work training, is made up of representatives from local authorities, health authorities, voluntary organizations and the private health and welfare sectors. CCETSW is represented as an 'other body' in the consortium along with other validating organizations already involved in social welfare and health service training. If the validating organizations such as CCETSW wish to validate courses which lead to a National Vocational Qualification then they must conform to the principles and standards established by NCVQ. The consequence, as Hall notes, will be that:

> Professional influence will (also) be diminished by the revised role of examining and validating bodies. . . . Many employers have let lecturers get on with the task of sorting out standards because they have not had the time, the inclination nor the experience to do it themselves. Under the new system the standard setting bodies will be given great power to dictate exactly what should be taught and tested by the appropriate examining body.

(Hall 1987: 296–7)

Local authorities are responding rapidly to the opportunities being afforded by NCVQ. In the north-west of England, for example, the ADSS has initiated a major review of all social services staffing, allocating to the various posts what they consider to be the appropriate level of training using the NCVQ framework. For many day and residential care staff this exercise recommended a significant reduction in their training requirements. There was particular controversy over the recommendation that heads of residential facilities did not require professional social work training (*Community Care* 3.12.87: 7). It is now envisaged that this work will be extended to the whole of England and Wales through a unit based in Manchester, controlled by the ADSS. Once again this would appear to be a 'fast track' development contrasting sharply with the QDSW review process.

In these developments the government is not only giving the green light but also urging speed; it is impatient for action. Furthermore, it is now pushing NCVQ to extend its framework beyond the pre-professional level 4 into professional and higher education. While this was always intended as the long-term strategy, NCVQ itself had not envisaged that it would be considering so quickly developments in those sectors of education. However, negotiations have started to see how professional qualifications above level 4 can be brought into the NCVQ mould.

Under the banner of practice competence and relevance NCVQ will almost certainly undermine CCETSW and transform professional social work education. The Central Council in any event has been substantially weakened by the government's rejection of *Care for Tomorrow* and is clearly losing ground in the NVCQ race to a range of other validating bodies. It is now the case, with the recent entry of the Business Training and Education Council's validation of social care certificate courses in many colleges of further education, that CCETSW's monoplistic position has been broken with respect to validating a range of courses in the social work field.

The extension of the NCVQ framework across all levels of social work training and education will both consolidate the influence and control of employers. It will also satisfy the government's objectives of reducing the power of welfare professionals and its roots in liberal higher education. There will undoubtedly be some hiccups in this transformation. Some institutions of higher education may for a variety of reasons, such as a commitment to liberal education or even elitism, refuse to participate. However, the new Education Act with its emphasis on income generation, 'contracting for work' combined with the 'enterprise' initiative in higher education, might create the sort of higher education environment desired by the Thatcher government.

Conclusion

At the time of writing it is evident that the government's strategy is making progress. Professional social work education continues in crisis. The divisions between practice and courses remain as sharp as they do between CSS and CQSW. It is a gloomy period. However, it is not without hope. The New Right ideologues are in part correct to note that within the liberal professions, such as social work, there are groups of people with influence who do not share the Thatcherite project. Now that the time-consuming period of review is over it might be possible that some of these oppositional impulses might come to improve a range of existing CQSW and CSS courses. The review did, however, bring together, often for the first time, a wide scattering of social work educators and practitioners who shared a commitment to a progressive and liberatory model of social work. Some of these groups are now at work planning short courses, shifting existing curricula and creating new patterns of training.

Such small-scale initiatives are of great value at this time in keeping alive important aspirations and concerns. But they are unlikely to be sufficient. What is desperately needed is a new case to be made for professional social work education. A case which avoids the arrogance and oppressive features of the past. The unpopularity of social democratic expertise and professionalism is clearly illustrated by the lack of popular or even semi-popular support for existing CQSW or CSS provision.

It will be insufficient to argue only for professional social work education. A much broader campaign which challenges the New Right project of restructuring and transforming all forms of liberal and professional education is what is required. This government is clearly committed to rooting out intellectual and ideological opposition amongst the professional middle classes. Until social work realizes that it is part of this wider project its own prospects will remain gloomy.

References

Bailey, R. (1988) 'Poverty and social work education', in S. Becker and S. MacPherson (eds) (1988) *Public Issues, Private Pain*, London: Social Services Insight.

Ball, C., Harris, R., Roberts, G. and Vernon, S. (1988) *The Law Report: Teaching and Assessment of Law In Social Work Education*, CCETSW Paper 4, 1, London: CCETSW.

Becker, S. and MacPherson, S. (eds) (1988) *Public Issues, Private Pain*, London: Social Services Insight.

Benton, S. (1987) 'Death of the citizen', *New Statesman*, 20 November.

CCETSW (1975) *Annual Report*, London: CCETSW.

CCETSW (1987) *Care For Tomorrow*, London: CCETSW.

De Ville Report (1986) *Review of Vocational Qualifications in England and Wales*, Report by the Working Group, London: HMSO.

Gilroy, P. (1987) *There Ain't No Black in the Union Jack*, London: Hutchinson.

Hall, V. (1987) 'NCVQ and further education', *Coombe Lodge Report*, vol. 20, 5.

Jones, C. (1978) 'An analysis of the development of social work education and social work 1869–1977', unpublished Ph.D. thesis, University of Durham.

—— (1983) *State Social Work and the Working Class*, London: Macmillan.

Jordan, B. (1988) 'Poverty, social work and the state', in S. Becker and S. MacPherson (eds) (1988) *Public Issues, Private Pain*, London: Social Services Insight.

Lewis, R. (1988) *Anti-Racism: A Mania Exposed*, London: Quartet.

Novak, T. (1988) *Poverty and the State*, Milton Keynes: Open University Press.

Oppenheim, J. (1987) 'Falling apart at the seams', *Insight*, 20 November: 10–11.

Rossetti, F. (1987) 'Whither social work education?', *Journal of Education Policy*, 2, 1: 43–58.

Steinfels, P. (1979) *The Neoconservatives*, New York: Simon & Schuster.

Townsend, P. (1970) *The Fifth Social Service*, London: Fabian Society.

Walker, A. and Walker, C. (1987) 'The growing divide', *Community Care*, 2 July: 24–5.